life *of a restaurant

life *of a restaurant

tales and

recipes

from

la colombe d'or

helen studley

CROWN PUBLISHERS, INC.
NEW YORK

Published by Crown Publishers, Inc., 201
East 50th Street, New York, New York
10022. Member of the Crown Publishing
Group.
Random House, Inc. New York, Toronto,
London, Sydney, Auckland

CROWN is a trademark of Crown
Publishers, Inc.

Manufactured in the United States of
America

Library of Congress Cataloging-in-
Publication Data
Studley, Helen.
    Life of a restaurant : tales and
recipes from La Colombe d'Or /
  by Helen Studley.—1st ed.
    Includes index.
    1. Colombe d'Or
(Restaurant) 2. Restaurant
management.
    3. Cookery, French—Provençal
style. I. Title.
  TX945.5.C59S88 1994
  641.5'09747'1—dc20   93-8738 CIP
  ISBN 0-517-58313-5

10 9 8 7 6 5 4 3 2 1

First Edition

TO JONATHAN
AND ALEXANDRA

ACKNOWLEDGMENTS

Writing this book took twice as long as I had anticipated. No wonder I was discouraged at times. Not so my editor, Erica Marcus, who said I made garbage collection sound interesting. Erica was not only a meticulous editor, but a tireless cheerleader, and I thank her for her unwavering enthusiasm, her infinite patience and tact. Also at Crown I'd like to thank art director, Ken Sansone for coming up with the title of the book, and Nancy Kenmore for her lovely design. Bob Markel, my agent, who had always loved the restaurant, believed in the book from the beginning and was a staunch supporter.

My heartfelt thanks go to the chefs who reigned in the kitchen while I was working on the book: foremost Naj Zougari, who guided me through the most complicated-sounding recipes, making every dish seem simple to prepare by following his rule of prep; Mark May, who taught me the importance of the well-garnished plate; and Wayne Nish, who initiated me into the subtle art of flavoring. There was sous-chef Hal Kennedy, who taught me knife skill, and the line cooks Carlos and Moises, who saw me through most of the recipes and never tired of my endless questions.

I am grateful to the members of the dining room staff who taught me how to write a dupe, about table positions, and the intricate rhythm of pickup. Special thanks go to Ronald Metzger of Seagram Chateau & Estates Wines for his help and assistance in the wine suggestions.

Outside the domains of the restaurant I am indebted to Nahum Waxman, of Kitchen Arts & Letters in Manhattan, who was always available for advice.

CONTENTS

acknowledgments
. . . . .
000

foreword
. . . . .
000

introduction
. . . . .
000

PART ONE
tales
. . . . .
000

1
the concept of
la colombe d'or
. . . . .
000

2
staffing the kitchen
. . . . .
000

3
managing the
restaurant
. . . . .
000

4
how we serve a meal
. . . . .
000

5
the suppliers
. . . . .
000

6
behind the scenes:
the regulators
. . . . .
000

7

the clientele

. . . . .

000

8

promoting
the restaurant:
reviews and
the media

. . . . .

000

9

special events

. . . . .

000

10

when we eat out

. . . . .

000

11

from our kitchen to yours

. . . .

000

PART TWO

recipes

. . . . .

000

12

recipes from
la colombe d'or

. . . . .

000

glossary of
dining room terms
and kitchen jargon

. . . . .

000

index

. . . . .

000

conversion chart

. . . . .

000

FOREWORD

. . . .

The dream of someday owning a restaurant is not unlike a sexual fantasy : Most people don't really want it to come true. Nevertheless, the idea of running a business based on the pleasures of good food and drink and conviviality occurs most often to those who, poor souls, don't know what they're getting into. Ironically, such Pollyannas very often make the best restaurateurs, and their starry-eyed fancies can result in the best restaurants—places maintained by people for whom the ups-and-downs of a backbreaking business are balanced by uncountable moments of high drama, narrow but hilarious escapes from disaster, and, finally, a realization that running a restaurant on a day-to-day basis is still among the most exciting businesses in America. At the very least, it's never dull.

All of this makes Helen Studley's honest portrait of her restaurant, La Colombe d'Or, as much a warning and encouragement to like-minded dreamers as it is a nuts-and-bolts textbook for restaurant management. For the story of La Colombe d'Or has a great deal to do with passion, commitment, and standards of excellence that need to be reassessed constantly in the face of changing times, mores, fashions, and economies.

La Colombe d'Or may be the first restaurant opened in an effort to save a marriage. Usually it is the frustrations of running a restaurant that break one up, but in the case of the Studleys, the idea of a mid-life career change brought the two back together in a sink-or-swim dependency that might have destroyed two weaker souls.

The trajectory the Studleys followed—from loving to eat in fine restaurants to opening a place of their own—was among the quirkier forms of entrepreneurial chutzpah to come out of the 1970s. Before then, restaurants were usually opened by those born into the business, more often than not first- and second-generation families who had some experience cooking or serving. Italians opened pizzerias, Greeks opened diners, and French people opened bistros. With a little luck, they survived, thrived, and enlarged or upscaled their eateries into white tablecloth restaurants, maybe even creating a small chain. Well-educated people were just not groomed to go into the restaurant trade, which was at best considered a six-day-a-

1

week job where profits were modest and prestige was somewhere around the level of a louvre-door salesman.

But the great interest in food and restaurants that developed among college-educated Americans in the late 1960s and early 1970s—which ranged from a post-hippie fascination with ethnic foods to a pre-Yuppie infatuation with nouvelle cuisine—was fueled by a strong dollar that allowed an enormous number of people the opportunity to eat out in the finest restaurants in Europe. Traveling Americans not only fell in love with places like Moulin de Mougins, Taillevant, and La Coupole, but, being Americans, they wanted to bring it all back home with them, just as the Rockefellers, Carnegies, and Vanderbilts had brought back European culture a century before.

For many young Americans, the splendors of Provence were the most alluring of all destinations. They were the crucible of dreams for highly educated travelers like Alice Waters, who opened Chez Panisse in Berkeley, Susan and Barry Wine, owners of the Quilted Giraffe in New York, and Robert and Karen Pritsker, proprietors of Dodin-Bouffant in Boston—all of whom left other professions to go into the restaurant biz.

As readers of *Life of a Restaurant* will learn, this is pretty much how La Colombe d'Or was born in 1976: frequent trips to Provence stoked a passion for French cuisine and a delight in French style, as exemplified by restaurants like Bijou Plage on the beach near Antibes, Le Cagnard on a hillside in Haut-de-Cagnes, and the breathtaking La Colombe d'Or in St.-Paul-de-Vence.

Back in New York the pretentious conceits of deluxe *nouvelle cuisine* were fast making waves and headlines at restaurants like Chez Pascal, La Folie, Le Plaisir, and others whose chic design and dazzling style drew customers away from those douce clones of the famous Le Pavillon, Henri Soule's stuffy salon that defined the New York French restaurant at that time. Many, like Brussels, Le Chambertin, Le Marmiton, and Le Madrigal, couldn't survive the challenge of nouvelle upstarts. Others, like Lutèce, La Côte Basque, and La Grenouille, took up the slack and nurtured a regular clientele who thought little of paying fifty dollars a person for dinner.

But New York was always home to a remarkable number of little neighborhood French bistros—many of them convenient to the theater

2

district, like A la Fourchette, Du Midi, and Pierre au Tunnel. Intimate, quaint, and friendly, such places all looked the same and served the same Franco-American clichés like onion soup, *bœuf bourguignon,* coq au vin, and *crème caramel,* with little of the regional flavors of the kind George and Helen Studley had come to love in their eating forays along the Riviera.

To a large extent, then, La Colombe d'Or pioneered *that* Provençal cooking in America—since become all the rage—and was hailed early on as a delectable step up in the bistro genre. The premises were ~~colorful,~~ cozy, casual, full of fresh flowers and pretty prints, and the kitchen, throughout a whole slew of chefs, maintained a remarkable consistency from year to year.

It is testament to the Studleys' fortitude and stubbornness that La Colombe d'Or—through nearly two decades of changing chefs, changing tastes, and changing styles—has endured without too much deviation from their original concept. It is still a friendly, never stuffy, neighborhood bistro serving wonderful food with real regional character. But it is a greater tribute to La Colombe d'Or and its owners to say that it is a restaurant that seems always to have been there, wedged in the basement of an old building on East 26th Street. In fact, when I read in these pages that La Colombe d'Or dates back only to 1976, I was surprised.

Somehow it seemed to me that the little restaurant with the pretty awning and the wrought-iron banisters had been part of my own salad days when I'd take a girl from NYU out for a date after a folk concert or drop in for a big plate of steaming cassoulet on those winter nights when New York vies with Chicago for the title of Windy City. Apparently I just *want* to remember La Colombe d'Or that way, because it does seem so much a part of an earlier, more innocent time when two people could scrape together a few bucks, clean out a basement, change the grease traps, and open up a little place serving good, hearty, wonderfully seasoned dishes no one else around town was then doing.

That La Colombe d'Or has evolved into one of the most beloved of all New York restaurants, with a following that stretches from California to Cologne, makes the Studleys' story all the more remarkable. For all the frustrations, heartbreaks, tears, and exhaustion chronicled in this lovingly written book, I came away with the inescapable feeling that Helen and

3

INTRODUCTION

When I started writing this book, I thought I knew all about the restaurant business. Blessed with a three-star rating, riding the wave of a booming economy, I assumed this was as it should be, the result of fifteen years of hard and dedicated labor. Then the chef left; the nation went into a recession. Business was so bad, I thought we might have to close. No restaurant, no book. I couldn't tell what pained me more.

Of course, we did not go under. I say "of course" now, because it's one-and-a-half years later, and we are still in business. That's the nature of restaurants: things are forever changing. Chefs come and go; clients adore you one minute and forget you the next. A money-is-no-object spirit is followed by penny-pinching. Provençal food is all the rage or totally out of fashion.

Owning a restaurant is not for the fainthearted. Maybe that's what attracted us to it in the first place—high risks and good food. It takes guts, stubbornness, and a slight touch of lunacy to stay with it. At times, it can be exhilarating.

La Colombe d'Or exists because my husband, George, and I are in there together. We have been from the beginning: taking care of the restaurant, molding it, agonizing over it, rejoicing in it, sticking with it—euphoric, downhearted; cheering each other on, propping each other up.

It keeps us young, engaged, and well fed.

Writing this book taught me a number of things. The first was that, in order to tell the whole story, I had to understand the business end of the operation, which had been solely George's domain.

My part in the restaurant was, and still is, the glamorous one, the one that people fantasize about when they think how great it would be to own a restaurant one day: playing hostess, planning special events, arranging dinner parties and wine tastings, writing press releases and the restaurant's newsletter.

But that part is only half the story. To write about the other, I had to learn how to calculate profit and loss formulas, determine a weekly food-

and-liquor budget, understand about licenses and building permits, insurance claims and labor laws, plus a multitude of codes and regulations. It made me wonder how George could deal with all of it and helped me understand why he didn't always show the same enthusiasm for the restaurant as I did.

By the time I finished the first draft, I had a better understanding of the operation. By the time I finished the last draft, I had become familiar with most of our purveyors, knew the ins and outs of the New York State Liquor Authority, could project sales figures and operate a point-of-sale system. Having worked in the kitchen alongside the pros, I had acquired new skills that enabled me to execute their recipes. All of this gave me great satisfaction and boosted my confidence. It also made me a better partner.

It took three years to finish the book. That posed some logistical problems. While the fundamentals of the restaurant operation stayed the same, things were changing as I wrote. Chefs, for instance. I would write one chapter while we had one chef; three chapters later there would be another. The same with sous-chefs, pastry chefs, and hostesses. When I began the book, they played an important role, but now, bowing to a restrained economy, they are gone. In the interest of continuity, I left the chapters the way they were.

Recounting chef Wayne Nish's and manager Joe Scalice's unexpected departures, I was very bitter. That changed when Joe sent a letter to George after their restaurant, March, received three stars. Joe thanked George for having taught him how to run a restaurant and have fun doing it. Joe and Wayne invited us for dinner, and they displayed such pleasure in seeing us that all my anger melted away.

In some ways this book is a family chronicle: vignettes of former chefs, cooks, and managers, who blossomed under our tutelage and then, like children, left to go their own way. The one thing that remained constant was our commitment to the restaurant and to the standards we had set for it from the beginning. Like the restaurateurs who inspired us in the past, we now uphold a tradition.

Life of a Restaurant celebrates that tradition.

tales

1

The Concept
of
La Colombe
d'Or

"*Ordering hot: one monk, one salmon, two bouillabaisse.*"

"*Pick up table twenty.*"

"*Table twenty coming up: one green, one escargot, one
quail.*"

"*Ordering hot.*"

"*Now I want a pasta, a cassoulet, one special duck.*"

"*Pasta ready when you are.*"

"*Carlos, I'm waiting for that liver.*"

"*We've got a duck, a pasta, and a salmon.*"

"*Keep a tab on the salmon!*"

"*Pick up table forty.*"

"*Carlos, you got two pastas, one salmon.*"

"*Ordering hot.*"

"*Right guys, let's go: one chick, one salmon.*"

"*Two salmons left.*"

"*Okay, let's go—follow me with two more scallops, one
duck, one salmon.*"

"*One salmon left!*"

"*Ordering.*"

"*Two salmons, one scallop.*"

"*Two salmons. Jesus, where have you been?
Unbelievable! One salmon; that's it.*"

"*Eighty-six salmon. Eighty-six!*"

9

$\mathcal{The}$ sounds of La Colombe d'Or's kitchen at the height of dinner service. Music to our ears. Sheer gibberish not too long ago.

It's hard to say when our desire to own a restaurant began. Perhaps it started on our wedding day, celebrated at Café Chambord, then New York's finest French restaurant. Years afterward, we could recall the delicate texture of the *sauce vin blanc* served with sole Véronique, but were hazy about who was at the wedding party and what the weather was like. The desire received a boost each time we took our annual transatlantic crossing on the SS *France*, the flagship of the Cie Générale Transatlantique, which Joseph Wechsberg called the finest French restaurant afloat. Undaunted by high seas, we feasted on *bisque de homard, terrine de volaille, rognons de veau,* and *filet de bœuf bressane.* We dove into the *plateau de fromages* and savored spoonfuls of *crème brûlée, mousse au chocolat,* or *soufflé glacé.* We became intrigued by the workings of the restaurant operation, carried out with the skill and perfection of a finely tuned orchestra.

The restaurant bug certainly took firmer root during our repeated travels in France, where we systematically ate our way through the country's restaurants and bistros, starting in Normandy and, inevitably, ending up in Provence. We became so enamored of that part of France that we decided that George would take a sabbatical from his real estate business so that we could spend a year there.

We rented out our New York apartment and, in the fall of 1970, sailed for Cannes with Jonathan and Alexandra, our young children. First we moved into an apartment in Golfe-Juan; later, we rented a villa in Antibes. In a way, it was a homecoming. George had been born in Belgium and gone to school in Nice; I came from Germany. Hitler's persecution of Jews had uprooted both of us. By living in Europe, we were trying to recapture our shortened childhood and experience Europe as displaced adults.

We set up house. I did the marketing, often accompanied by George and the children. We filled our baskets with pâté, sausages, goat cheese, tomatoes, farm bread, rosé wine, and went on picnics. George and I talked to fishmongers, vintners, farmers, and restaurateurs. Inspired by *Mastering the Art of French Cooking,* I took cooking lessons with Simone Beck, Julia Child's collaborator, who lived in nearby Plascassier. Soon, my repertoire included fluffy omelets, lamb roasted with whole cloves of garlic, and piquant *tartes au citron,* all of which we consumed on our terrace overlooking the Mediterranean.

Our ground-floor apartment in Golfe-Juan was across from Tétou, which, as far as we were concerned, served the best bouillabaisse east of Marseille. Their presentation always took our breath away; we nodded approval at the enormous oval platter, laden with poached fish that looked as appealing as a floral bouquet and smelled even better. The waiter would ladle out the pungent broth, adding dollops of vibrant *aïoli,* and keep refilling our plates till we bade him stop. Then came the main event: with the skill of a surgeon, the waiter would bone and clean the Mediterranean bounty—*lotte,* red snapper, striped bass, halibut, and lobster. We could hardly wait.

It always was a lengthy meal. Fortunately, the children were content to play in front on the beach, rejoining us for Madame Tétou's delectable strawberry tart, whose recipe, she said, she would take to her grave, and, eventually, she did.

A short ride into the backcountry brought us to Auberge des Seigneurs in Vence. No matter what the season, we sat close to the hearth and watched Monsieur Rodi, *le patron,* roast *poulet de Bresse* over aged olive wood. The aroma was intensified by vintage eau-de-vie, with which Rodi liberally doused the birds, and by the pistachio nuts he tossed into the fire with abundance. While the birds were turning on the spit, Rodi amused his guests by sending windup toys through the dining room or by telling dirty jokes, preferably to elderly ladies. By the time our chicken arrived, we had put away a hefty *pistou,* a *tian* oozing with rosemary oil, the *petite salade,* and were well into our second bottle of Rodi's house red.

We frequently went for lunch to Moulin de Mougins in Mougins, then just a simple one-star restaurant outside Cannes. On one occasion it started to snow, an unheard-of occurrence in this area. By the time we had finished our entrée, the cypress, palm, and olive trees were masked in snow. George and I were the only people in the dining room. But not for long. Roger Vergé, the owner-chef, joined us at the table, bringing an apple tart, still warm, and a bottle of a local wine. When I asked what was in the zucchini-and-tomato casserole that had accompanied our rack of lamb, he volunteered to give us the recipe.

Bijou Plage was a modest diner on the beach halfway between Antibes and Juan-les-Pins. We had passed it often on our shopping trips to Nice. One day, we decided to stop and have lunch. It was close to three o'clock. The middle-aged *patronne* was *desolée*. The kitchen was closed; everyone had gone home. Yet she insisted that we stay. "I'll be happy to serve you a cold lunch," she said. "As an innkeeper it would pain me to let you go away hungry." George and I sat in the spankingly clean diner by the sea, feasting on homemade pâtés, *saucissons*, Bayonne ham, mussels in remoulade, and canned tuna, accompanied by French baguettes and a bottle of Tavel.

"Would you like to see the bathrooms?" Madame asked after the meal.

Not particularly, we said. Madame seemed distressed. As we were paying, she confessed that she had assumed we were Michelin inspectors. "They put great stock in the cleanliness of an establishment's bathroom," she confided.

For sunset dinners, we liked to drive up to Le Cagnard in Cagnes-sur-Mer. Actually Le Cagnard was located in Haut-de-Cagnes, a hillside village perched high above the sea. On previous visits, we had driven up the steeply winding roads with our little Fiat. This time we came with our new Citroën. As George was trying to make another turn into the ever-narrowing streets, the Citroën got stuck on a turn between two houses. We could move neither forward nor backward. Faces popped out of every window. Toothless little old ladies commented on our stupidity; children squealed with delight. Fortunately, the Citroën was a masterpiece of engineering. Following the instructions in the manual, George dismantled the two side fenders over the rear wheels, and, cheered by a round of applause, we made the turn, arriving half an hour late for dinner.

Less complicated destinations included the untold local bistros and waterfront haunts to which we returned again and again.

But, without a doubt, our favorite restaurant was La Colombe d'Or at St.-Paul-de-Vence. Sitting on the pebbly terrace, surrounded by passionflowers, olive trees, umbrella pines, Légers, Matisses, and Picassos, sipping local rosé and lunching on the spectacular hors d'oeuvres was our idea of heaven. Like Yves Montand, Simone Signoret, and James Baldwin, we became quasi-regulars. After lunch, we watched the men play boule, waited for the Léger or the Maeght museums to open, or dropped in on the potters in Vallauris.

Every so often, we visited the *vrai* Provence—Avignon and Aix, Remy, Roussillon, and Châteauneuf—getting our fill of Roman ruins, papal palaces, poppy fields, and lavender, while anticipating the meals at the great eating establishments of the area: Oustaù de Baumanière in Les Baux, Auberge de Noves in Noves, and Hiély in Avignon.

The children, however, clamored for hamburgers. It took some time, but, eventually, I came up with the right mix of chopped meats to re-create the all-American burger. The children were thrilled; so were their new French friends. For a while we toyed with the idea of opening an American restaurant. But, since even the smallest transaction at a French post office took hours, we realized that we were not cut out for daily dealings with the French *fonctionnaires.*

In fact, as much as we enjoyed our sabbatical in Europe, we discovered that we were more Americanized than we had thought. Europe, we decided, was a nice place to visit, but we didn't want to live there.

In the spring of 1972 we returned to New York. Once we settled into our familiar routine, we were not happy there either. George hated the wheeling and dealing of his profession. Besides, the commercial real estate market in New York was suffering from a recession. The children, glad to be back in an American school, started to socialize. I was restless and searched for activity. George and I were at odds with each other. Our marriage was coming apart. With the help of family counseling, we managed to muddle through the difficult period and hit upon an ingenious solution: instead of giving in to midlife crisis, we would embark on a midlife career change. We would do a French restaurant in New York. We studied our scrapbooks, accumulated menus and recipes; we looked at the pottery from Vallauris, the Provençal fabrics, the olive-wood trays, and the copper pots. Without having formulated a definite theme, we knew we were on our way.

To celebrate our personal triumph and properly launch our monumental undertaking, we decided on a last weekend fling in Paris. After we'd settled down in our seats and accepted a glass of red wine from the Air France stewardess, George turned to me: "What should we call the restaurant?"

13

I was ready with my answer. Relishing the moment, however, I stalled for a few seconds before I said, "La Colombe d'Or." George was not in the least surprised. By the time we got off the plane, we had practically created our restaurant.

We had little money left and no experience whatsoever. But we knew what we wanted : a friendly, informal restaurant we would enjoy—welcoming and stylish without being fussy, with good food, an imaginative wine list, fair prices, and consistency.

George, after fifteen years, quit the real-estate-brokerage business and enrolled in the restaurant school at Brooklyn Community College, where he took restaurant-management courses and cooking classes. Neither one of us wanted to be the chef. We reasoned, however, that to operate the restaurant properly, we should be familiar with every aspect.

Eating out now, we decided that every restaurant experience had to count. We avoided hard-to-get-into places like the Quilted Giraffe or The Box Tree and never made it to Vienna 79. Michel Fitoussi's Palace was neither in our vision nor within our budget. But the Four Seasons continued to impress us with its understated elegance and immaculate service, while Lutèce and La Côte Basque came closest to our idea of haute cuisine. Dining at Café Argenteuil brought back pleasant memories of dishes we had enjoyed in the French provinces.

Almost every Sunday evening found us at La Rôtisserie. Located in the East 50s, this fairly large and oddly decorated restaurant served roast chicken accompanied by heaping portions of perfectly executed French fries and delectable spinach, all of which was so good we forgave them the rancid butter and inferior wines. Dinner averaged $15 for two—a bargain even in those days.

Among the small restaurants in New York that we particularly enjoyed was Le Veau d'Or on East 60th Street. We liked its bourgeois fare, and professional staff, and we felt comfortable in the intimate surroundings. At Trattoria da Alfredo in Greenwich Village, we delighted in the simple Italian dishes prepared by chef-owner Alfredo Viazzi. He was a jovial man, dedicated to his métier. We told him about our fantasy. Viazzi encouraged us to proceed. He was generous with advice. Among his many sound suggestions, buying, rather than renting, our location proved the best.

George combed the market, following every lead. It took months to find a spot we could afford. But one day he discovered it : a run-down, semi-abandoned, small restaurant, Gloria, in a hundred-year-old brownstone on East 26th Street in Manhattan. The owner had passed away, and her daughter was selling the restaurant and the building. I rushed down to take a look. A fifteen-watt light bulb illuminated overturned chairs, dirty ashtrays, cat litter, broken sinks, and empty beer bottles.

"This is it?" I was appalled.

"You'll see," said George. "One day, there will be limousines lined up in front."

Meanwhile, there were primarily prostitutes doing a brisk business servicing clients in cars with mostly out-of-state license plates.

In April 1976 we took the plunge and bought the old four-story building. The price, including the thirty-seat restaurant, was $94,000, with $15,000 down. We were anxious to open as soon as possible. But where to start?

Soon after, driving to the Bowery to buy a secondhand bar, we made a wrong turn and wound up on Mulberry Street in Little Italy. The stunning storefront of an Italian restaurant caught our attention. Il Cortile. We stopped for an espresso. The interior gave the illusion of a courtyard in a Tuscan country house : warm lighting, tile floors, groupings of fern trees, sconces mounted on a mahogany wall, terra-cotta sculptures, white-marble tables, sparkling glass, flowers.

"This place feels real," said George. "Whoever designed it is our man."

George asked the bartender.

"See the guy with the big mustache? He's the man. His name is Antonio."

Antonio Morello was not only delighted to meet us, he invited us to join him for lunch. He was born in Argentina and had studied architecture in Italy. Il Cortile had been his first major commission since his arrival in New York. We told him about our vision of creating a Provençal restaurant that should look as if it had always been there.

"What are we waiting for?" said Antonio. *"Andiamo."* We headed for 26th Street. Antonio paced up and down the narrow space of our new

15

restaurant. He smelled and sniffed. He paused. And then, with the speed of a panther, he pounced at the wall and tore the faux wainscoting away with his bare hands. Underneath were beautiful old bricks, beams, and a fireplace.

"Fantastico," he cried. "Stupendous! And look at the tin ceiling!"

He rubbed his hands. "When do we begin? I will create, for you, a most beautiful restaurant."

And so he did. Using old doors, sconces, Amish farm implements, French fabric, handmade tabletops, Mexican rush chairs and tiles, plus our personal collections, Antonio Morello and his partner, Donato Savoia, working as Morsa Studio, transformed the grimy space into a charming restaurant very much in the spirit of our beloved Provence.

The job took three months and cost $6,500. We always kidded that Windows on the World, the restaurant on top of the World Trade Center, which opened around the same time we did, cost $6.5 million.

It was time to look for a chef. We put an ad in the *New York Times*. Not too many people applied. Among the few that did, Jaclyn V. seemed right. She was a young woman of French-Italian background who had run her own catering business but wanted the challenge of a chef's job. She presented an intelligent menu, handwritten on parchment paper. We asked her to cook dinner for us at our apartment. Her meal consisted of a *salade niçoise* and chicken breasts wrapped in blanched bacon, accompanied by Provençal tomatoes and Niçoise potatoes. She had brought a homemade pâté and lemon tart. We hired her.

Before the official opening of the restaurant, we gave a party for everyone involved in putting the place together: carpenter, electrician, plumber, handyman, the Morsa boys, and our staff, which consisted of chef Jaclyn; her assistant, Dinkins; Marco, the dishwasher; and two aspiring actors who said they had experience as waiters. In a gesture inspired by some forgotten movie, I brought salt and bread for the occasion. George made a speech. Sitting at one long table, we feasted on pâté with cornichons, shared a Duc de Provence wine, and felt ecstatic.

We opened La Colombe d'Or on September 10, 1976, five days before George's forty-sixth birthday. That first week we were packed. Every relative and friend showed up. After that, we stood around and waited. I remember a Saturday night when one single couple walked into the completely empty dining room. I was embarrassed and felt I had to apologize.

The chef of Il Cortile, who had been most gracious with advice, came for dinner. George stopped by his table.

"Wonderful place you got!" the chef said. "I would make two suggestions: get a new chef and replace the waiters."

We didn't have the nerve. Also, we were too much in love with our creation. True, we didn't care for Jacyln's stuffed eggplants and found her *fricadelle* extremely heavy, but Jaclyn insisted that they were authentically prepared and suggested that, anyway, it was a matter of personal taste. We didn't argue. After all, she was the chef, and we were neophytes.

At any rate, we seldom had time to sit down and eat. George took care of all the paperwork and tended bar at lunch and dinner. After 10:00 P.M. he worked in the kitchen, preparing a limited supper menu that we served till midnight. I hosted in the evening, kept up with inventory, ordered the wines, arranged the flowers, and daily picked up dessert from Bonté, one of New York's fanciest *pâtisseries*. We stayed till it was time to close and take out the garbage. By then it was 2:00 A.M.

There were a few patrons who liked the place well enough to come back two or three times in a row. Among them was a lady too stout to squeeze onto our banquettes. She was an enthusiastic diner, friendly and interested in everything.

One Wednesday morning, George received a phone call from a fact checker at the *New York Times*. Our restaurant was scheduled to be reviewed on Friday by the paper's reviewer, Mimi Sheraton, the lady of the banquette.

We thought of nothing else for the next two days. One star, we figured. She will give us one star. She liked our place. We were euphoric. We had been discovered! We had made our imprint on the New York restaurant scene!

Thursday night, George dashed to Times Square to get the first edition of the paper. The review was there. We read it over and over, too stupefied to comprehend it all at once:

Two other of the city's restaurants are not recommended at all. The first is
La Colombe d'Or.... Inspired by the enchanting Provence restaurant of the
same name in St.-Paul-de-Vence, this version is also enchanting in appear-
ance, with brick walls, natural wood, hanging plants and a beautiful blue
French provincial print used on upholstery. There are a few really delicious
things to eat here too, including excellent coarse, hard-crust bread, butter
aromatic with herbs, excellent Brie and chevre cheese and pastry from Bonté.
But those are the only features to be recommended, and outside of a fair fish
soup, all prepared dishes bordered on the dreadful. But because of the charm
of the decor and the publicity such a place is likely to come in for, a caveat
seemed in order.

We couldn't believe it; the blow was too hard. Trying to protect our feelings, we hung on to the shreds of positive observations and quoted things out of context: "enchanting in appearance ... beautiful ... print ... a few really delicious things to eat here ..."

We were glad for our friends at Morsa. "Unfortunately, we are a restaurant, not a designer's showroom," said George. As for the few delicious things? Store-bought, all of them.

What had gone wrong? Where had we been? I was shattered. Tomorrow morning everyone would read it in the paper. And what about the business, our investment, the dream?

"The honeymoon is over" said George. "Let's talk to Jaclyn."

Jaclyn was enraged. The reviewer was wrong, she insisted. The menu was authentic. The food was excellent. She refused to discuss changes.

The two of us sat at table four and had a glass of wine.

"It's now or never," said George. "We need a real pro in the kitchen."

"Will you tell her?"

"Yes."

"When?"

"Saturday, after service."

I was scared, but felt better. Maybe we could turn things around.

During dinner service that Saturday, I was so nervous that I could barely remember table numbers or who had ordered what drink. With a few reservations and a couple of walk-ins, we finished early.

George went into the kitchen. I stayed behind.

Jaclyn did not take the dismissal lightly. Packing her knives, she shouted and cussed, her voice carrying into the dining room. I joined George in the kitchen and watched as Jaclyn began to wrap up five tins of pâté.

"What are you doing?" asked George.

"I'm taking the pâtés home," said Jaclyn. "They are mine."

"Let her take the pâtés," I whispered.

"No," said George. "They belong to the restaurant. We have paid for the ingredients. We have paid for your labor. The pâtés stay."

And so they did.

Firing Jackie was a painful experience—the first of many difficult decisions we had to make to stay in the restuarant business.

2

Staffing
the
Kitchen

Chefs come and go. In seventeen years, we have had thirteen chefs. Some lasted three months; others five years. Some chefs quit; others got fired. Kai Hanson, our first great chef, was murdered. That was on October 28, 1977, a day engraved in our memory. Kai, who was our second chef, had been with us just a year. Within that short period he took our restaurant from an amateurish dream to a professional establishment.

Kai came to us through an employment agency specializing in the hospitality industry that George had contacted after our first chef's forced exit. Among Kai's references were a glowing letter of recommendation from the owner of a fish restaurant in Copenhagen, Kai's hometown, and an equally strong endorsement from Restaurant Associates, at whose Chicago restaurant Kai had worked for two years. Most recently, he had been a captain at Maxwell's Plum, then one of New York's most flamboyant dining spots. Kai told us he was aching to get back into the kitchen.

Looking at our menu, he said, "Nothing wrong with it. It's good. If you like, I will cook my version of it for you at your house."

We invited Antonio and Donato, our architect friends. Kai arrived at five o'clock. Three hours later, the four of us sat down and sampled the entire La Colombe d'Or menu, *à la Kai*. At the very first taste of ratatouille, we looked at one another and smiled; we smacked our lips at the fish soup and could hardly wait for Kai's roasted lamb with beans. It was our old menu, come to life with new, exciting flavors! We hired Kai that evening. He would start that Monday—December 13, 1976.

Kai did not wait till Monday. On Sunday he appeared at the restaurant and looked over his domain. He walked around the tiny kitchen, tested the equipment, shook his head, or rubbed his hands.

"No dishwashing machine?" he asked George.

"No. Marco takes care of the dishes, as well as the prep. He is a hard worker—a terrific guy from Peru."

Kai nodded. He took out a yellow pad and made notes to change the positions of the burners, the cold, prep, and waiters' pickup stations.

By seven o'clock that first Monday morning, Kai was on the phone with suppliers. He knew many of them by first name; in fact, he seemed to know everybody in the industry, particularly the chefs, cooks, managers, and captains connected with the vast empire of Restaurant Associates, which in those days included the fanciful Forum of the Twelve Caesars, Trattoria, Zum Zum, and Four Seasons. One of Kai's old buddies, Gary Reynolds, had been manager at La Fonda del Sol, one of the most colorful operations of Restaurant Associates. Gary came to La Colombe d'Or as a cook. Four months later, he became our manager—the position he really wanted, for which he was eminently qualified.

To watch Kai run the kitchen was a lesson in organization and leadership. While receiving and checking supplies, prepping the food, and maneuvering his three-man crew in the cramped quarters, he wasted not a word or a motion. Prepping took place till half an hour before service. At twelve noon, Kai changed into a clean uniform. Then he positioned himself in front of the stations. Short and stocky, with blond hair and a small, bristly mustache, giving orders in a thick Danish accent, he looked like a Nordic version of Napoleon poised for battle.

Cooking was in his blood. Without having been to France, Kai captured the essence of Provençal cuisine. Garlic sausages with warm lentils appeared on our menu; rabbit stew, infused with mushrooms and wine; roast pork with fennel; sweetbreads braised in white wine. His desserts were equally inspired: apple-raisin fritters, pears poached in brandy, hazelnut tarts, fig mousse, and a chocolate cake, the *gâteau Victoire*, that was to become our signature dessert.

We couldn't wait to sample Kai's dishes. Often, the minute we sat down to eat, Kai would come running out of the kitchen with yet another creation. "Try this. What do you think?" Twirling his mustache, he stood waiting for a response. "Tripe. Good, no? And I got it at a great price." The next time it would be monkfish, blood sausage, or fresh sardines, stuffed with bread crumbs, olives, and anchovies.

Bringing fresh herbs from the country one Monday morning, Kai placed the herb bouquet in a jar of olive oil. He also used them to flavor vinegars and vodkas—a novel concept in those days.

"Kai is like liquid sunshine," said one of our friends.

He was a perfectionist. Most of our wait staff were sweet young people, wanting to be dancers, actors, or models. Kai insisted that as long as they were in the restaurant, being professional waiters should be their first priority. He could be rough. A spotted plate, fingerprints on a glass, poorly arranged garnish, and unclear communication drove him crazy. Some waitresses were afraid of him.

Kai had his dark side. At times he could be as obscure as the Prince of Denmark. He was superstitious. A full moon made him uneasy. In one instance, he claimed that a particular waitress made the cream turn and insisted that she leave the kitchen. Interviewing new kitchen staff, his interview consisted of only two questions: "What's your favorite color?" and "What's your sign?" He had amazing success in picking winners.

I kidded him about his astrological approach and tried to find out what the magic combination was. Kai wouldn't say. But one thing was clear: George and I obviously passed muster. The three of us had an excellent rapport and enjoyed one another's company.

Occasionally, we went out together for dinner. We called it a field trip, seeing what we could learn from other people's operations. We sampled the lusty northern Italian fare at Da Silvano, a smartly trim storefront restaurant in Greenwich Village; marveled at the sleek decor at Mr. Chow, but decided we preferred the Chinese food in Chinatown. When Alain Chapel appeared as guest chef at the Four Seasons, our meal ended with Kai trading stories with Chapel. On his day off, Kai liked to take us to the Market Dining Rooms & Bar. The restaurant was located on the concourse of the World Trade Center, but its down-to-earth atmosphere and food reminded us of the restaurants around Les Halles in Paris.

At our own restaurant, Kai frequently would join us after dinner to talk shop. We were thrilled; this was what being restaurateurs was all about: picking dishes, discussing flavors, matching wines, watching trends, making plans for the future.

That future looked bright when the restaurant reviewers rediscovered us. Florence Fabricant, then the food writer for *New York* magazine, was the first.

"Despite sub-street level premises, the new Colombe d'Or does its best to suggest the setting of its charming namesake ..." read the headline in a full-page article that appeared on January 17, 1977. Praising the strong, colorful culinary accent of Provence, both in food and decor, the review stressed the informal spirit of the restaurant: "Owner Studley greets you in a sweater in the evening, jeans at lunch. No need to stop at Bloomingdale's before coming here. No need to stop at the bank, either.''

Mimi Sheraton, of the *New York Times*, was exuberant. ''Oh, what a difference a chef can make!'' she started her second review of La Colombe d'Or. Among the dishes that ''overwhelmed'' her were ''gently spiced and garlicked roast lamb with white beans, . . . cassoulet with goose, lamb and sausage, . . . choucroute garni, enriched with juices of sausage, pork, and lean streaky bacon,'' and ''the really sensational bouillabaisse.''

She gave us two stars. The famous La Côte Basque, reviewed on the same day, received one.

Business was so good that we decided to enlarge. Kai helped us design an expanded kitchen; the Morsa team set about duplicating the warm decor of our dining room on the ground floor of the adjacent store, which we leased for $250 per month, with an option to buy the building. The expansion space was in the worst possible condition—the brick walls were crumbling; the floors were giving way; the cellar was unexcavated; plumbing nonexistent. It would have been easier to build from scratch.

While the renovation was going on, we closed for the month of August, and Kai came with us on a tasting holiday in southern France. We started in Nice and worked our way across to Aix-en-Provence, via Marseille. We ate and compared every bouillabaisse, cassoulet, bourride, daube, and sorbet; noshed cheese and *socca* at the markets, and drank cassis in local bars.

We returned to New York with new ideas for the fall menu. Leo Lerman heralded our return in his dining-out column in *Vogue* magazine: ''The place to eat now is La Colombe d'Or.'' It caused a stampede, bringing Governor Carey, Mayor Koch, Betty Comden and Adolph Green, Leslie Caron, Michael York, James Beard, and members of the Kennedy family.

One month later Kai was dead. Knifed, in his apartment above the restaurant. One of our cooks, concerned when Kai did not show up at his habitual hour, discovered his body. George called the police. No light was ever shed on the murder. The shock was so shattering we thought of closing. We formulated no particular plans; we sat in the dining room and were gradually joined by the lunch wait staff. The gathering was like a wake, with everybody crying and talking about Kai. How little George and I had known about him! Supported by the dedicated staff and a fully booked house, we decided to stay open for dinner. All evening long we served the food Kai had previously prepared. None of our clients knew about the tragedy. Whenever somebody complimented me on the food, I had to run to the bathroom to hide my tears.

Around midnight George and I sat down and opened a bottle of Kai's favorite wine. Without discussing it, we knew that we would go on. We were utterly committed to the place—Kai had made us professionals.

Kim, our sous-chef, postponed his plans to relocate to San Diego and agreed to temporarily take charge of the kitchen.

In looking for a new chef, we wanted a Frenchman. We reasoned that a French chef would give our cooking added authenticity, while enabling us to speak French again. We hired Jerome and soon discovered that being French was no guarantee of excellence. Actually, Jerome was a fine cook. He came from the old school, had a solid classical background, and was very comfortable with our menu. Unfortunately, he spent more time running after waitresses than running his kitchen. For that, he relied on our sous-chef, Joe M.

Joe had a passion for food. His job application read: "My ambition is to be one of the world's great chefs." After a few months, we gave him that chance. We dismissed Jerome and made Joe chef.

Joe's food was gutsy. His greatest strength was his sauces; his beurre blanc was masterful. Jay Jacobs, the restaurant reviewer of *Gourmet*, gave La Colombe d'Or his wholehearted endorsement, waxing enthusiastic over our "toothsome *rillettes*, . . . celestial example of *soupe de poisson, morue à la provençal* and *Poussin rouennaise,*" among many other dishes.

Our problem was, Joe was disorganized; we could never be sure when the orders would come out of the kitchen. The climax occurred the day we had booked a special party for a coq au vin lunch. Twenty people were sitting at one long table, waiting for their coq au vin. They staved off hunger with bread and wine. Two hours later, there was still no coq au vin. George went into the kitchen. The coq au vin—a slow-simmering stew that needs at least three hours to cook and thus is always prepared ahead—was being cooked *à la minute*.

When Joe, an avid outdoorsman, toyed around with relocating to Alaska, we wished him luck and off he went. A year later, George got a call from a man who said, "I own the best French restaurant in the Yukon." What did we think of Joe's abilities as a chef? Joe got his reference.

A good man may be hard to find; it's also impossible to keep one down. The more ambitious and talented the chef, the more that holds true.

Our next chef of note was Kurt H. Kurt came from Zurich. Correctness, order, and protocol were part of his makeup. His kitchen ran like the proverbial Swiss watch: on time, consistent, predictable. Kurt restored order, and we breathed a sigh of relief.

But Kurt, who had a young wife and child, dreamed of a job with shorter hours and a pension plan for his family. When he received an offer to be chef at the Tower Suite, to handle their private lunch club, he left. We were sorry to see him go, but realized that the new job admirably suited him.

Chef Rick Steffann was with us the longest. He was a sweet and lovely man, a wonderful teacher and born cook. His Provençal specialties included *crêpes d'aubergines* (thin eggplant crepes filled with ricotta and spinach). *frisée aux lardons* (chicory salad with warm bacon drippings), *poulet-romarin* (chicken breast with rosemary, artichokes, and pearl onions), *boeuf en daube* (Provençal beef stew), in addition to cassoulet and bouillabaisse. His biggest dessert hit was Paris-Brest, an eye stopper of a mountainous pastry crown, filled with praline butter cream and sprinkled with grated almonds. Rick was always modest about his accomplishments —"Piece of cake," he would say.

Rick took great interest in the careers and advancement of his crew members. He often came to George saying that Tom or Peter had progressed way beyond being a line cook and was ready to move on. Rick helped them find chef jobs and stayed in touch with them.

Rick was also a Good Samaritan. He had been a medic in Vietnam and could be counted on to heal every burn and cut that needed attention. Humorous and good-natured, Rick was liked and respected by everybody in the restaurant—a considerable accomplishment, since there usually is a rivalry between the kitchen and the dining room.

Rick was generous to a fault: he paid for his girlfriend's medical studies even after she had left him; took care of his brother's hospital bills, and looked after the children of another brother. The one person he neglected was himself. He suffered from severe back pains, which seriously affected his ability to work. Ultimately Rick elected to have a tricky operation that required a very long recovery. When he was finally able to work, he decided to pick up and start fresh in Washington, D.C.

After a series of ho-hum chefs, we hired Wayne Nish. Wayne had been Anne Bass's private chef. Prior to that, he had trained at the Quilted Giraffe. He had been out of a job for four months when George's ad in the *New York Times* caught his attention. "Wayne Nish?" said our outgoing chef. "Grab him. He is tops." Years before, the two had worked at the "Quilted."

Wayne started in May 1988. In the beginning, he wasn't happy with our menu, and we weren't too happy with his cooking. While Wayne strained to develop his culinary style, we wanted to continue our classic Provençal menu. It took time for us to trust one another's abilities and intentions. We waited patiently. And then, in mid-August, Wayne cooked his interpretation of our annual Corcisan Napoleon dinner. We sat up and took note. From *chausson de légumes, macaroni à la stufatu, gigot d'agneau* with polenta, spinach, and chestnuts, on to a *sorbet au pastis* and *tarte au citron*, this was a lighter, modernized version of Corsican peasant food that would have sent the little general into battle singing.

Meanwhile, business was slow. We felt it all the more because we had to have major repair work done on our buildings, including a new roof, a face-lift for the facades, and pavement repair. The cost was prohibitive. Although Wayne cooked masterful dishes, few people knew about them. Food cost was high; morale low.

When we learned that Wayne's wife was away during August, we invited him to spend a weekend at our summer place in Sag Harbor. Just before his arrival, our Sag Harbor friend Phyllis Wright invited us for dinner. We told her we had a houseguest, namely our chef. "That could be fun," said Phyllis. "One of the other guests is Craig Claiborne."

"Craig Claiborne?" I said to George. "Maybe we shouldn't go. It sounds as if we planned it."

Of course we went, bringing Wayne, bread, and desserts from the restaurant.

Phyllis is not only a good cook, she is a clever hostess. She sat Wayne and George next to Claiborne. We ate, drank, talked into the night. Way past midnight, and after quite a bit of wine, George asked Craig how one went about getting the *Times* to review a restaurant. Bryan Miller, the *Times* restaurant critic for the past four years, had never been to our place. We were anxious to have Miller review us at this stage in our career.

The following Saturday night, Bryan Miller appeared at La Colombe d'Or. After his customary three visits, he gave his verdict on September 16, 1988: three stars!

Once again, La Colombe d'Or became an overnight hit. Three weeks after the review, Wayne gave way under the pressure. He walked out of the kitchen at the height of lunch service. "I can't do it," he said, "keep up this volume and maintain standards."

"If you leave, you're through here," said George. "No one walks out during service."

They thrashed it out, two strong people with different temperaments and ideas. By early evening, Wayne was back on the line.

With the holiday season, the pressure increased. Wayne learned to cope with success without having to compromise his culinary integrity. If anything, his cooking became even better. Clients reserved tables far in advance, anxious to taste our grilled quail with goat-cheese-and-noodle frittata or steamed shrimp with zucchini-cream and basil *pistou*.. They savored roast cod with lima beans, monkfish with eggplant and prosciutto, and braised and sautéed duck with sweet and aromatic spices, among many other menu items. We still featured ratatouille, bouillabaisse, and cassoulet, although Wayne would have preferred to take them off the menu.

Tall, handsome, erudite, Wayne glowed at the adulation of clients. Struck by the glamorous aspect of chef stardom, fueled by the media's attention, he strained for more. Four stars, the highest rating—that was his dream.

It did not coincide with ours. In fact, it clashed with our concept of La Colombe d'Or. A four-star restaurant automatically calls for a dress code and formal service. It means tablecloths, opulent flower arrangements, and Baccarat glasses. It demands a substantial wine cellar, a sommelier, an emphasis on luxury foods with prices to match.

It was clear to us that, ultimately, Wayne would seek a more appropriate stage upon which to fulfill his aspiration. We figured on a year. We got two.

Unfortunately, Wayne's May 1990 departure was marred by negotiations that had gone on behind our back. We couldn't understand Wayne's need for secrecy; his plan was so logical that we would have been the first to encourage him. He was going to open his own restaurant. His restaurant was going to be called March, because that's when the idea had become a reality.

Excited, Wayne had told the press, and then, a few hours before the story would break, he told us. Not surprisingly, he took two of our cooks with him.

Fortunately, this time, the economic situation had changed, and there were many more talented chefs out there than seasoned restaurateurs. Not just in New York, but all over the country. With money getting tight, people were going out less. Restaurants that had been the height of fashion a short while ago closed—partly because they could not afford the rent, partly because people shunned trendy places in favor of value. For the first time in many years, top chefs were out of a job.

It was tempting to hire one of them. But we decided against it, because the obvious choice was standing in the wings like the proverbial gifted understudy waiting for the reigning diva to take sick. Mark May, our talented sous-chef, who had been running lunch for two years, was more than ready.

Mark was most familiar with our menu; in fact, a number of dishes and garnishes had been his contributions. Like us, he was an ardent Francophile. Born in Lexington, Kentucky, Mark had perfected his culinary skills as chef at Château de la Chèvre d'Or, the one-star Michelin-rated restaurant in the hillside town of Eze in southern France, and at La Salière, a bistro-style restaurant in Monte Carlo. While cooking at La Salière, Mark had spent extra hours "clerking" in Alain Ducasse's legendary kitchen of the Louis XV, the ultimate restaurant showcase, at the Hôtel de Paris.

Among the many applicants for sous-chef we chose Hal Kennedy. Hal had recently returned from an extended stay in Indonesia. He impressed us with his refreshing modesty and a no-nonsense attitude toward cooking.

29

"There are only three restaurants in New York I want to work for," he said. "This is one of them." We didn't ask him about the other two. Our instinct was right: the self-trained Hal was a talented and most imaginative cook.

After having tried a number of pastry chefs, we settled on Joyce Wong. Looking like a porcelain doll, Joyce had the stamina of an ox and the patience of a Buddha. Her physical strength was bolstered by the karate lessons she took; her patience was tried as she vied with the morning cooks for precious oven space. Sugarplum fairy that she was, Joyce could always count on her walnut squares and chocolate triangles to melt the heart of any cook, including chef Mark.

After a year of this glorious triumvirate it became obvious that this was a luxury we could no longer afford. The economy had gone from bad to worse. Business now was down by 40 percent. With food and labor costs as high as ever, we started losing more than $10,000 a month. Reluctantly, we let Joyce and Hal go. For a while Mark carried the load by himself, working both lunch and dinner shifts. It was hardly his idea of a chef's bliss; nor did we think it was right for him.

George, who had a special fondness for Mark, offered him a piece of the business, trusting that times would change. Mark was flattered, but declined. Without ever having fought, we had an uneasy peace. No one was happy. We waited for Mark to make a move; he waited for us. George and I had two topics of conversation: our dwindling finances and Mark May.

"It's not working out," said George. "We'll have to look for another chef."

When we told Mark, he was relieved. He had been looking at various spaces to open his own place.

Again, George put an ad in the *New York Times*. "... well-established French restaurant is looking for a chef ready to do the impossible: work long hours, create high-quality food while maintaining a realistic food cost."

Out of five plausible replies, that of Najib Zougari stood out. Born and trained in Tangier, Najib had worked as sous-chef to Gray Kuntz at the Peninsula Hotel. Prior to that, he had worked with Jacques Chibois and Jean-Michel Diot at Maxim's. After a preliminary interview, George suggested Najib have lunch at the restaurant and study the menu. Next, we asked him to cook his idea of a lunch at our house. Najib appeared at the appointed hour. Taking nothing for granted, he brought his own equipment, every item of food, and a bottle of wine.

Our apartment kitchen is minuscule, tailored exclusively for our need for breakfast. I watched Najib work. He was precise, fast, and meticulous. When he asked me about the oven, I realized that it had broken down about a year ago, and, since I never use it, I had not bothered to have it fixed. My neighbor agreed that we could use her oven. By the time George came, lunch was ready. Najib, who had helped me set the table, handed us his menu:

Chilled Tomato Soup with Crabmeat and Chives
Braised Baby Artichokes tossed with Coriander
Fillet of Salmon with Spring Vegetables
Fresh Strawberries with zest of Lime

It was the perfect summer meal: elegant, light, and beautifully flavored. The salmon was overdone by one minute. I never told our neighbor.

By the time we had tasted the artichoke salad, George and I knew that Najib was our man. We told him after the dessert.

"Najib," said George. "A beautiful name, but hard to pronounce. Would you mind if we called you Naj?"

"I don't mind. Naj sounds good."

"There is one other thing," said George. "I assume you are a Muslim. Helen and I are Jewish. Is that a problem?"

"No problem," said Naj.

"No problem" could be Naj's middle name. Working double shifts, coming in on Sunday, training new people, preparing high-quality food without undue delay, responding to special requests, listening to suggestions, willing to experiment, cheerful, and respected, nothing is ever a problem with Naj.

Supporting Naj is the rest of the kitchen brigade. Over the years, an army of unsung prep and line cooks have served us faithfully. Some, like Peter Hoffman, have opened their own restaurants. Others, like Jean, succumbed to the classic French malaise of *le foie*, said to be caused by too much drink.

Jean's background was obscure. Because he was called Jean le Bourguignon-Burgundian by his cronies, we assumed he came from Burgundy. Joel, one of our fleeting chefs, had met Jean at one of the French bars that used to line 9th Avenue near the pier of the French Line. Rumor had it that Jean had jumped ship. He was a middle-aged man, whose weatherbeaten face was dominated by a massive, glowing red nose. Jean was practically illiterate, but he possessed a shrewd peasant wisdom that served him extremely well. He always started his morning shift by hurling a string of profanities at the ovens.

"Once I straighten them out, they listen to me for the rest of the day," he told George, whom Jean respectfully called Monsieur George.

George had a weak spot for Jean, who, by George's own admission, made him feel like a *patron* in a Jean Gabin movie. When Jean, who lived exclusively on beer without ever showing signs of being affected, was hospitalized, George visited him regularly. Shortly before his death, Jean presented George with the only memento he had kept from his past: a rather ugly-looking wooden replica of a life-size gull, which is now sitting in George's office.

Moises and Carlos have been line cooks ever since Rick taught them to cook. Both work the grill: Carlos in the morning, Moises in the evening. I am so used to their flawless timing, I can tell when another cook has prepared my grilled meat or fish. Knowing our repertoire by heart, the two of them have provided much needed continuity during the comings and goings of our illustrious chefs. In a pinch, they'll jump in and assist at other stations.

The kitchen is divided into three basic stations: grill, sauté, and the cold station. The lineup, meaning the cooks who line up or work at these stations, requires a minimum of three cooks: one for each station. The grill cook also mans the fryer and the two ovens; the sauté cook operates burners —twelve in all—the salamander, and the steam table. The salamander is used for broiling; the steam table keeps the sauces warm. The cold-station cook, also called garde-manger, is in charge of handling all cold dishes, as well as putting the finishing touches on desserts. In addition, there are two microwave ovens, used to quick-heat anything from a cassoulet to a chocolate dessert.

During our banner years, the lineup consisted of a sous-chef, four line cooks, four prep cooks, two dishwashers, plus the pastry and the executive chefs. Wayne and Mark seldom worked on the line. They either expedited —calling out orders that had to be fired, restaurantese for "prepared"— or they walked around the dining room. Dressed in whites, their name embroidered on their jacket, they exchanged information with clients and accepted their compliments. The kitchen crew worked one shift each—one crew for lunch, another for dinner.

In leaner times—like today—the chef works the line, usually at the sauté station, from which he also expedites. He and the cold-station cook work double shifts. Since the grill station is the hottest and toughest station in the kitchen, grill cooks work one shift only.

Everybody preps, including the dishwashers and Julio, our steward and butcher. Julio started as a dishwasher eight years ago. From dishwasher he moved to prep, where it soon became apparent that Julio was a born butcher. Good butchering means two things: obtain the most tender cuts of meat, fish, and fowl; and strive for a minimum amount of waste. Bent over a large fillet of salmon, extracting stray bones with a pair of pincers, Julio looks like a surgeon concentrating on his task. To watch Julio tackle a slab of calf's liver or a side of beef is akin to observing a sculptor carving shapes from stone. Everything is done at record speed; half an hour into cutting up chicken and ducks, the kitchen pans are overflowing with legs, thighs, breasts, wings, necks, and carcasses for future stock. Every portion of salmon is weighed, wrapped, and stored in the walk-in. The same with other fish and individual meat cuts. The cooks depend completely on Julio's *mis en place*.

Julio comes from San Salvador. When he smiles, which he does frequently, he displays an impressive set of gold teeth—worth a small fortune, according to George.

Julio starts his shift before seven o'clock in the morning. While waiting for deliveries, he scrubs and cleans, minds the stockpots, and has been known to bake an occasional cake or two. When our dishwasher didn't show up one Saturday, Julio brought his kid brother, José. George hired José on the spot. That was about a year ago. Like his brother, José is bright, thorough, and fast. Naj has already given him some evening prep shifts. Moises, our Bolivian grill cook who started his rise in similar fashion, keeps a benevolent eye on José.

La Colombe d'Or participates in the New York Restaurant School's externship program. Similar to the internship of medical students, the externship requires advanced students of the Restaurant School to work a total of 280 hours in a professional kitchen to gain practical experience prior to graduation. It was Wayne, an alumnus of the New York Restaurant School, who knew about the program and initiated the exchange. Students may express preference where they would like to work. We are always in great demand. The reason for our popularity is based on our reputation for really teaching. Far from just letting students prep vegetables, our chefs take them through the entire gamut of kitchen operation, from making fresh pasta to turning out a well-executed veal chop.

We, in turn, benefit from these students. For one thing, they provide an extra pair of hands, particularly appreciated in today's tight market. It also gives us first crack at a promising future cook. By the time we get a student, his or her aptitude for the profession, or lack of it, is apparent.

So it was with Greg. Greg, a skinny young man from Queens, came to us during the fall of 1991. From the way he peeled shallots to his grip on a sauté pan, he showed promise. But he looked sloppy.

"You want to be a cook?" George asked him.

"Yes, sir," said Greg.

"Then don't wipe your hands on a clean apron," said George. "Here." George handed Greg a clean kitchen towel. "Learn to use these. There are plenty of them around."

The next day Greg showed up with a spanking-clean uniform, two kitchen towels tucked at his apron.

On his last day of internship we offered him a job. He now works on the line as garde-manger.

"Let me show you," he says to Anna-Maria, our new student from the Restaurant School. He adjusts one stray leaf of arugula and wipes the rim of the salad plate.

Anna-Maria nods approval. In her two weeks with us, she has shown definite potential.

"I want to be a chef," she says.

3

Managing the Restaurant

Managing La Colombe d'Or is an unending task. It starts early in the morning and ends after midnight, and, as George says, "Sometimes not even then." He refers to the times when the restaurant's alarm system goes off during the middle of the night. Usually it's nothing. But then again, we never know. The one time we decided against using the alarm, burglars came in from the roof and walked out the front door with a four-hundred-pound safe.

The management routine includes preparing the payroll and bank deposits; drawing up operating manuals for special events and private parties; making weekly schedules; supervising maintenance of equipment; keeping track of china, glass, and flatware; ordering disposable items, from toilet paper to dishwashing detergent; and keeping an up-to-date list of everything in the restaurant. This list, with close to three hundred food items, helps the kitchen to establish what we have to have in the house at any time on any day.

A similar inventory is kept of liquor, wine, and nonalcoholic beverages. Carrying one hundred different wines, with at least one case of each in-house, plus three to five cases for the more popular ones, means keeping track of more than one thousand bottles of wine, in addition to the spirits.

The bartenders tally up all wines and liquors sold during their shifts. Those sales are deducted from the latest inventory every morning—a job that may be carried out by the day bartender, the maître d', or whoever is assigned that post. George or the beverage manager keeps the wine list up to date and does the reordering.

Our wine cellar is in the basement. It is an attractive space with exposed brick, a wooden header, and a domed ceiling. When we had it excavated, we had visions of holding intimate wine tastings there. I had imagined candlelight. It never happened. We are far too busy keeping up with deliveries, checking all incoming orders, and storing them properly.

We stock a three days' supply of red wines in wine racks next to the bar. A three days' supply of champagne and white wines are kept in the basement cooler. Wine cellar and cooler are under lock and key. The bartender on duty has the key; we keep a spare one in the safe. Once Mike Adams, our day bartender, took the key home. George, the only one who, besides the bookkeeper, knows the combination to the safe, had just left.

37

We persuaded clients to drink red wine till we could reach either Mike or George to unlock the whites.

George, who lives closer, was the first one to arrive. Not too happy either. The next day he initiated a different security system.

Is there a mistake we haven't made? Sometimes we wonder.

No doubt, the most crucial task in restaurant management is to establish the restaurant's break-even figure and to keep within that budget. For no matter how good the food, or how pleasant the ambience, if the business doesn't exceed break-even, it will not survive.

As the term implies, break-even is that weekly number reached after deducting fixed costs (such as rent, labor, power, fuel, and so on) and cost of sales (such as produce, fish, meat, and wine) from gross sales (gross receipts less tax and tip. . . . . cost is $15,000. The equation for our break-even . . . . . .

$$\frac{\text{Fixed Cost}}{\text{Total Sales}} = \frac{\text{Gross Profit \%}}{100\%} \text{ or } \frac{\$15,000}{\$21,500} = \frac{70.25\%}{100\%}$$

WEEKLY SALES

FOOD	(75% of sales)	$16,125
BEVERAGES	(25% of sales)	$ 5,375
TOTAL SALES		$21,500

COST OF SALES

FOOD	(29% food cost)		($ 4,676)
BEVERAGES	(32% beverage cost)		($ 1,720)
less TOTAL COST-OF-SALES	29.75%		($ 6,396)
GROSS PROFIT	70.25%		$15,104
less FIXED COSTS			$15,000
NET PROFIT (LOSS)			$ 104

The chart tells us that we need to sell $21,500 at a 30-percent cost of sales to meet our break-even of $15,000. If our cost of sales increases from 30 percent to 32 percent, we would have to sell $22,058 to cover our overhead. If, on the other hand, our cost of sales went down to 28 percent, we would make a profit.

George makes his food-budget projection every Monday. He bases it on how many covers—meals served—he estimates we will do that week, including scheduled parties. Taking our $41-check average into account, he comes up with his budget for the week. Posted on the bulletin board, and carefully explained, it tells the chef how much money he can spend on his purchases for that week.

But a restaurant's objective and a chef's point of view do not necessarily coincide. While we try to run a business that at least should pay all our bills, chefs want to shine. They dream up dishes that call for New Zealand baby lamb, exotic mushrooms, and truffle oil, luxury items that can send the budget through the roof. We could be packed every night and lose our shirts.

It is within this area that a chef earns his stripes: knowing what's in the house and utilizing it imaginatively; taking advantage of local produce; purchasing wisely; having the purveyors on your side. Given the proper training and a certain aptitude, anybody can be a good cook. Beyond being a good cook with flair and imagination, a chef has to demonstrate strong leadership ability and possess a solid business sense.

Even more crucial, it takes a very levelheaded businessman to see a restaurant through periods of glory as well as hard times. George is such a man. But even his projected sales figures can be off. A snowstorm on a Saturday night, a rave review of another restaurant in the area, an important social or political event, immediately throw the projected sales out of line. Clients don't show up, often without canceling, leaving the chef with much perishable food.

That's why private parties are such a blessing. Booked in advance and held under deposit, they present some stability in a fickle business.

Nothing can be taken for granted, however. Just when everything seems under control, something unforeseen happens: the compressor breaks down, Con Edison has a major blowout, somebody forgets to put the heat on overnight and the pipes freeze.

Sometimes I feel I'm married to a doctor who is on call twenty-four hours a day. I'll be dressed, ready to meet George at a concert, when the phone will ring.

"Sorry, the Krauss party arrived with so many extra people, we'll have to put them downstairs. I can't leave now. Go on ahead. If I can, I'll meet you in the lobby during intermission."

Once, we were packed, ready to take the seven o'clock flight to Paris, when George called from the restaurant.

"Gary is sick. He just went to the doctor. I don't know how serious it is. There is a chance we may have to postpone the trip."

We never took that trip, because Gary, who was our first manager, returned with the news that he would have to go to the hospital. We were not sure about the nature of his illness. He died of AIDS a year later.

We have had three managers: Gary Reynolds, Joe Scalice, and our son, Jonathan. Each had his strong points and left his mark. Gary was unruffled and calm. Elegant and meticulous, Gary was as concerned with the restaurant's appearance as with his own. He had a wonderful rapport with the staff and acted as their spokesman. Slightly cynical, even arrogant at times, he maintained a certain aloofness; he did not fraternize.

Under Gary, there was a marvelous feeling of solidarity—a sense of family, of caring. We functioned like a mini–feudal society; everybody was in his or her place; everybody fitted into the system and was taken care of.

Gary, who had a background in show business, loved arranging parties for the "family." Every August, there was a big outing: two summers in a row we went sailing around Manhattan on a reconstructed commercial schooner. The kitchen supplied the food and the dining room staff brought beer, wine, and picnic gear. At another time, we went to Atlantic City on a gambling spree. One summer, George and I invited the "family" to our house in Sag Harbor, where we staged a picnic, boat rides, nature walks, a fiercely competitive baseball game, and a clambake. Once we went apple picking on my brother-in-law's farm.

When he learned that our prep cook, Emilio, a passionate soccer player, was playing in a soccer match, Gary rented a minibus that took us to Long Island to root for Emilio. On Oscar night, when Hollywood presents its award extravaganza, Gary staged a late-night Oscar party at the restaurant, with lottery prizes for the one who, by secret ballot, had predicted the winners.

In all matters Gary had the assistance of Leila, our maître d'. Leila had come to us fresh from Paris. In her early days, Leila looked more like a Toulouse-Lautrec dancer than a chic Parisian. From the very beginning, however, there was something special about her. Leila's openness, her work ethic, and her stamina were contagious. Leila blossomed as she went from being a waitress to hostess to maître d'. She worked at La Colombe d'Or twelve years, till she could finally afford to give up her daily one-hour commute to and from New York, two years after she and her husband had bought a house in Morristown, New Jersey.

Leila not only took care of "her" staff and "her" clients, she physically took care of the restaurant. She sewed curtains and made the banquette covers with Provençal fabric sent by her mother; she painted the bathrooms, stenciled the tiles, made flower arrangements, and acted as official restaurant photographer. Extremely kindhearted, she looked after her girls. When Georgina, our West African cook, became pregnant, Leila took her in until Georgina could figure out what to do about her vagrant lover and her coming child. When one of our waitresses who had been dismissed for using drugs needed a temporary home, Leila provided it. Leila lent money as well as moral support to everybody who asked for it.

At the same time, she ran a very tight dining room and never lost track of the fact that her loyalty was with the house. It was Leila who told us that Rick's back problem was so acute that he barely was able to function at times. Gary would never have faced up to the problem. Taking care of unpleasant tasks or troubleshooting was not part of his makeup. Faced with a difficult situation, Gary withdrew and became passive.

It frustrated George.

"Do I really need Gary?" he often wondered. "We could save a lot of money."

But George knew that Gary provided stability. Living in the apartment above the restaurant, he acted as our eyes and ears. His presence enabled us to take our trips to Europe and spend weekends in Sag Harbor, confident that the restaurant was running smoothly.

41

When Joe Scalice first appeared, he had only minor experience. But he was ambitious and eager to prove himself. He learned fast and was so eternally cheerful that we called him Mr. Sunny Provence.

As Gary's health deteriorated, Joe, who by then had become a valuable waiter, took over more and more of Gary's responsibilities. Joe threw himself into the job; the bigger the challenge, the more he liked it. George barely had to mention what needed to be taken care of, and it was done. Kitchen and dining room ran harmoniously. When the restaurant rose to overnight fame, thanks to that three-star rating, Joe was up to it. George liked Joe immensely and depended on him. His unexpected departure was particularly painful.

Our son Jonathan's willingness to come back East to help us out meant a great deal. Jonathan had been food-and-beverage manager of a big motel chain in Portland, Oregon. He had all the right qualifications for the job. He was strong and confident and, as always, fun to be with. The year he spent with us was filled with fondness and respect.

Jonathan was an unmistakable doer, but sometimes more in words than in deeds. Talking about a problem and suggesting a remedy, he could just as easily convince himself that just talking about the problem would solve it.

Jonathan and Mark got along well; both had the same sense of humor. Without it, they might easily have been at each other's throats, because there is a constant pull between operational reality and artistic ambition.

As a matter of routine, Jonathan used to call Mark early in the morning to discuss the kitchen that day. If supplies, kitchen staff, and equipment were operating normally, Mark arrived after lunch, which was run by the sous-chef. At the slightest signal of a problem, Mark got on his motorcycle and appeared within five minutes.

Mark loved his motorcycle, a Yamaha, with its 120 horsepower, capable of doing 180 miles an hour.

"Gives me nightmares just thinking of Mark driving such a powerful machine in this city," said Jonathan.

"Sour grapes," according to Mark. "Jon would give his right arm to own one these machines."

Jonathan loved action. He also had a flair for drama.

"Crisis?" he said. "You want to hear about crisis? It is part of my routine. I'll be busy verifying yesterday's cash and charge slips, tabulating the credit-card slips for payment, when I find out that the ice-making machine broke down. Or I'll be in the middle of checking invoices, when the coat-check girl calls in sick, the air conditioner goes on the blink, or I get hit with a flood in the basement."

Jonathan's strength was with people. Presidents of major companies and timid elderly ladies responded equally well to his attention. He excelled at arranging private parties and went after them aggressively. He kept a manual of past parties, noting special requests, and stayed in touch with the people involved. He knew what menu worked best for any given occasion and how to orchestrate the event. Efficient with business parties, Jonathan sparkled when faced with the challenge of a special event.

"People are spending a lot of money on a feeling," he said. "They may be celebrating a once-in-a-lifetime occasion. It's up to us to provide that experience, to make it come true."

A bit of a showman himself, he made surprise parties his forte. Among his proudest achievements was Dr. Nichols's party for his wife's birthday. The surprise scheme was as follows: while on their way to visit friends for dinner, the couple's car would "break down" in front of la Colombe d'Or. Dr. Nichols would ask his wife to go into the restaurant to call AAA. When Mrs. Nichols walked into the restaurant, she would be directed to the pay phone on top of the landing, right in front of the Napoleon Room, where twenty-four of her assembled friends would shout "SURPRISE!"

To ensure the success of the party, Jonathan picked his crew carefully, trying to match the efficiency and temperament of the waiters with the tone of the evening. And the Nicholses' surprise was a triumph.

But every so often the best-laid plans come undone. It happened when a party of twenty-six was celebrating the tenth anniversary of their company. The serving team was Jeff and Pamela, ace waiters who work particularly well together. Elflike in appearance, Pamela moved like a ballet dancer. She was as fast as a weasel and small enough to squeeze between the tables. Jeff, on the other hand, was built like a football player. Called Big J by the staff, he could balance an overloaded tray on one hand while tackling a dozen dirty dishes with the other.

"It will be an easy party," Jonathan had told them. "The same menu for everybody and champagne throughout the evening."

Champagne it was for everybody, including Jeff, who, in the seven months he had been with us, had never been seen to touch alcohol. Pamela watched anxiously as Jeff bumped into chairs, slammed down plates, and wove in and out of the room.

"I think we have to take Jeff off the floor," Pamela alerted our hostess, Jackie.

With a full house and guests arriving, Jackie had neither time nor waiter to spare. Still, she followed Pamela upstairs. Jeff had taken off his tie and loosened the buttons on his shirt collar.

"Hi, Jackie," he shouted. "Have a drink."

Jackie gently nudged Jeff out of the room and down the stairs, worrying that Big J might lose his balance and come crashing onto her. Safely downstairs, she pressed the intercom to Jonathan's apartment upstairs. Jonathan, who had put in thirteen hours of work, put on jacket and tie, ready for action. He put Jeff into a cab, telling him to pick up his gear the next morning.

The people at the party never noticed that there had been a problem. But Jonathan had to reevaluate his staff. He also had to hire a replacement for Jeff.

Hiring waiters, we follow a standard procedure. It starts by placing an ad in the *New York Times*. We used to advertise in the *Village Voice*. The result was a deluge of phone inquiries, few of which ever resulted in a waiter or waitress with the proper experience or personality to work at our restaurant. Advertising in the *Times* we receive half the number of calls, but considerably more qualified people. After the initial telephone screening, we schedule appointments. We do not necessarily look for an impressive restaurant portfolio, but for friendly people with a good attitude and reasonable intelligence. Presentability and poise count a lot.

The acting manager or maître d' does the preliminary interviewing. Each applicant fills out a questionnaire. Part of the questionnaire contains common restaurant terms that we ask applicants to identify. It's amazing how many people claim solid dining room experience but do not know the most basic menu and kitchen terms. Frankness is a prerequisite. George,

44

who has a gift for seeing people's true natures, prefers to hire a novice to an arrogant experienced waiter.

Every waiter, no matter how experienced, starts by trailing. "Trailing" literally means following a senior waiter, becoming his shadow and observing how we do things. Next, the trainee trails and assists the food runner, which enables the new waiter to become familiar with the mechanics and rhythm of our service. Following this period, the trainee spends a few shifts in the kitchen, watching how the chef plates each dish. Then it's back to the dining room for a stint at the dessert-and-coffee station.

Before we hire a new waiter, we ask our established crew what they think about him or her. Their observations and gut feelings most definitely influence our final decision.

Even with all these precautions, the process is not foolproof. Some waiters are whizzes in setting up tables, but are tongue-tied with clients. Others have a great rapport with clients, but forget to place orders, can't remember who gets what, and pour water into wineglasses. Ace waiters have lost their cool at the height of service, throwing a fit because they have to wait for a drink order to be filled or a check to be processed.

Waiters quit. Some realize that, contrary to what they thought, New York is too much for them. For others, working as a waiter is just a way of making money, a stepping-stone toward their chosen career. A few leave because they can make more money at a restaurant with higher volume.

It takes a lot to be a good waiter: skill, strength, a sense of humor, and empathy for people. The wishes of clients—from special requests to speed —often clash with the priorities of the chef, or the policy of the house. Even violence happens. Years ago, one client, actor Ed Asner, got so impatient, he grabbed his waiter by the tie and, nearly choking him, yelled, "Where is my food? You better bring it now!" The poor waiter was so shaken, he decided that waiting on tables was not for him.

Waiters used to tell us horror stories about what was going on in some restaurants: how a chef would not warn a waiter he disliked that the plate he was about to pick up was scalding hot; that waiters, in turn, would take revenge by pouring pepper into a dish before serving it to a customer. I remember a scene at La Caravelle, years before we owned La Colombe d'Or, in which the captain and a customer were ready for a fistfight, apparently over a misunderstanding about the tip.

Part of the manager's job is making up the weekly schedule for the dining room staff, which, according to Jonathan, "can be more complicated than planning a presidential campaign." Requesting special stations, preferred shifts, more hours, fewer hours, staff members have been known to act like prima donnas. As a rule, senior people get the more desirable shifts, such as evenings, when tips tend to be higher, and weekends, because there is more volume.

Our wait staff, including the bartender, share equally in the tips—a system that pleases them and assures that everyone will do his or her share. Those who do not, do not last long.

On a busy night, waiters can easily make $125 in tips. From their point of view, the fewer servers on the floor, the more tip money. From the management point of view, the more waiters on the floor, the smoother and more efficient the service. The trick is to strike a just balance.

George strongly believes in giving people responsibilities, what is now called employee empowerment. He has a good instinct about people's potential. Over the years, coat-check girls have become hostesses; waiters have become wine stewards or maître d's. Each is put in charge of his or her station. George calls it depth of management.

"I don't want to be a slave to the cash register," he says. "Once I realized that I could separate myself from it, I had more fun."

His trust usually pays off. The people in responsible positions pride themselves in doing their job. We depend on them.

When people ask him how he can possibly absent himself from the premises, he says, "My presence is felt."

And is it ever! According to the staff, it's George, not God, who is in the details. Sometimes they imitate George's morning routine: straightening out the coat hangers, making sure that cooks wear clean Band-Aids covered with protective gloves, pouring salt on the dining room floor to prevent our Provençal tiles from becoming slippery. George is equally bothered by a crooked hanging picture or a waitress's stray hair. Occasional lipstick marks on glasses are a problem.

"Today's lipsticks stick like glue," he says. "The chemicals in the dishwashing machine can't always get rid of the stains. Besides, wineglasses should not be so sanitized that they smell like a hospital." Cham-

46

pagne glasses are even more difficult to clean. Ideally, George would like women customers to wear neither lipstick nor perfume.

"Strong perfumes overwhelm the subtle flavors of most dishes, while the oil of lipstick kills the sparkle of champagne."

Before each service, all glasses are hand steamed over a coffeepot with boiling-hot water, then towel dried. The job takes two waiters at least half an hour. Watching them forever having to double-check those glasses, I understand the practice of smashing used glasses in Imperial Russia—it's one way of not having to deal with finger marks or lipstick.

At that, the life span of a glass is short-lived: four weeks at most. Some glasses break on their way to or from the dishwasher; most casualties are caused by the waiters. Not just one glass at a time, but an entire trayful —an occurrence that happens most frequently on slow nights when waiters tend to get sloppy.

George has a theory that dishes and glasses seem to disappear whenever a server gets a roommate or moves to another apartment. I can't believe it. But George should know; he okays the reordering and pays the bills.

Before each shift, the maître d', George, or I inspect the staff. Nothing can be taken for granted.

"Emma, your apron has spots. Please put on a clean one.

"Kevin, roll down your sleeves.

"Xavier, your shoes are dirty."

It reminds me of when our children were little and had to be told to blow their noses and wash their hands.

Every evening after service the kitchen is scrubbed down until it could pass Marine inspection. Germs, health, and safety are constantly on George's mind.

Once a month we prepare the entire premise for the exterminator. All glasses, china, and silverware are removed; tables stripped; liquor, wines, coffees, and sundry food or drink items stashed away.

Our contract with the exterminator guarantees that we will be roach free for the next thirty days. Four days later, as I present the dessert to two women at table three, I see a cockroach crawling up the banquette. One of the women sees it too.

47

"Oh, my God!" she cries.

I don't blame her. I offer to comp her meal. She accepts. According to our contract, the exterminator will reimburse us. We have rarely exercised that option. First, because such incidents do not happen often, and second, we hate having to substantiate our claim.

Some clients show remarkable understanding. "It's New York," they say.

"It's a nightmare," says George.

Years ago George initiated the practice of providing comment cards to clients at the end of the meal. Reading them gives us a fairly good idea of how our public sees us. It also helps pinpoint weak features and alerts us in case there is a problem.

"Dear Helen and George—we love your restaurant. This is our third visit. The food was superb. Our waitress was a delight. We will be back soon."

"Best bouillabaisse in town."

"The cassoulet was too dry."

"Why did you drop the monkfish from the menu? It was my favorite dish."

"The mussels were sandy."

"Great meal. We particularly enjoyed the mussels."

"Formidable!"

We average fifteen comment cards per service, most of them complimentary. We realize, of course, that clients who do not enjoy their meal may not bother to tell us about it. We wish they would, because every complaint brought to our attention is followed through by George. He first finds out what actually happened on the floor or in the kitchen and then communicates with the client. If there is a serious grievance, George will invite the client to return as our guest.

Occasionally, a client will call and complain that one of our dishes caused him to be ill.

"I had your pasta with mushrooms and rabbit sausage and was sick all night."

George expresses concern and promises to get back to the caller. Although we sold fifteen pasta dishes, this is the only complaint. George talks to the chef: the sausages had been delivered that morning. George calls the sausage maker.

"We are under closer scrutiny by the USDA health inspectors than anybody in this business," says the sausage maker. "Maybe the lady wasn't used to eating so much at night. Happens, you know?"

George is not about to tell that to the woman when he calls her back. "I am very concerned," he emphasizes, "but there seems no cause for alarm. What can I do to make you feel more at ease?"

"It's okay," replies the woman. "Actually, I feel much better. Maybe I ate too much." She returns a week later and signs up with our Frequent-Diner Program.

The Frequent-Diner Program was George's idea, inspired by the airlines' frequent-flier program. The decision to initiate our own program, however, was a reaction to the discount charge-card companies, among them IGT, LeCard, Travel World Leisure Club, and Transmedia, which lure diners with tempting discounts. To have us participate in their program, Transmedia offered to prepurchase ten thousand dollars' worth of meals from us for their members. In exchange, we would give Transmedia meal credits for twice that amount. Transmedia cardholders would be billed by Transmedia, which would give them a 25 percent discount, exclusive of tax and tip, on every meal consumed in a participating restaurant.

It sounded tempting: we could use the offered sum toward advertising. Still—"Two for one?" said George. "On top of it, we compete with everybody else. Advertising reaches too broad a market. Maybe we should target a discount program directly to our clients."

We started our Frequent-Diner Program in October 1991. George printed application cards. "Our plan is simple," the card read. "With every meal that you buy at La Colombe d'Or, you earn 10% of your net check. You can redeem this bonus in increments of $50.00 towards lunch or dinner."

"What a nice idea," said our clients.

Within three months we had more than eight hundred applicants. Today we have three thousand frequent diners on our list; the number keeps growing. Many customers have already cashed in three or four bonuses. We are delighted.

Entering names and keeping track of clients' accumulated bonus earnings keeps a clerical assistant occupied a few hours a day. But George loves computers. He enters his calculations, makes projections, assembles data, revises the menu, updates the wine list, prints out the reservation sheet, sends personal letters, writes memos.

"Look at this," he'll say.

He'll show me a spread sheet with drafts in three different colors. I am impressed, but not engaged. Statistics are not my strength. I am good with our public, cultivating the social aspect of the business. It's what George likes least. He does not mind the endless hours he puts in taking care of anything from drawing up a special marketing campaign to meeting with a kitchen repairman. Unless there is a special event, big party, or personal engagement, come seven o'clock in the evening, George likes to go home.

"I must have spoken to one hundred and fifty people," he'll say. "Now it's your turn."

I'll have been home all day, working on the book, writing articles, composing our newsletter, researching recipes, preparing seminars, occasionally reviewing a cookbook. I am ready for action. Greeting people, making them feel welcome, explaining our dishes—I think I have the fun job. By the time I return home, George wants to hear how the evening went. Vibrating with excitement, I used to spill everything: "We overbooked; people had to wait half an hour for their table. It was a nightmare." "Twenty no-shows; we must have turned at least fifteen people away! I think we should ask people to reconfirm." "The new waiter hasn't been sufficiently briefed on how we write the dupes. He really fouled us up."

Over the years I have learned to restrict my stories to the more positive ones, leaving grievances and complaints for the morning. Over breakfast, we talk.

"I think it's time to change the garnish on the salmon. Any suggestions?" asks George.

"People seem to be eating more meat. What do you think about including a pork dish on the menu?"

"I want you to try the venison tonight. Tell me what you think."

"Eric was very abrasive last night. A bit off-the-wall."

"Did you straighten him out?"

"There really was no time. What do you think about serving the fettuccine without the sausage? People keep asking for a vegetarian dish."

"I want to hear about Eric. What about him?"

I don't have an answer. George is annoyed. Fortunately, not for long.

"About the fettuccine—it's one of our most popular dishes. As for the vegetarians, we are not a health-food restaurant." George checks his watch. "I'll have to leave. The accountant is coming. Do you have the release for the Valentine's dinner? It should go out today. Also, let's start working on the next newsletter."

"Okay. What about the benefit for God's Love? Who do you think should be the guest of honor?"

"I don't know. Maybe Paula Wolfert. What do you think?"

Sometimes I worry that all George and I ever talk about is food. Are we turning into food dodoes? I wonder.

But then again, food is constantly on my mind.

It's Sunday morning. George and I are sailing on Long Island Sound. I stretch out on the deck, catching a cool breeze, and watch the overhead clouds. I recall a sail while living in Antibes. We anchored in front of Eden Roc on Cap d'Antibes and had lunch. I wouldn't swear to it, but I'm sure we started with mussels.

In my mind, I am planning another trip. The southern part of Brittany, perhaps. All those unknown restaurants to visit; all that marvelous food to taste. New cookbooks, new people.

I can't wait.

4

How We Serve a Meal

$\mathscr{The}$ word "restaurateur" comes from the French *restaurer*—"to restore." That's why people eat out—to be indulged, to be restored. This is the contract between a restaurateur and the public. We are accountable to our clients; so is every member of our staff. Together, we are a team, performing like a theater company. George is producer; the chef, the director. The players are divided into two sections: those that work in the back of the house, or the kitchen, and those that work in the front of the house, the dining room. Combined, they consist of chef, sous-chef, pastry chef; four line cooks, one steward, two prep men, two dishwashers; two bartenders, two hostesses, two coat-check girls, eight full-time waiters and waitresses, two extras, two runners. The script is our menu.

Show time begins at twelve noon Monday through Friday for lunch, and again at six o'clock for dinner, seven nights a week.

At lunch, the restaurant resembles a club, frequented by publishers, editors, and advertising executives who work in nearby offices. Many come two or three times a week, bringing their clients. On some days almost every table is cluttered with manuscripts and contracts, making it difficult for the waiters to find space for the bread, butter, and tapenade that we serve before the meal.

Since most lunch guests like to be out in fewer than two hours, service has to be speedy.

Bartender Mike Adams fills the drink orders that waiters prop at the spindle at the bar. Mike reaches for champagne glasses, mixes Kirs, shakes martinis, pours Bloody Marys, fetches Pellegrino, Perrier, and Evian waters, uncorks bottles of Nerin Blanc de Blanc and of Château la Fontaine —our house pouring wines—smiling most of the time.

Six feet four inches tall, blond with blue eyes, he looks like a Viking. Half a year ago, he had a mild heart attack and spent four weeks in the hospital. We all took turns visiting him and bringing food. Mike couldn't bear to be idle. It drove him crazy. When he finally received the doctor's permission to return to work, he appeared with a new shirt and tie and presents for everybody.

His spirit is undiminished. Before service, he has already lugged the ice from the ice machine in the basement; stocked his beers and bottled waters; filled the juice containers; stacked the bar refrigerator with the

53

most frequently requested white wines and champagnes; checked the level of the soda guns; cut lime, lemon, and orange slices and lemon twists; and lined up olives, pearl onions, and black currants for the garnished drinks. By 11:00 A.M. he has hung up the water, wine, champagne, brandy, martini, and pony glasses in the wine rack above the bar, scrutinizing each glass for a spot or blemish. During the course of a busy lunch, he will use two hundred glasses, two dozen bottles each of Pellegrino and Perrier, sell a few beers, mix about fifteen Bloody Marys and twenty martinis.

Whoever claimed that people have cut down on their martini consumption obviously didn't check with Mike.

Alain and Marcella work in the "old" room, the one that predates our extension. The old room has fifteen tables, which can be put together to accommodate large parties. The two round tables, numbers seven and thirteen, snugly placed at opposite corners, are our coziest tables. Whenever possible, we reserve them for couples. Rose, our lunch hostess and an incurable romantic, is thrilled when her hunch about people pays off. Seating dating couples at those tables, she considers herself a regular Cupid.

Alain, who owned and lost two restaurants in his native France and has been a waiter for more years than he cares to remember, does not go in for romantic speculations. To him, a table is a table.

Clients do not necessarily agree. Aside from requests for a table in the smoking or nonsmoking section, they request "a round table," "a quiet table," "the same table we had last time," "a table in Alain's station." Requests to sit in the section of a specific waiter or waitress are common.

"Pamela, what are the specials today?" The two women at table thirty-three come so frequently that they don't bother with the menu.

"A herb-tomato consommé with chanterelles, and *confit* of rabbit with polenta."

One of the women hesitates. "*Confit* of rabbit? Should I have it? What do you think, Pamela?"

"Have it," says Pamela. "You'll like it."

Pamela knows what she is talking about. She tasted the dishes at the family meal. The entire morning crew eats together at 11:00 A.M. at one long table set up in the dining room. The evening crew repeats the procedure at five o'clock. Family meals are put out buffet style and include a

meat or fish dish, vegetables, salad, desserts. The idea is to feed the staff as well as the guests—how else can they generate honest enthusiasm? Years ago, we used to serve family meals after service. It had a serious drawback: the waiters got so famished describing dishes, they munched a piece of bread, cake, or whatever else they could put away quickly.

They still manage to do so. As A. J. Liebling, former staff writer of the *New Yorker* and author of *Between Meals,* observed: "All waiters love to eat.... Many have learned to eat so that their cheeks and jaws do not move; they can eat in the middle of the dining room and no one knows."

If the chef knows, he makes no issue of it. Meeting the waiters before service gives him an opportunity to explain the specials and to go briefly over the menu.

Louis is taking the order at the next table next to Pamela. Pencil poised, he notes in prescribed menu language:

1 quail ①
1 fish soup ③
2 ragu 2 4
2 mixed green ⑤ *6*

---

2 lamb ① *(m) 4*
2 duck ③ *1(w)* ⑤   # /
1 cannelloni (entree) 2
1 cassoulet 6

This translates into 1 grilled quail with eggplant pancake; 1 *soupe de poissons;* 2 ragouts of sweetbreads and morels; 2 mixed-green salads; 2 racks of lamb, 1 medium; 2 ducks, grilled breast and *confit,* 1 well done; 1 cannelloni of *daube de bœuf,* entrée portion; 1 cassoulet. Orders above the line are appetizers; orders below are entrées. The numbers that follow each order refer to our seating code, indicating who ordered what. A circled number means the client is a lady and should be served first.

Louis heads for the kitchen, skirting around Billy, who comes out with a basket of bread. Except for an emergency exit, there is only one door in and out of the kitchen—a situation that would give a traffic cop nightmares.

"Ordering." Louis slips the white and yellow copies of his ordering form, called the dupe, at the end of the ordering line, keeping the pink copy.

Sous-chef Hal takes the white dupe: "one quail; one fish soup; two ragu; two mixed greens; two lamb, 1 medium; two duck, one well done; one cannelloni, entrée portion; one cassoulet."

The information sets off a chain reaction. Appetizer orders are filled immediately after they are called and served as promptly as possible. Entrées will be cooked à la minute and plated when called again, except for cassoulet, which takes twenty minutes to warm through.

I stick my head into the kitchen.

"I want you to taste this," says Hal.

He spreads a mousselike mixture on a crouton and hands it to me.

"Mmm! Nice combination of flavor and texture. What is it?"

"Monkfish liver, mashed with capers, olives, fresh thyme. Glad you like it. I'm considering it for tomorrow's special. If you like, I'll send some to your table."

1:00 P.M. Every table is taken.

Alain walks through the dining room carrying a tureen of additional broth for bouillabaisse, weaving a trail of the aroma of the heady fish brew. It mingles with whiffs of cassoulet, truffle oil, wild mushrooms, lamb encrusted in Provençal herbs—a gamut of fragrances that envelopes the two dining rooms.

The waiters, with five to six tables each, pop from one table to the next, answering questions, refilling water, pouring wine, removing crumbs, bringing additional bread, clearing plates, and, above all, keeping in close communication with Curtis, perhaps the most important person on the floor.

Curtis is our runner—the person who runs the food from the kitchen to the dining room. A runner is an ace waiter who knows how the dining room works; a runner is an expediter who understands kitchen operations. A runner is the middleman between the front and the back of the house. The waiters depend on him to keep the dining room rhythm going; the chef counts on him to coach the kitchen through its most hectic hours. Curtis has been with us for two years. Standing in front of the line, aching to get the food to the tables, he is the picture of calm. Actually he has an ulcer, which he nurses with pills and warm milk. The way he balances three to four hot plates on his arm, making sure that nothing spills and that he does not bump into waiters coming into the kitchen, he could be a star performer in the circus.

The waiters keep a running communication with him.

"Curtis, table six is ready for their entrées."

"Curtis, the entrées for table eleven."

"Where is my duck for table two?"

To inform the chef which tables are ready for their entrées, Curtis moves the appropriate dupes from the far end of the ordering line to the front.

"Chef, pick up table six. Pick up table eleven."

"Fire." Hal calls the orders for tables six and eleven: "one bouillabaisse; two lamb, a medium-rare; one special; two salmon."

"1:20 P.M., tables 6 and 11," writes Curtis on the kitchen tile with a crayon, meaning the entrée orders for table six and eleven went into production at 1:20. This bit of personal bookkeeping helps him keep track of the next orders to go out. It also keeps track of the actual timing for those occasions when customers complain that they have been waiting for their food "for hours."

By 1:30, plates of garnished pasta, tuna, cod, scallops, liver, lamb, cassoulet, and bouillabaisse crowd every inch of the pickup station. Hal strikes the brass bell at the end of the table, the equivalent of a three-alarm fire. It tells waiters "Food is dying in the window. Drop what you are doing. Come and get it out!"

Marcella, on her way to refill the water pitcher, and Pamela, who is about to clear table thirty-three, leave those chores and appear in the kitchen, followed by Curtis. They take three plates, cover them with copper *cloches*, and, checking the dupes, march into the dining room. Rechecking the dupes, they place the appropriate plate in front of each client. Plates in place, they remove the *cloches* and, voilà, reveal the beautifully plated dishes.

"It doesn't always work," says Marcella. "We don't always have the same system of writing down the seat numbers. So there can be mixups."

Which is one of the reasons George and I like them to remove the *cloches* with as little fanfare as possible. After all, the idea of the *cloches* is just to keep the food warm on the way to the dining room. Curtis agrees. Having polished those copper domes every morning as part of his daily routine, he sees them as just another dish. To Billy, however, removing the *cloche* is like lifting a theater curtain.

1:50 P.M. A party of two walks in.

"We are the Irvings," they say.

Rose looks at the reservation book. No Irvings are listed. In fact, she doesn't show any reservation for that time. Every table in the house is taken. Three people are seated at the bar, waiting for their table to clear. Besides, the two o'clock people have not even arrived.

It's a tricky situation. Everybody makes mistakes. Perhaps somebody forgot to enter the reservation. Perhaps the Irvings made the reservation for another day. Perhaps they never made it at all.

"I am sorry," says Rose. "There must be a misunderstanding. Please bear with me. I'll see what I can do."

Some people are nice; others are not. If the fault is ours, they have every right to be furious. But people have also been known to bluff their way into a restaurant. We try our best to accommodate everyone.

"How long a wait?"

"I'll know better after two o'clock," says Rose. "Would you care to wait at the bar?" The Irvings are most agreeable.

Sure enough, there are two no-shows.

No-shows are a problem, particularly on weekends when we turn many customers away because we are fully booked. We are grateful when people who cannot honor their reservation call to cancel. Chances are we can rebook that table.

Louis appears at the bar with two portions of phyllo-dough apple tarts, filled to bursting with rum-soaked apples, nuts, and raisins, for which he needs cinnamon ice cream.

"Oh, my God," cries the man at table twenty-three, closest to the bar, "that looks fabulous! Please save me one."

He is not the only one who goes gaga over sweets. Our desserts are showstoppers. Even clients on a diet who want salad without dressing and ask that their grilled fish be served without sauce succumb when faced with desserts.

Marcella does her dessert act for table twelve.

"This is our walnut tart. It is made with walnuts, honey, and caramel and served with vanilla ice cream. This is our raspberry gratin, a pastry cream with Italian meringue, raspberries, and pine nuts, served with *crème anglaise* and honey-caramel ice cream. And this is my favorite: our chocolate galette, with a hazelnut praline in the center. We serve it with chocolate sorbet."

With her deep voice and heavy Italian accent, Marcella could make railroad ties sound irresistible. She writes the dessert orders on the back of the pink dupe and is off to fill those orders.

At the espresso station Dundy, our coat-check girl who jumps in when needed, prepares espresso and cappuccino without losing sight of customers ready for their coats, umbrellas, and checked parcels.

2:40 P.M. A couple walks in.

"Are we too late for lunch?"

"Let me check with the kitchen," says Rose.

One minute later she returns and takes the couple to table forty. Knowing that the kitchen is anxious to break down the stations, she takes the order herself and rushes it into the kitchen.

"Chef, ordering. One cannelloni, one ratatouille..."

Rose has been with us for six years. She is so efficient that she could handle an entire room by herself. She greets regular customers by name, remembers their birthdays, likes, and dislikes.

Rose's wardrobe seems unlimited. I have never seen her wear the same outfit twice.

"Not so," says Rose. "Occasionally I repeat. But my figure hasn't changed since high school, and I have kept all my clothes since then."

There's a bit of the schoolteacher in Rose. The younger waitresses look up to her. They could not have a better role model.

The dining room begins to clear. Mike is totaling up checks. He fills out credit-card slips, counts cash payments, and gives out change. He starts balancing the cash and the charge slips with the register total. He counts the cash tips, to be equally divided, and notes the charge tips, to be put on the sales report and paid out at the end of the week. He is waiting for table forty to settle its bill so that he can close the books.

The couple at table forty, however, is oblivious of time or place. Holding hands, they look at each other starry-eyed. Their dessert is untouched, and their coffee ice-cold. Louis's offer to bring fresh coffee has been waved aside.

"You go home," Pamela tells Louis. "I'll take care of them. I'm working a double anyway."

Curtis clears the dessert station and cleans the runner's refrigerator, which holds the butter and tapenade for each service. Marcella and Alain scrub their tables with a mild solution of water and vinegar and place clean napkins on the tables. With all chores done, they sit down, have a cigarette, coffee, call a friend, and make plans for the rest of the day. They leave around 3:30, running into the evening waiters who begin to drift in.

4:15 P.M. Dressed in uniform of white shirt, red bow tie, black pants or skirt, long dark-blue apron, the evening wait staff take their posts. Steve and Robbin fold napkins, a favored chore with every waiter.

"Very relaxing," according to Robbin. Eric and Mireille wipe the silverware and hand steam the glasses to make them sparkle. Everyone helps set the tables, checking with the evening hostess to see how many deuces, fours, fives, and bigger parties are on the books.

5:00 P.M. Family dinner has been put out. The chef holds his briefing session.

5:30 P.M. Nuts, olives, and pouring wines in place, Mike Osley, the evening bartender, opens his bar. At the bread station, Eric cuts thick slices of bread from the huge loaves, delivered twice a day from Tom Cat Bakery in Long Island City. Next, Eric fills twenty crocks with butter and tapenade, enough to serve the early diners. Mireille brings out fresh desserts and arranges them at the dessert station, placed at the entrance to the old dining room.

Dinner service is about to begin.

In the kitchen it is quiet. Moises and Jim, the line cooks, finish the *mis en place:* checking sauces for seasoning, frying artichokes, whipping up mashed potatoes. They organize their station: pulling out all food items that can sit at room temperature: chopped parsley, chives, and dill; the *brunoise*, roasted pepper, and shallots; the mustard glaze; and flavored bread crumbs. They double-check that the lowboy refrigerator under the line is stocked with enough butchered meats and fish for the evening.

6:30 P.M. Orders start coming in. At seven o'clock the kitchen gets hit.

"Ordering."

"Ordering cold: one *socca*, one artichoke, one soupe du jour."

"Ordering."

"One cook soup, one fish soup."

"Ordering hot."

"Two chix; two 'bouilli'."

"Pick up table thirty-three."

"Chef, I'm missing an escargot."

"Like hell you are. I don't see an escargot on the dupe."

"No problem. They all like my fish soup."

"Hot plate, watch out!"

"I need the special birthday cake."

"Ordering cold."

"Get those orders moving. Where is the runner?"

John O'Sullivan, the evening runner, is standing in front of the cold station, legs in sprinting position, shoulders slightly hunched. He lifts his plates stacked with sizzling steaks, poached cod, and steaming cassoulet and all but flies out of the kitchen, careful not to collide with incoming waiters placing new orders.

"Wait!" cries Mark. "There is no liner under the cassoulet!"

"Pick up table forty."

The orders for table forty are lined up at the pickup station. Each plate is a meticulously thought-out composition: slices of rare duck breast beside tomato, poached pear, and asparagus stalks; monkfish fillets draped over fennel compote, fava beans, and a dollop of *aïoli*; black trumpet mushrooms, sprigs of coriander next to chunks of pink lobster; medallions of browned sea scallops and cool seedless-cucumber moons.

"Jim, you got two pastas, one salmon."

Jim pours some clarified butter into a preheated pan, waits for the butter to bubble, then tosses his pasta into the pan. Next, he takes mushrooms, precooked in a butter-garlic sauce, and adds them to the pasta. He seasons the dish with salt and pepper, puts it on a plate, sprinkles the top with chopped chives, and turns his attention to the salmon order. Salmon is a big item; so is cassoulet—our best-sellers.

The dining room is packed; there is a private party in the upstairs Napoleon Room. People are waiting at the bar. The phones keep on ringing.

"Sorry, we're fully booked."

We'll probably serve one hundred and seventy-five dinners tonight.

Six waiters are on the floor, backed by one runner, the manager, maître d', and coat-check girl.

The kitchen lineup is: chef Mark May, sautéing and expediting (calling out the orders, directing the traffic); Moises at the grill station; Jim at the cold-and-pastry station; Armando, prepping and last-minute butchering; Victor manning the dishwasher.

Mark is thirty-two. Five feet eight, with a deep dimple in his chin and a ready smile, he has boundless energy and enthusiasm. An avid sailor and skier, he runs his kitchen as if it were an Olympic team.

"Let's go: one house-smoked salmon, two shrimps, two quails, one *socca.*

"How are we doing upstairs?

"Ordering two salads, one no dressing.

"Jim, two quick greens. Let's go."

Jim doesn't know what to do first. Four separate orders hit his station simultaneously, and now the chef wants two extra greens. On top of it, he is running low on vinaigrette. As always, it was prepared this morning: one liter of olive and walnut oils, red wine, sherry and balsamic vinegars, salt and pepper. Jim plates the two greens, arranges one tuna carpaccio, and starts whipping up a new batch of vinaigrette.

"Chef, the lady on table forty-one wants to know if there is garlic in the pasta special."

"No garlic in the pasta."

"Ordering hot!"

"Fire one lamb, one bouillabaisse."

Moises grabs a frying pan, preheats it, adds clarified butter, seasons a rack of lamb with salt and pepper, sears it briefly, turns the lamb over, brushes it with mustard glaze, sprinkles it with Provençal herbs and bread crumbs, and puts the pan in the oven to finish. Time for Mark to prepare the garnish. He heats a portion of zucchini chutney, sautés julienne of red and green peppers, and arranges the garnish on the plate before handing it back to Moises. Moises slices the top part of the rack of lamb, centers it on the plate, sauces it with pan drippings, and wipes the rim with a clean napkin. The order is ready for pickup.

Mark checks the clock above the kitchen entrance. The party upstairs must be ready for its entrées.

"Jon, we need the counter space. Clear the bread station."

Jon stashes the breads in the cold station underneath the bread counter. Jim lends a hand in lining up twenty-two dinner plates.

"Pick up Napoleon Room."

"Right, guys. Here we go. Lobster. Pick up lobster."

Moises and Jim transfer broiled lobsters onto the plates: twenty-two of them, split in half, claws cracked. Mark, black trumpet mushrooms in tow, arranges them next to the lobsters. Armando follows with fried baby artichokes.

Jonathan, on duty tonight, stands by, ready to assist in running the food.

Mark hits the bell.

"Get the lobsters out! Everybody move those lobsters."

Jonathan, white napkin draped over his arm, leads a group of lobster-carrying waiters through the dining room, up the stairs, and into the Napoleon Room.

"Ordering."

"Ordering."

Mireille and Lucia appear simultaneously. "Terrific night." The busier the floor, the better the performance. It's on slow nights that things go wrong. Mark puts on a clean uniform and goes into the dining room to check on the pastry display. He's stopped by the people at table six who want to know how he smokes his salmon. On the way back to the kitchen, he spots a napkin on the floor and picks it up.

"Ordering hot!"

"Ordering two pasta, one no sauce."

"What do you mean, 'no sauce'? Who doesn't want my sauce?" Mark throws up his hands. "Sick."

Mark is not only proud, he is fond of his sauces, particularly his *jus de poulet.*

"Next to my wife, I love my *jus de poulet* best."

He is serious. *Jus de poulet*, a form of chicken jelly, is a twice-reduced stock that, by adding various flavoring agents, forms the basis of many of our sauces. We prepare five gallons of it twice a week. All other sauces are prepared every morning, using the fish, chicken, and duck stocks that are forever simmering in mammoth stockpots. Forty gallons of basic stocks are reduced to about five to six quarts. Nothing goes to waste. Lobster shells, fish heads and bones, duck carcasses, veal bones, chicken and meat trimmings are braised, boiled down, strained, skimmed, reboiled, and strained again. It's part of prepping, a task that goes on all day, using the help of everyone in the kitchen, including the chef and the dishwasher.

On any given day, sixty to seventy pounds of fish are cleaned, twenty chickens butchered. One gallon of butter is clarified. Twenty-five pounds of vegetables are peeled, sliced, and chopped. Stems are plucked from bunches of fresh thyme and rosemary; lobsters are knifed to keep the tails from curling, making them easier to work with.

Pastries, desserts, and petits fours have been made in the morning by our pastry chef, Joyce Wong. In order to secure oven space, Joyce starts early in the morning.

We only have two ovens. Both are usually occupied: roasting duck, chicken, or beef bones for the various stocks; vegetables for garnish; game birds and the like for specials. Preparing her pastry creations, party cakes, and the two hundred miniature cookies that we present to clients with our compliments at the end of the meal, Joyce has to negotiate for equal time.

The prepping station is adjacent to the kitchen. Here are the industrial Hobart mixer, the Buffalo chopper, KitchenAid mixer, food processor, blender, and the walk-in refrigerator, which holds about one week's supply of staples. Freezers and additional refrigerators are in the basement.

11:00 P.M. The last orders are coming in. The temperature in the kitchen registers 110 degrees. Moises has consumed six bottles of Coke. Jim swears by bitters and sodas.

64

Mark is ready to do his ordering. Clipboard in hand, he calls his orders into the purveyors' office on their answering machines. To make sure those orders are coming in correctly, Mark leaves a copy on Julio's station for tomorrow morning.

Jim plates one more order of raspberry sorbet before returning the macerated grapefruit sections to the walk-in.

11:30 P.M. Moises, Armando, and Victor are breaking down the kitchen. All meats, fish, and other perishables are repacked in fresh containers, covered with saran wrap, with the date written on top, and put into the main walk-in. All surfaces, refrigerators, shelves, lids, stove tops are washed with soap and water, leaving the kitchen clean enough to pass Marine inspection. The floorboards are picked up, and the floor scrubbed down.

Mark has changed into T-shirt and jeans. He sits at the bar, sipping an Absolut with cranberry. Mike Osley joins him with his favorite after-service nightcap port: a 1977 Niepoort Colheita.

Time to close.

5

The Suppliers

One question customers frequently ask is if we go to the Fulton fish market to buy our fish. The answer is a resounding no. Years ago, when we actually tried, someone broke into our car and made off with fifty pounds of fresh fish while we went in search of soft-shell crabs. For us it makes more sense to deal exclusively with purveyors. We count on them to provide us with quality fish, meat, produce, and dairy items, the finest oils, the best vinegars, wild mushrooms, and tender greens, delivered directly to our doorstep.

We deal with about twenty purveyors. Some are large companies that carry a wide range of products. Others, equally large, deal in one product only: fish, meat, fowl, produce, dry goods. There are suppliers who specialize in luxury products of which they are exclusive agents. And then there are the small, independent producers and growers who sell to a limited number of restaurants.

Most of our suppliers are located in or around New York; all others are a fax or an 800 number away. Some make daily deliveries by truck; others ship via airfreight. A few come to New York in their station wagons, once or twice a week.

The trick is to pick the best. That's one of the marks of a good chef: his knowledge of suppliers and his rapport with them. Buying wisely, getting consistent quality at the best market price, enables him to function day after day while giving him ample opportunity to be creative. That also means never to take anything for granted.

"If you don't watch them carefully, they may send you inferior stuff," according to Naj.

Most unlikely. Nevertheless, Julio, our steward, who receives the morning deliveries, is a fierce watchdog. Leeks, lettuce, zucchini, onions, eggplants, he checks every crate. He weighs all meat and fish deliveries and makes sure each item is choice.

In some cases we deal with two or three purveyors of the same merchandise. Why? For one thing, it sets up a healthy competition. It also enables us to switch from one supplier to another without having to miss a beat. Since lunch and dinner service depend on split-second timing, we can't wait for a delivery because somebody goofed or a truck broke down. Beyond that, some purveyors do not deliver on weekends; others insist that

67

orders have to be placed before 3:00 P.M. to guarantee delivery the next morning. And, most important, one purveyor frequently has an edge over his competitor for one specific item. We want to be sure to be in on it.

Amazing Foods is one of our top purveyors. They daily deliver the fish for our bouillabaisse: shrimps, lobsters, clams, mussels, salmon, cod, monkfish. Once a week they add eighty pounds of fish bones for fish stock. One call to Amazing Foods will bring rouget from Hawaii, halibut from Iceland, Dover sole from Holland, occasional sea-urchin roe from Japan, and squid ink. Squid ink, which we need for our squid-and-fava-bean salad with a squid-ink vinaigrette, is a costly item: sixty dollars for one pint. Fortunately, a little squid ink goes a long way, also leaving permanent stains on any garment it comes in contact with, as I discovered.

Amazing Foods also supplies us with Vidalia onions, squash blossoms, yellow pear tomatoes, champagne grapes, and other exotic items so cherished as contemporary garnish. What's even nicer, Amazing Foods can be counted on to come through in a pinch. When we're caught short, they'll make that extra trip to help us out.

"I am in this business as much for love and respect for fine food as for money," says Patrick Cummings, one of the founders and partners of the company. Expecting a shipment of wild Atlantic salmon, caught off the Icelandic coast, Pat will call us. It's suppliers like Patrick who make trips to the Fulton fish market unnecessary. Dealing directly with growers from all over the world, he is a better shopper than we are. Possibly also more economical.

"This is a very volatile and highly competitive business," says Patrick. "That's why we operate on a small margin and choose our clients carefully."

That statement refers to a client's ability to pay on time, which usually means within thirty days. Restaurants, too, operate on a small margin; many are way over their head in debt. Stories of high-profile restaurants going under while owing large sums to their purveyors are not uncommon, particularly in the difficult economy of the 1990s. Having established a reputation as a solid customer over the past seventeen years has paid off in our relationship with purveyors. Some of them have been with us from the beginning.

Among them is Bill Ricci. Bill is our florist. His contribution to the restaurant is as important as that of any purveyor. Bill started doing our flower arrangements back in April 1977. He has been doing them ever since. He comes every Tuesday morning bearing multicolored asters, pompons, carnations, birds-of-paradise, peach and almond blossoms, daisies, lilies, and lupines.

Bill's arrangements are artistic without being overwhelming. He concentrates on cut flowers that have a decent shelf life and are suggestive of sunshine. Bill returns every Thursday to make necessary touch-ups.

Presently, we contract for three individual arrangements. At the height of our three-star fame, we were up to nine arrangements a week.

"You are not the only client who had to cut back," says Bill. "February 1992 was the turning point for most restaurants. What can you do?"

Bill is a sweetheart. Occasionally, George will invite him and "the wife" to have dinner at the restaurant.

In dealing with the food purveyors, ego, personal contact, likes, and dislikes play a role. Chefs like to work with New York's establishment purveyors. To buy meat from De Bragga & Spitler, considered the Tiffany's of meat purveyors, gives a chef status. Not only does he get the finest New Zealand–raised lamb, he gets the same lamb served at Le Cirque, the Four Seasons, and other top New York restaurants. Besides, it helps to be on good terms with Marc Sarrazin, one of the owners of De Bragga & Spitler, because he also operates an informal personnel agency for chefs.

Purveyors, too, take pride in being represented by certain clients. We buy veal knuckles, backs, and necks, kidney, liver, and such specialty items as beef blood, pigskin, fatback, beef shank, sweetbreads, and caul fat from London Meat, which carries "anything that a French restaurant needs," according to owner Fred Fields. "Only chefs trained in the French tradition know what to do with some of it." Caul fat, for instance, which is the thin, fatty membrane that lines the stomach of pigs and sheep, resembles a lacy net and is used to wrap and hold certain foods. The fatty membrane melts during the cooking process and keeps the food especially moist. We use it to hold our medallions of monkfish together. Fatback is the unsmoked and unsalted layer of fat that runs along a pig's back. It's vital for cassoulet, as is pigskin, which we use as casing for our homemade sausages.

Fish and meat account for 55 percent of our weekly food bill, with fish gaining steady ground: at this point three to one. A few years ago, it was the reverse. Today, we have five permanent fish entrées on our menu, in addition to a fish appetizer and one or two daily fish specials. Salmon is a best-seller. We use 140 pounds of salmon a week, twice the amount of either monkfish or tuna, our two other most popular fish. Main Ingredients and Pescane regularly supply us with the bulk of our fish.

Duck, enough for about 145 orders a week, comes from Long Island Meat, as does chicken. During the course of a week, we'll use 72 chickens, 200 pounds of chicken bones, 35 pounds of calf's liver, 60 dozen eggs, and 150 loaves of bread.

The bread, baked by Tom Cat Bakery in Long Island City, is delivered twice a day. It is a classic French *bâtard*, more specifically a *fendu*, referring to the deep split in the middle of the torpedo-shaped loaf. Noel Comess, owner of the bakery, attributes the unique quality of his breads to the stone-deck ovens in which they are baked. Although Tom Cat offers various kinds of bread, all equally good, we chose the fat, two-pound round loaf for dinner service because we enjoy its peasantlike style. To supplement lunch and private parties, we order Tom Cat's elegant *levain* rolls, and, to honor a special guest, Tom Cat will bake their hand-shaped *miche* for us, decorated for the occasion.

With the exception of ice cream and sorbets, which we buy from Ciao Bella, we make all our desserts. That means French Valrhona and Callebaut Belgian chocolates, praline paste, cocoa powder, vanilla beans, and crystallized flowers, which we buy from De Choix Specialty Food Company. A division of Amazon, De Choix also supplies us with French cheeses and various Corsican products, which we need for our annual Napoleon dinner.

Since Provençal cooking is based on olive oil, we use gallons of oil—different ones for different dishes. Our most precious oil is white truffle oil, imported by Urbani Truffles USA from Umbria. The fragrance of that oil is so intoxicating that the entire dining room takes note whenever we serve our wild-mushroom ravioli laced with white truffle oil. To dress *mesclun* salad, we use Sida extra virgin olive oil, a delicate, beautifully balanced oil produced in the Agnana Calabria region of Italy. L'Olivier from Provence has just the right texture and pungency for hearty Provençal dishes.

Colavita is our workhorse oil; canola and grape-seed oils are used for deep-frying. We also prepare our own infused oils—predominantly basil and mint—which are part of our fish garnishes.

Coinciding with the quest for ever more remarkable products, some American purveyors burst upon the food scene with domestic delicacies cloned from France's haute cuisine ingredients. Arianne Daguin, creator of D'Artagnan in New Jersey, helped broaden the scope of New York restaurant fare by providing chefs with local fresh duck and goose foie gras as silken and tender as those her famous restaurateur father would likely find in Gascony. Thanks to D'Artagnan, quail, squab, rabbit, and smoked duck breasts became part of our menu, with foie gras appearing as occasional holiday fare.

Coach Farm, started by Miles and Lillian Cahn in the Hudson Valley, put goat cheese firmly on the New York food map. Their goat cheese enhances our salad, while their goat curds go into our gnocchi. Shipments arrive twice a week. Occasionally Miles or Lillian travels to New York and stops by the restaurant to say hello.

Fresh & Wild, in Vancouver, Washington, is our primary wild-mushroom purveyor. Fresh & Wild operates under the motto "Direct from the mountains and forests of the Pacific Northwest to your kitchen without delay." Orders are shipped by airfreight, guaranteed to arrive within twelve hours. Charlie Novy, the company's founder, is not only a passionate mycologist, but an excellent cook. I met him in Portland and had a chance to taste his wild-mushroom-and-cheddar-cheese dish, which would have done any restaurant chef proud. Charlie will get on the phone and tell us about the arrival of particularly beautiful shiitake, morels, or white chestnut mushrooms. The white chestnut crop is small and has a limited season. To be offered a shipment is an honor that we are not about to ignore.

I met Hans Johansson, a New York State forager, at the annual Marketplace Tasting, organized by the New York chapter of the American Institute of Wine & Food. I was impressed with Hans's mushroom selections and told him about our restaurant. The next morning, Hans sent us a box with samples of hand-picked chanterelle, hedgehog, black trumpet, and *porcini* mushrooms. Our chef created a mushroom special around the bounty, and Johansson's company became one of our purveyors.

When George met Marc Buzzio, a second-generation sausage maker and partner of Salumeria Biellese, George was so impressed by the quality of Marc's sausages that he decided to let Marc make the *saucisson d'ail* for our cassoulet and also the rabbit sausage, which is part of our pasta dish.

When we decided to test clients' readiness for *boudin noir*, we bought ten pounds of the classic blood sausage from Les Halles, a competing neighborhood restaurant that also features a *boucherie*. We plated the sausage with homemade applesauce, mashed potatoes, and Dijon mustard. Featured as a special, the dish sold out within the first hour of service.

"Great sausage you have there," we told Jean-Michel Diot, one of the owners of Les Halles.

"You bet," said Jean-Michel. "It comes from upstate New York. A place called Natural Meats. If you are interested I'll give you their number."

That's how we met the farmer/sausage maker Anne Roberts, whose sparrowlike appearance could qualify her as an Edith Piaf lookalike.

"My goodness," says Anne in her heavy French accent, "all the farmers around Cooperstown were going broke with dairy products they could not sell. My husband and I decided to go into the meat business, particularly pork."

Finding herself with a lot of leftover pigs' blood, Anne, who grew up in a farming community in Normandy where nothing was ever wasted, got in touch with the U.S. Department of Agriculture. Having pored over the *Code of Federal Regulations*, considered the bible of the DA, Anne was able to convince the authorities that there was no law against using fresh pigs' blood and received permission.

"We make the old-fashioned *boudin de table*," says Anne. "Meat from pigs raised without hormones, clean blood, *le panne*, the fat around the kidneys, lots of onions, and natural casing. Makes all the difference in the world."

Naj agrees. As frugal as an old-fashioned housewife, Naj abhors waste. If it were up to him, he would happily dispense with expensive, out-of-season products and concentrate on whatever is available. Passing by Murray's Cheese Shop in Greenwich Village, he noticed that their goat cheese is cheaper than the one we buy from Coach Farm.

"I also like it better," says Naj. "It's younger, creamier, and has more flavor."

Problem is that Murray's does not deliver. On top of it, that lovely goat cheese is not always available. So we stuck with Coach Farm.

No question, Naj loves to go shopping. He regularly checks out the produce at the Greenmarket on Union Square, located a few blocks from the restaurant. This is where the farmers, dairymen, hunters, and foragers from upstate New York, the Hudson River Valley, Pennsylvania, and New Jersey bring their products. They are an earnest, dedicated group that takes great pride in producing food of the highest quality while respecting the environment.

New York chefs love the contact with these farmers. In fact, around ten o'clock on Wednesday, Friday, and Saturday, market days, the Greenmarket looks like a meeting place of New York's most prominent chefs.

Naj is right there. "Kale is good now," he says. "Also mustard greens and turnips."

The truth is that La Colombe d'Or is a Provençal restaurant, albeit situated in New York, where sunshine is at a premium come November. However, from our flower arrangements to the menu, we maintain the illusion of Provence, where mimosa and almond trees blossom in February. Although we may slip in a turnip garnish for our smoked-duck salad in red-currant vinaigrette and serve braised red cabbage with a grilled salmon dish, we need year-round tasty tomatoes for many of our dishes.

Luckily, Sun-Ripened Tomatoes, a New York–based company operated by the Marcelli family, supplies freshly picked, vine-ripened tomatoes year-round. For nine months their tomatoes come from Florida by tractor-trailer, driven by the brother-sister Marcelli team. For the remaining months, the Marcellis follow the crop up the East Coast, collecting New York– and New Jersey–grown tomatoes in August. The trucks are kept at a temperature between fifty-five and sixty degrees at all times.

"Anything above or below that damages the tomatoes' natural flavor," says Lucky Marcelli, who handles the marketing. Lucky feels so strongly about proper temperature control that she'll come to the restaurant to supervise storage.

"The wine cellar is the best," she says. "Also the safest." She laughs at the thought that her tomatoes are precious enough to be kept under lock and key.

During the summer, we bring herbs from our garden in Sag Harbor. But our bounty is hardly enough. Besides, we need fresh herbs year-round, and for that we depend on Fines Herbes Company, located in downtown New York.

When I decided to give a seminar on Provençal herbs for members of the New York Women's Culinary Alliance, I asked Peter Goldstein, one of the owners of Fines Herbes, if he could help me out with some additional herbs. On the day of the seminar, Peter delivered a box with enough herbs to supply every French restaurant in New York. Two fellow members of the Alliance and I made herb garlands and draped them around mirrors, paintings, and sculptures in the Napoleon Room. Next, we made thirty herbal bouquets, one for each participant. Still finding ourselves with leftover herbs, we constructed an herbal tree that became the centerpiece at the table. The aroma of rosemary, tarragon, thyme, chervil, mint, lavender, and sage was so heady, it made us dizzy. Dinner guests followed the scent the way dogs sniff out truffles and came upstairs. The seminar was a success.

Of course, all is not roses with the purveyors. Delivery mix-ups occur. We'll get a shipment of zucchini intended for round-the-corner Les Halles. Another neighborhood restaurant signed for our capons. Every so often we get stiffed with improper weight. Hard to say whose fault that is. However, we do not suffer it lightly, which is one of the reasons we deal with many purveyors.

"Tell them about the instances when I leave a message with my order on their machine, and they don't call back to tell me that that particular item is unavailable," says Naj.

It happens. Naj leaves his orders on the answering machines with the various suppliers every evening after dinner service. The purveyors, who start filling these orders around four o'clock in the morning, send their trucks rolling at 6:00 A.M. By 8:00 A.M., Julio will have received, inspected, and signed for most of our orders. Naj arrives around 10:00 A.M., confident that his orders have been filled. Then he discovers the salt cod for our *brandade* is missing, or his request for additional monkfish has been ignored. Naj, normally a model of patience, loses his cool. His hollering, interspersed with French and Arabic curse words, reaches up to the office.

A chef's frustration. It drove Vatel, the famous French chef in the era of Louis XIV, to suicide. Poor Vatel. If he were a chef today, he'd simply call another supplier.

When all else fails, George goes shopping. Asked to float gold specks in champagne for a golden anniversary celebration, George discovered edible gold sheets in one of our neighborhood Indian stores. He bought a package, and, with the help of a waitress, he tore off tiny pieces of the thin sheets and put them into the champagne glasses.

George's favorite store is Dean & DeLuca, where he loves to pick out merchandise that will add the finishing touch to a particular party: selections of French cheeses, assortments of jams, pink peppercorns, Nyons olives, and spelt, a grain said to be the poor man's wheat in the Haute Provence that costs a fortune here. We needed the spelt for a Provençal food festival that we did jointly with Food and Wines from France. To make the festival as authentic as possible, we also asked a friend who happened to be visiting the Haute Provence to bring us a bottle of *crème de myrtilles,* a tart blueberry liqueur traditionally served in rosé wine.

Alcoholic beverages, including liquor, constitute about 25 percent of our sales. Compared with alcohol sales in other restaurants, that is relatively low. But since our bar can accommodate only four people, we do little bar business. We could, of course, have built a bigger bar. But that's not what we wanted. George and I have never enjoyed hard liquor. Besides, we like to think of La Colombe d'Or as a typical French restaurant where wine and food are equal partners.

We buy liquor primarily from two big houses. Depending on the public's response to advertisements, some name brands outsell others. Absolut vodka, Dewars, and Glenlivet are a case in point. Beyond that there are the standard varieties that we must have in house at all times. We keep at least three bottles of each. To please steady clients, we keep a bottle of their preferred drink on hand, although they are the only ones who ever ask for it : Strega for Dr. and Mrs. Johnson, chilled kirschwasser for Mr. Freund, and Punt e Mes for my favorite single and nameless client. In the case of Pellegrino and Evian, our special waters, we keep at least ten cases each. Occasionally we run out.

"What, no Johnnie Walker Black label? What kind of a place is this?" Clients are outraged.

What kind of place indeed? Should we tell them that : (a) due to a truckers' strike there has been no delivery, (b) twice a year all warehouses close for two weeks because they take inventory, (c) the company that represents Pellegrino did not receive a shipment themselves, (d) much as we would like, we do not carry their favorite sherry, vodka, or scotch because it is not represented by the purveyors we deal with, that to start ordering a specific brand from another distributor means having to order at least one case, and that we'd have to hire an extra bookkeeper to keep track of all those vendors?

Our relationship with the wine and liquor purveyors is quite different from that with our food purveyors. Since the State Liquor Authority stipulates that wine and liquor purchases have to be paid within a three-week period, the question of payment never comes up. Consequently, all our dealings tend to be gentlemanly and, in most instances, very personal.

We deal with about fifteen different wine houses. Some, like the Seagram Chateau & Estate Wines Company, are very big and have an impressive portfolio; others, like Grand Cru Inc., are boutiquelike. Many suppliers are importers as well as distributors. All have been approved by the State Liquor Authority, including the salesmen, who have to get a yearly permit.

These salesmen are a remarkable group of people. Most are highly educated, urbane, with a passion for wine. Peter Martin, who represents Winebow, is a good example. Peter's introduction to wines started at Oxford University, acknowledged as having one of the finest cellars in Europe. When Peter recommends a wine to us, we listen. He understands our food and knows who our clients are. Peter visits us once or twice a month, bringing new wines or vintages to taste. Studying our wine list, he may discover niches that we have overlooked. He may suggest a wine of excellent quality that is attractively priced from a small producer. When a winegrower whose wine we carry, or are considering carrying, comes to New York, Peter might bring him for lunch. Often we will join them. When Peter introduced us to François Perrin, whose family owns Château de Beaucastel, the cordial lunch, strengthened by Monsieur Perrin's wines, resulted in our putting Beaucastel on the wine list and an invitation from Monsieur Perrin to visit his domain and stay as his guests.

Peter, who could talk wine all day, occasionally conducts wine tastings and training seminars for our staff. For a restaurant like ours, without a sommelier, that is most helpful.

Blake Johnson represents Robert Chadderdon Selections. Chadderdon's selection is predicated on the palate of Robert Chadderdon, who has befriended some of the finest vintners in France. When Blake told us that Chadderdon's motto is "When you know the man, you know the wine," George and I thought "What bunk." That evening we drank a bottle of Mercurey '86 Sazenay that Blake had left for us. It was an elegant Burgundy, beautifully crafted.

"What's Monsieur Sazenay like?" George asked Blake the next morning.

"Ah, you should meet him," said Blake. "He is one of the most cultivated, elegant wine makers I've ever met. What did you think of his wine?"

The house of Chadderdon is very particular about with whom it will deal. It took us years of courting before they agreed to take us on, with certain conditions at that. While most purveyors will gladly ship us one case, Chadderdon insists on a minimum of five cases. Since most of their selections are high-priced wines, that means paying a hefty sum of money all at once. Also, exquisite as a particular Burgundy or Bordeaux may be, at $65 a bottle, it is not exactly a best-seller. Still, we are proud to carry their wines, and many of our clients are glad that we do.

Taking his cue from Robert Chadderdon, Blake acts as consultant rather than salesman. He and George spend hours talking about *châteaux*, crus, vintners, restaurants, and sights in St. Emilion, Châteauneuf-du-Pape, or the Loire Valley. Actually, one of those talks had us so fired up, George and I decided it was high time for us to return to Bordeaux. Blake took full credit for our decision and helped us with valuable recommendations and introductions.

Iris Ashkinos was a singer, bent on a career in opera, who, by her own admission, knew nothing about wine. Frustrated in her pursuit as artist, Iris landed a part-time job with Paramount Brands, a division of Paramount Distiller Inc. What attracted her to the business were the flexible hours and the constant exchange between people. Paramount sent Iris to take Harriet Lembeck's comprehensive wine course. That was twelve years ago. Today, Iris is one of Paramount's ace salespeople.

Paramount is a medium-size company whose portfolio runs from simple country wines to Veuve Clicquot. In addition they carry most standard brands of liquor. That is important to us, because we can satisfy many of our needs with one phone call. There are other advantages. Paramount, or rather Iris, acts like a friendly neighbor. Need something in a hurry? No problem. They'll come and deliver. Small or big orders, it makes no difference. Iris can also be counted on to supply our waiters with yet another dozen corkscrews. By now a confirmed enologist, she still likes to talk music.

"Did you hear Kathleen Battle last night?" she asks. Once we went to the opera together.

To complement our Provençal food, we seek out wines from the southern region of France, particularly the Haute Provence, southern Rhône, and the Languedoc-Roussillon areas, which are studded with small estates or cooperatives that produce delightful, affordable wines.

Alain Junguenet, owner and distributor of Wines From France, is a true maverick. Born in Lyons, holding a degree in chemistry, a former race-car driver, Alain has literally "sniffed" out some wonderful vineyards and has become the most tireless wine ambassador of southern France. George and I enjoy his company and that of his Kentucky-born wife, Elaine. Occasionally we'll have dinner together. Alain will show up with new selections. His enthusiasm for each one of his wines resembles a father's pride in his children.

"You'll have to taste this," he says, producing a chilled bottle of Muscat de Frontignan from his carrying case. The golden, highly aromatic sweet muscat is as good, if not better, than the higher priced, much lauded Beaumes-de-Venise.

"Of course," says Alain. "Your president liked it so much, he ordered a few cases from our ambassador."

"The president! What president!" says George. "Bush! Clinton!"
Alain turns to his wife. "What president am I thinking of!"
"You are thinking of Thomas Jefferson," says his wife.

Following Thomas Jefferson's example, we ordered one case. Served slightly chilled, a glass of muscat heightens the pleasure of any dessert. We frequently offer muscat with our compliments. It is a nice way to acknowledge favorite clients, to make amends for an overly long wait, or simply to familiarize a client with the wine. In this fashion, we have made many converts to muscat. Alain now can barely keep up with our demand.

That, in general, is one of our pet peeves with the wine distributors. No sooner have we put a wine on our list, featuring it as an ideal match with a certain dish, when, on the next order, we are told that that wine sold so well that there is a wait for the next shipment or, worse, it's no longer available.

In addition, mishaps occur. Instead of receiving a case of '83 Bordeaux as ordered, we get '85. Since we do not necessarily open the case immediately, it might take a few weeks before we discover the error. Occasionally, an entire shipment may have suffered en route and gone bad. Sometimes, one bottle, out of dozens, will have turned.

Fortunately, there is never a problem in sending a bad bottle or a case back. Of course, we may be out of that wine for quite a while—sometimes we'll have to take it off our list.

Which is not to say that, just as with our food purveyors, we don't change or add new wine distributors from time to time. George and I attend many wine tastings, seminars, luncheons, and dinners given throughout the year by individual growers, wine associations, or the distributors themselves. When we come across a wine that pleases us particularly, one that would be an asset on our list, we consider taking it on, sometimes as a replacement for a similar wine, sometimes in addition. In this fashion we become acquainted with the portfolio of a distributor we had not dealt with before. We meet their salesman—bright, proud of the wines he represents, filled with enthusiasm and romance, the very stuff wine is made of.

6

Behind the
Scene:
the Regulators

$\mathcal{A}$ *restaurant* is closely supervised and accountable to innumerable city, state, and federal agencies, codes, and regulations. Among them are

The New York State Liquor Authority (SLA)

The Federal Bureau of Alcohol, Tobacco,
  and Firearms (BATF)

The New York City Department of Health

The New York City Water Department

The New York City Department of Sanitation

The New York City Fire Department

The New York State Tax Department

The New York City Environmental Protection Agency

All agencies collect fees from us, which go toward the city, state, and federal departments' revenues. Some of these agencies are efficient; others are not. Most are understaffed and antiquated. The New York State Liquor Authority is a case in point.

The SLA was created in 1934, after the repeal of Prohibition. Its objective was, and still is, to regulate alcohol distribution in a fair and legal way by controlling the importing and licensing of all wines and spirits bought and sold in the state. The SLA was mindful of guarding the public against mob control, harmful spirits, and excessive drinking, and its early rules were necessary and made a lot of sense. To safeguard the industry against organized crime and similar forms of monopoly, the SLA stipulated that wholesale and retail operations could not be in the hands of the same owner. To see that people avoided excessive drinking, it insisted that any public place where liquor was being consumed also had to serve food. In a bow to churches' and schools' sensibilities of the 1930s, it ruled that no one could sell or dispense alcohol within two hundred feet of a church or a school.

Sixty years later, with teenagers peddling drugs in schools and church-yards, the SLA still operates under the same old rules.

Those rules are tough when applying for a liquor license, which every restaurateur, retailer, importer, and distributor must obtain in order to

81

sell wines and liquor. Going through the application process was an early introduction to the bureaucratic shenanigans with which, by now, we are all too familiar.

In order to obtain our liquor license, we had to hire a lawyer who specializes in SLA matters. As was recommended to us, the lawyer was a retired SLA commissioner, knowledgeable in the ways of the authority and therefore in a position to help expedite the process. Before that process could begin, George, as principal owner, was investigated. That meant he had to supply proof of the origin of the funds used to open the restaurant, furnish character references, and post a bond. In addition, he was finger-printed. We also had to pay for our pending license. Today it costs $5,100 for a three-year license, lent to the state at no interest.

We received our original license within three months—lucky, since the process can drag on for a year, particularly now, when drastic budget cuts have left the SLA even more shorthanded.

Together with the license, we received copies of the SLA's laws and bylaws. Rule number one states that we can only deal with SLA-approved wholesale vendors; under no circumstances may we buy from approved retailers or other sources, although they frequently offer more attractively priced merchandise than the distributors. No wonder restaurant wine prices occasionally baffle customers. Seeing a Chablis ler Crus for thirty dollars on our wine list, they remember that their neighborhood liquor store sells that same wine for $14.99. Are we highway robbers, out to make a whopping profit? The fact is that, having bought one case of that particular wine from an approved wholesaler, we paid $159.95 a case, or $13.33 per bottle, to which we added a customary markup. The retail store most likely bought an entire container, holding anything from sixty to one hundred cases of the same Chablis, at who knows what discount. Since large retail stores make their profit on volume, they work with a minimal markup.

A high-volume restaurant or different restaurants with the same ownership might operate under similar conditions: they'll order a container of a certain wine under their own label—a practice known as private filing—which gives them the advantage of gaining a considerable degree of prestige, at a great saving.

The SLA's rule number two states that all alcoholic beverages must be consumed on the premises, which means if a customer does not finish his bottle of wine, he cannot take it with him. This may make sense in some cases, but not always. At least not to Mr.F, who, up to that moment, had been a very good customer.

He and a friend had finished their bottle of a Château Haut-Brion '79 1er Grand Cru. Still lingering over their entrées, Mr. F ordered a second bottle, of which they only drank one glass each. With the wine at $100 a bottle, Mr. F was not about to leave the restaurant without that Bordeaux. He recorked the bottle and tucked it under his arm. Greatly alarmed, our bartender explained the situation and suggested Mr. F return tomorrow and finish his wine. Mr. F said he would not. There was a confrontation. We are sure our bartender showed too much muscle. We assume Mr. F felt put-upon and cornered. Whatever the case, the upshot was that, in spite of George's most personal follow-up the next morning, Mr. F has not been back, and the Haut-Brion is still waiting for him.

Rule number three concerns payment. Like every restaurant, we were assigned a paying cycle, giving us the date by which our vendors have to be paid. We are in cycle four, which means that all our liquor and wine bills are due the first week of the month after we receive the merchandise. If we are late, we are in trouble, no matter what the reason.

It happened not too long ago. Frederick Wildman, one of our wine vendors, had moved his offices. Our bookkeeper sent the check to Wildman's old address. Not receiving payment on time, Wildman reported us to the SLA as being late. The SLA instantly put us on COD with all vendors until we convinced the SLA that we had paid all our bills promptly, and they, in turn, notified the vendors that we were "clean."

The Federal Bureau of Alcohol, Tobacco and Firearms, to whom every restaurant owner has to pay an annual fee of $250, acts as the nation's liquor watchdog. It regulates imports and supervises all state liquor authorities, as well as the manufacturers and wholesalers of alcohol, tobacco, and firearms. Sometimes the bureau issues a statement that throws the industry into turmoil. Among the BATF's latest disclosures was the release that, when drinking wine, consumers ingest a minute amount of lead. Although members of the wine industry immediately pointed out that there is more lead in legumes than in wine and that billions of people have been enjoying wine for thousands of years without a lead problem, the consumption of wine dropped, at least for a month, until the media breathlessly reported that, according to recent scientific findings, red wine "may have potential" to lower cholesterol.

The New York City Department of Health charges $350 for a restaurant's annual license, which must be posted for all to see. The department's vigilance is laudable in many ways. Health inspectors appear periodically to inspect the premises. They look for improper handling of food, poor storage, bad refrigeration, inadequate dishwashing facilities and water temperature, infestation, filth. There are different levels of violations. Some have to be corrected immediately; others have to be corrected by a given time.

On February 14, 1986, we received a violation. Having been informed that there were mouse droppings under one of our basement freezers, we were told to eliminate this problem by a certain date. When the inspectors came for reinspection, they found fresh droppings.

In those days it was customary for the health department to notify the city newspapers of their findings. The *New York Times* made those reports public every Sunday. Checking that *Times* page was the food establishment's favorite sport. We could hardly believe that our restaurant was mentioned on that page. It was little solace that another restaurant, one of New York's most elegant places, was also mentioned. George's mother, shocked to the core, called from Florida. She was not the only one. Business suffered, although George immediately set up our own daily inspection team, thanks to whose vigilance the entire premise would pass Marine inspection. We never got another violation.

Months later the department stopped making public announcements. It had become known that there was rampant corruption within the department. It had been common practice for inspectors not to write up a legitimate violation if properly rewarded, or they would fabricate violations to receive bribes. In 1991, the department had been sufficiently overhauled and resumed public notices of inspections. The main focus was now on areas where the public health was at greater risk—"cracked eggs rather than rodent doo-doo in a far corner," as the new deputy health inspector announced.

As before, the department still requires that a restaurant's owner, manager, or chef—any one of them—take a fifteen-hour course in food handling. Although they advise restaurateurs to wash lettuce in a Clorox solution, it is a helpful course, particularly for newcomers.

The New York City Water Department is less efficient. A year ago, they forced us to install a $2,000 electronic water meter reading outside the premises, so that they didn't have to come inside the restaurant to read the meter. We installed the device. But since the department so far has not gotten the electronic reading equipment, it's reading the indoor meter as usual. Our latest water bill was $5,000 for the year.

Reasonable, compared with the garbage. It's amazing how much garbage a restaurant generates. Thirteen hundred dollars' worth of garbage a month, paid to a private carting company. Years ago, the New York City Department of Sanitation used to pick up all garbage. But as the city grew, the task became overwhelming, and the city decided to let businesses take care of their own garbage disposal. For a while, a mafia got into the act, putting their contractors on specific routes. Nobody else would touch that route. Today, garbage collection seems more open, with rates for carting services set by the city according to bulk.

Peculiar things have happened. Shortly before we opened the restaurant, we installed flower boxes and filled them with geraniums. Passersby shook their heads: "In this neighborhood! They'll never last." Sure enough, two days later the boxes had been ripped off the wall and stolen. We received a call from a woman who lived across the street. She had witnessed the incident: it had been perpetrated by a couple of men from a private garbage-hauling company. She remembered the name on the truck: Capone. George made a series of calls till he finally located a garbage-carting company in New Jersey under that name.

"I'll look into it," said the man in charge. "No hard feelings, I hope. It won't happen again."

The next day a truck pulled up with our flower boxes. Two men reinstalled the boxes, filled with additional flowers and ivy.

One might think that payment for the New York City Fire Department comes out of city taxes. But, as restaurant owners, we pay an additional yearly fee of $500 to the department. Firemen come periodically to inspect air-conditioning equipment, the date on the hand-held fire extinguishers in the dining rooms, the fire-prevention equipment on the hood over the stove, the roof, and anything else that might be involved in case of fire.

The automatic fire extinguisher, the Ansul system, is activated the minute the temperature above the gas burners reaches a certain level. When that occurs, the heightened temperature causes a lead fuse in the equipment to melt, which then automatically opens six nozzles that release a flood of chemicals to extinguish the fire, at the same time shutting off the gas.

In the summer of 1991, at a time when we were operating at a loss with barely enough money to pay suppliers, the fire inspectors informed us that the Ansul system, although still operative, was out-of-date. Installing a new system meant hiring an expediter to submit appropriate drawings and reports in order to receive a new permit from the building department. It also meant contracting a company capable of installing the system, plus buying the system. The estimated cost was $4,500. Our priority was to replace the kitchen exhaust system, a $15,000 project that takes out stale air from the kitchen via the stack to the roof. In September, the inspector returned. Not seeing the new system, they issued a fine and gave George a summons, to be heard at the criminal court. The installation of the new Ansul system took all morning, which meant we had to close for lunch.

When George appeared at court on two appointed dates, the Fire Department did not show on either date, and the case was dismissed.

In addition to adhering to city, state, and federal regulation agencies, there are many codes with which restaurant owners must comply : observing immigration laws, working with the Human Rights Commission, complying with the Disabilities Act, supporting the bottle bill and recycling requirement, and, now, enforcing New York's smoking policies. Under that law, any restaurant seating more than fifty people is required to establish up to 70 percent of its seating as nonsmoking, based on the customer demand.

Neither George nor I smoke. In fact, it bothers us when someone lights up a cigarette while we are eating. But we are not fanatical about it and dislike having to act as police officers in our own restaurant.

In some ways, that policy changes the entire character of our place. Suddenly there are requirements as to who can sit where, which often

86

knocks out requests for a preferred table or a favorite server. To complicate matters, people do not necessarily specify smoking or nonsmoking when making reservations. Dining out with friends, entertaining businesspeople, they themselves don't know the smoking habits of their guests. They arrive, two at a time, part of a party of six, happy with their table. And then, just as the couple at the adjacent table is digging into their cassoulet, one person out of the six starts smoking. The cassoulet eaters object. We now become arbitrators, diplomats, peacemakers.

Most people cooperate; some do not. It happened right at our table. We had invited friends for dinner, among them a famous food writer. As usual, we sat at table twenty-one, located in the room customers enter first. Since the bar is in this room, we had originally made this the smoking room. But when we realized that most clients asked to sit in the nonsmoking section, we switched rooms. With so few smokers occupying tables in the front room, at first glance the restaurant looked half-empty.

We had not seen our friends since that switch. Two of them arrived early.

"Good grief," they said, "people used to be able to smoke here. Don't you remember Robert is a chain-smoker?"

The smoking room was packed. A five-top table would not become available for another hour. In the upstairs Napoleon Room, to which we frequently direct smokers, a wedding party was in full swing.

"We are sure we can work it out," said George.

"You realize, I can't stay," said Robert the minute he arrived. "America is turning into a police state. They meddle in my affairs thousands of feet aboveground; soon they will tell me what I can and cannot eat. I have dedicated my life to celebrating the pleasures of the table. Nothing personal, you understand. Don't mind me. Enjoy your dinner."

I got so upset, I almost drank a whole bottle of Alsatian Riesling, despite the warning that it contained sulfites and, among other things, might cause birth defects.

Among 12,000 legislative bills that are introduced each year into the state legislature or the city council, only 650 are endorsed by the New York State Restaurant Association, an organization that represents the restaurateurs' interests and actively lobbies against overly harsh measures that, if passed, could seriously affect the restaurant industry.

"In some instances it's a matter of educating the public first," says Fred Sampson, the present president of the association. "Have them accept new laws and regulations."

He cites a recent ruling that wanted restaurants to prominently display the face masks (one adult size and one child size) and latex gloves that restaurants must carry in case of mouth-to-mouth resuscitation emergency needs. While the mask might protect the parties involved from AIDS (ridiculous in the first place), "seeing such equipment conspicuously displayed does not create a desirable ambiance." The association won its case; masks and gloves may be stored out of the restaurant goer's immediate vision.

Another bill presently under discussion is the "antidiscrimination" measure that would deny employers the right to set dress, grooming, and jewelry standards for employees. If passed, we could not prevent servers from wearing nose rings, tongue studs, or spiked purple hair. And while such a getup might fit into the atmosphere of some places, I just can't see it at La Colombe d'Or, Le Cirque, or at any restaurant where I'd care to eat.

The *Nation's Restaurant News,* a trade publication, was up in arms. "Restaurant operators should have the right to set dress and grooming standards for employees working on their premise," ran their editorial. "Frivolously applying discrimination laws diminishes society's seriousness about fighting bias.... Guaranteeing someone's right to wear a mohawk at the reception desk limits the rights of employers to set standards for the work place."

To keep on top of rules and regulations, tax payments, legal and other business matters, we keep two lawyers and an accountant on retainer and have a full-time bookkeeper and part-time clerical help.

Which leaves the matter of insurance. Between liability, fire, theft, and accident insurances, we pay yearly premiums of around $50,000.

There are other operating expenses. We easily go through 250 to 300 white napkins and tablecloths a day, about a dozen cooks' uniforms, and umpteen gray-and-white-striped aprons—part of the waiters' uniform. Our monthly laundry bill runs to $1,500. Once I tried to persuade George to switch to white aprons.

"That means adding three hundred and fifty dollars to our monthly laundry bill," said George. "Half of what we pay for flowers."

All of these fees and expenses hardly compare with the amount we pay to the credit-card companies: more than all the laundry bills, as much as the yearly garbage collection, more than insurance, easily twice as much as our yearly electricity bill.

About 90 percent of our business is paid by credit cards, a service for which the credit-card companies charge a fee. American Express's fee is 3.25 percent of the bill; Visa and other major credit-card companies' charges run from 1.9 to 2.2 percent. All fees are based on the total amount collected, including tips and tax. Of course the New York State Tax Department expects to receive and gets the full amount of tax collected, which we send to them promptly on the twentieth of every month.

What those fees and double deductions wouldn't buy! A new hood over the range, new upholstery for the banquettes, an extended wine cellar! Beyond that, restaurants that do not accept credit cards have a relatively free hand with their bookkeeping. In an all-cash transaction, who is to know how big the check, how generous the tip! It allows for skimming undeclared cash, which enables an owner to pay his staff off the book, something every employee from dishwasher to maître d' yearns for.

It would not work in our case. Aside from inconveniencing customers, a cash-only policy has negative sides. For one thing, it is risky having large amounts of cash on the premises. Holdups are common; cheating is tempting. Beyond that, checks may bounce, and check-approval companies charge fees. Credit-card charges are as much a fact as all other charges in restaurant operation.

Adding it all up, George has figured out that—even with a full house and an acceptable food cost—it costs us $20 for a customer to sit down before he or she has as much as ordered a glass of water.

7

The Clientele

"*There* are dozens of reasons, only remotely related to food, why people go to restaurants," wrote Craig Claiborne, former food editor of the *New York Times*. "They go to see and be seen, they go because a restaurant is a conversation piece or because it makes a convenient rendezvous."

I could add to Clairborne's list: they go to impress, to flex muscle, to challenge their partner, to relive a memory. And George's theory goes way beyond this. According to George, "People go to restaurants to recapture childhood; to feel nurtured, cared for, pampered, loved." It explains why people's reactions to the restaurant experience can be extreme; at times euphoric and at times furious.

As hostess I witness it daily: Mr. Y with an 8:30 reservation for a party of four acts like a disappointed child.

"Is my table ready?"

"Yes, it is." I point to table forty, located in the nonsmoking section, as requested.

"No." Mr. Y shakes his head. "That's not the table I requested." He points to table twenty. "I want that table over there."

"I explain that we cannot guarantee a specific table, particularly not on a weekend.

"How long are *they* going to be?" asks Mr. Y, referring to the present occupants of table twenty.

"Hard to say. Some people like to linger over coffee."

"What else can you give me?"

"I have one table in the other room."

The four follow me into the old room. The ladies in Mr. Y's party are delighted. Not Mr. Y.

"Isn't this your smoking room?"

I explain that since there have been many more requests for nonsmoking than smoking, we have designated this part of the room nonsmoking for this evening.

Mr. Y, who at this point is trying to prove to himself and to his party that he always gets what he wants, dismisses the table with contempt. "If that's the best you can do, we are leaving," he declares without consulting the rest of his party.

The woman at table thirty-three, on the other hand, is thrilled to be here. She consults me about the menu. She cannot make up her mind; everything looks wonderful. She loves every dish, coos over every morsel, worships the chef, and wants to kiss his hand. The husband tells her to cool it. Suddenly, the place seems hostile to her. She pushes her dessert away and complains of a draft.

I seat two men at table eleven. When I arrive a few minutes later with a party of three assigned to table twelve, I find that the two men have taken possession of that table instead.

"Don't worry," whispers the waiter. "They won't be here too long. They aren't planning to eat, they told me. They'll only have some wine."

I am dumbfounded. This really bugs me. I wish George were here; he'd know how to handle the situation. I march my party of three back to the hostess stand, asking them to please wait. Then I return to table twelve. I take a deep breath. "Gentlemen, you are welcome to sit at the bar where you may stay as long as you like. But I need this table for a party of three. I hope you understand."

Getting up slowly, the men linger at the table, discussing their next step. I'm anxious to have the table reset. At that moment, the runner approaches with three cassoulets for table ten. Since we block the aisle, he can't get past us.

"Excuse me, excuse me." Seeing the bottleneck, the runner takes the cassoulets back to the kitchen.

It's at moments like this that I either want to burst out laughing or stalk away.

"Go ahead," I am tempted to say. "Sit wherever you like. Don't mind me."

I wish I could sell our seats in advance just as they do in the theater. After all, our operation is not that different from the theaters: the play is the meal; the waiters are the actors; I am master of ceremonies. Selling seats would eliminate no-shows and assure each customer his or her rightful seat. Weekend seats would be more expensive, of course, and children under five would have to pay double at all times.

Within minutes, the crisis has passed. The men have developed an appetite, after all. They become pussycats: could they possibly have their old table back? The rescued party of three, happily settled at their table, find the whole incident amusing. They exchange pleasantries with the two men; I could bet they'll end up sampling one another's dishes.

Meanwhile, table forty-two is occupied by a middle-aged couple. Legs crossed, the man sits halfway into the aisle.

"What's in your bouillabaisse?"

I enumerate the ingredients, which include mussels, clams, and lobster.

"Shellfish?" The man is indignant. "I can't have shellfish. Maybe the chef can leave it out."

"Have the special," says his wife, knowing it's coq au vin.

"Coq au vin?" The man shakes his head. "You know I only eat breast of chicken, and it has to be boned."

"In that case, let me suggest our sautéed chicken with shallots and truffled mashed potatoes."

"I had chicken yesterday," says the man. He doesn't like fish and meat is out of the question because he had a hamburger for lunch.

"I don't know what happened," he says. "This used to be a good place."

He addresses himself more to his neighbors than to his wife, a good-looking woman who chats amicably to attract her husband's attention. The man does not listen. He is bored. I imagine he'd rather be home.

I see a lot of it: a power dance between two partners. Going out for dinner, particularly on a weekend, was undoubtedly his wife's idea. Perhaps it's her way of proving that her husband still cares about her; perhaps she wants to get even with him for paying more attention to his business than to her. At the end of their meal, the husband questions every item on the bill. He also informs me that our billing system is a disgrace and that our wine list should have a wider selection of rosés.

New people at the door. The Peters. Twenty minutes late.

"You changed things," says the man. "I don't recognize it at all. Is this under the same owners?"

I look at the Légers hanging on the back wall; the Caras next to table twenty-one; the Picasso plates, terra-cotta objects, copper pots, olive trays, flowers, and little doves all in their proper place.

"Nothing has changed," I say. "When were you here last?"

He doesn't remember. Six, seven, maybe eight years ago.

The comedian Jackie Mason used to do a bit about people who act as if they are partners in the restaurant they enter:

"Where is everybody tonight?"

"How come it's so crowded?"

"What's wrong with the air-conditioning?"

"I feel a draft."

"Who is the new bartender?"

"You call that a table?"

Usually I can handle the situation. Knowing the script gives me a certain advantage. Besides, I like the roles assigned to me, playing mother, sister, chum, appeaser, educator, authority, among others.

I seat a young couple.

"Can I get you something from the bar?"

"What will you have?" the man asks the woman.

"I don't know."

She looks at the man; she looks at me, hoping for some guidance. I know the symptoms—their first date. The woman may drink two martinis for lunch, but now she wants to make a good impression.

Sometimes it's the other way around. The woman is sophisticated; the man doesn't know a Burgundy from a Beefeater. The restaurant is a testing ground for the cultural potential of their romance.

Actually, quite a number of restaurant dates have led to matrimony. Jack Schwartz, now a book editor at *Newsday*, took his wife-to-be here on their first date one week after we had opened, back in September 1976. Ever since then, the couple has celebrated the anniversary of the date by booking a table at La Colombe d'Or.

Donald Broars, a surgeon at the Hospital for Special Surgery, proposed to his wife, Betty Jane, while dining at La Colombe d'Or.

"I remember I had the *confit* of duck," says Betty Jane. The Broarses come frequently. Whenever possible I seat them at table thirty-three, where the momentous event took place.

Breakups also take place over untouched salmon and Beaujolais Nouveau.

"Just take the plates away and don't ask any questions," I'll whisper to the waiter.

Women going out together have the fewest hang-ups—except occasionally for their appearance.

"What's the dress code?" they often inquire over the phone.

"Informal. But please don't come in sneakers," I am tempted to say. Quite a few women do. Nine out of ten times, sneaker-wearing women also insist on taking their shopping bags to the table and are unwilling to part with coats and umbrellas. Surrounded by all that paraphernalia, they look like homeless gourmets.

According to our coat-check girl, on Friday people arrive with so much paraphernalia, we could use an extra baggage room to store it all.

The coat-check girl operates independently and keeps all her tips. On a busy winter evening she might collect more than a hundred dollars, all in $1 bills.

Do people ever forget to tip?

Yes, it happens once in a while with foreign visitors, particularly the French, who are used to having the tip included in the bill. It's a delicate situation. We usually point it out. But in some cases it's obvious that their faux pas would cause them acute embarrassment in front of people they are entertaining. We let it go.

Tipping double the amount of the total tax, 16 percent, is considered a fair tip. Many clients leave 20 percent. That's the amount we add onto the bill for private dinner parties. Occasionally, the hosts or hostesses are so delighted with the way the party went, they will give the waiters a handsome sum of additional cash. Waiters love cash and boast about it to one another. Their combined cash tips are put into a kitty by the bartender. At the end of service the bartender divides the cash evenly among all servers, including the runner and himself.

Charge tips are paid out once a week, together with the weekly salary. Since the credit-card companies charge their 1.9 to 3.25 percent commission on everything, we deduct the appropriate amount from the waiters' charge tips. Not a popular concept with the staff. Besides, charge tips are an open book, subject to taxation. So are cash tips, of course. But who's to know how much was really made.

Occasionally a client will leave a big tip because it makes him feel good. Pat Cetta, owner of Sparks Steak House, entered our waiters' hall of fame back in 1976 when he left a $50 tip on a $28 check. Thinking it may have been a mistake, George asked Pat if he had meant to leave that amount. Pat, who in those days weighed three hundred pounds, threw his arms around George. "You bet," he cried. "Your restaurant is an exercise in perfection." It was the beginning of a friendship.

Not all friendships that originated in the restaurant started on such a high note. Irv and Roberta Schneiderman were disgruntled clients when we first met. George, eager to receive input from clients, had put a sign on every table that read: "If you have any comments, talk to George." Passing by a table, George was stopped by a customer. "Are you George?"

George nodded.

Pointing to his unfinished dish, the man said, "Well, George, this crust is soggy."

The dish was *bœuf en daube* baked in a phyllo dough. It was a challenge to which George responded with gusto. What followed was a discussion on how to avoid a soggy crust while maintaining a juicy stew. Mrs. Schneiderman ventured some suggestions. It turned out that she was a world-class cook as well as a cooking teacher who had earned her stripes in Diana Kennedy's kitchen. By the end of the evening, we had joined them at their table. Wine, food, and music were their passion. With so much in common, it was natural that we should become friends. Aside from seeing one another either at the restaurant or at one of their exquisite dinner parties, we have traveled together in France and stayed at their summer place near Grasse.

The Davids became friends because they could not pay their bill. Mr. David had made a reservation for a party of four. Shortly after Mrs. David and her guests arrived, Mr. David called to speak to his wife.

"Mr. David is delayed in his office," Mrs. David explained. "He will not be able to join us."

It was only after the meal that Mrs. David realized that having changed her bag at the last moment, she was without cash or credit cards. The people she was entertaining were business acquaintances of her husband. Mrs. David confided in George.

"Don't worry," said George, who had never met the Davids before. "Send me a check."

Two days later Mr. and Mrs. David booked a table for two, bringing a copy of Liebling's *Between Meals*. We became friends there and then.

Another friendship started on a peculiar note. Walking through the dining room one day, I noticed a woman whip out a tape measure from her pocketbook and actually measure the width of the table where she and her party of four were sitting.

"Twenty-four inches," I heard her say. "It should be at least twenty-seven."

Meter-maid mentality, I decided. Besides, who comes to a restaurant equipped with a tape measure?

Lois Brown, as I found out.

"I can't help it," she explained later. "I design place settings for restaurants. Your tables, if you permit my saying so, are too small for your oversize plates. Mind you, it's by no means a criticism; it's just an observation."

That's what I like about this business. There is always something to learn. Lois Brown gave me her card and said to feel free to call her if ever I needed information or advice. Sure enough, when we had a hard time locating martini glasses, I called Mrs. Brown. She gave me the names of two suppliers.

"If they can't help you, let me know. And please call me Lois."

We see a lot of Lois and her husband, who became regular clients. But I have never again seen a tape measure.

For a long time, Mr. and Mrs. Nielson were simply a nice couple who enjoyed La Colombe d'Or. Like clockwork, they arrived every Friday at 7:00 P.M. sharp.

"We're running away from our children," they explained jokingly. "Three boys, all teenagers."

I thought they lived in New Jersey; they assumed we lived near the restaurant. One evening we ran into one another at Carnegie Hall.

"Hah," said Mr. Nielson, "something else we have in common."

Mr. Nielson and George, it turned out, were alumni of the High School of Music and Art.

The Nielsons offered to drive us home after the concert.

"It will be out of your way," we said.

"It's no problem," they insisted. "Where do you live?"

That's how we discovered that we live across the street from one another.

Mrs. Nielson was thrilled. "I am giving a little dinner party next Sunday," she said. "If you are free, we'd love to have you come."

I readily agreed. "Mistake," George said later. "Remember the teenagers. Besides, how do you know she can cook?"

He needn't have worried. Two of the teenagers had gone on a ski trip, and Mrs. Nielson had engaged a Swedish cook who prepared a sensational smorgasbord. By the end of the evening, George and Mr. Nielson—now Carl—were swapping sailing stories, while the cook gave me her recipe for lingonberry mousse.

Perhaps my most endearing client is the elderly gentleman who comes every Thursday around six o'clock. I assume he is a widower. Walking slightly stooped, he shuffles to table twenty-two, which we keep ready for him. He keeps the menu close to his thick bifocals and inquires about the specials. His hearing is slightly impaired. Without his having to ask, I bring him a glass of Punt e Mes. He eats slowly, while reading a book. When it comes to the bread pudding, he puts the book down. By seven o'clock he's finished and gone.

Once, he purchased a copy of my chicken cookbook, displayed at the bar. I asked him if he cooked.

"When I go to my house in the Berkshires," he said.

That's as much as I know about him.

Over the years, we have seen a considerable number of celebrities at the restaurant. There were fellow restaurateurs, among them George Lang, owner of Café des Artistes; Joe Baum, now of Rainbow Room fame; Tom Margittai of the Four Seasons; Jean-Jacques Rachou of La Côte Basque; Roger Vergé of Moulin de Mougins, who came to eat and gave us the benefit of his experience. Drew Nieporent, now the owner of Montrachet, was a teenager when his parents first introduced him to our restaurant.

"You were my inspiration," says Drew.

Marc DiGuilio and Peter Meltzer, who later opened the bistro Quatorze, were such steady customers that we felt they were family. Eating at Quatorze now, we see many La Colombe d'Or touches.

Among the people whose visits we particularly treasured were James Beard and Roy Andries de Groot. James Beard, who suffered from gout, came in bedroom slippers. De Groot, author of *The Auberge of the Flowering Hearth* and, at that time, food editor of *Esquire,* came with his Seeing Eye dog.

Jeanne Moreau came trailing glamour; Leslie Caron came with Michael York. Liv Ullmann could not be seated.

The Swedish actress arrived by herself. She had no reservation. The restaurant was packed; there wasn't a chair to sit on.

"Miss Ullmann, can you wait?" asked George. "I'll give you the first table that becomes available."

Ms. Ullmann shook her head. "Anyway, I can't have garlic," she said and left.

Winston Churchill's daughter Sarah got tipsy. Using a chair as a prop, she charged through the dining room in a simulated bullfight, crying "Olé!" Barry Manilow's mother acted the superstar when she started to sing at the top of her lungs. When George asked her to tone it down, she was indignant: "Young man, don't you realize I am Barry Manilow's mother?"

The various members of the Kennedy family, including Jackie O., did not have to identify themselves. Everyone in the restaurant recognized them. The same with Peter Jennings, one of our former steady clients. The minute his secretary called, we would chill his favorite wine: Châteauneuf-du-Pape '89, Grand Tinel.

My favorite client is too young to drink. Kate Richard has been coming to La Colombe d'Or ever since her parents brought her for her second birthday. Usually we do not encourage parents to bring young children. But Kate Richard proved to be a Mozart of the palate. She began her meal with roasted peppers and buffalo mozzarella, polished off her sole meunière, and lapped up a big portion of chocolate-banana tart. Returning on her third birthday, Kate switched from sole meunière to monkfish in saffron sauce and from the chocolate-banana tart to the *gâteau victoire.* When the aftermath of chicken pox prevented Kate from celebrating her fourth birthday at La Colombe d'Or, she asked her parents to please pick up the chocolate-banana tart and the *gâteau Victoire* from the restaurant.

Kate has just celebrated her eleventh birthday.

What did she eat?

Confit of duck.

"It's wonderful," she declared. "Please, don't ever take it off the menu."

Our oldest steady client, Joshua Myron, came to the restaurant on his doctor's orders. Recovering from anemia and sundry ailments, Mr. Myron's doctor recommended a weekly dose of liver.

"La Colombe d'Or serves the best liver in town," said the good doctor.

It's been ten years since Joshua Myron followed his doctor's advice. Experiencing good health, as well as a good appetite, Mr. Myron, who just turned ninety-two, has sampled every one of our dishes. These days he concentrates on our bouillabaisse.

"The best this side of Marseille," he said. "I recommended it to my doctor."

The restaurant's medal of honor for enduring patronage goes to two people: Barbara Petroske and Luise Roberts. Both came the day we opened. Barbara remembers it vividly: "I live around the corner and couldn't wait for you to open. This neighborhood was a culinary wasteland."

She walked by every day to watch the progress. On opening day, she came with a friend.

"The place took our breath away," she recalls. "It was so cheerful, so light and comfortable—the banquettes with their Provençal fabric, the pictures and the flowers. It was like instant sunshine; a breath of fresh air."

Barbara even remembers what she ate: pâté, roast chicken, and *tarte tatin*. She cannot even guess how many meals she's had at La Colombe d'Or since.

"Sure, there have been occasional upheavals," she admits. "But by and large, you have been very consistent."

Luise Roberts, a retired dancer and choreographer, used to be a regular client at Gloria, which occupied our space years before we bought it.

"Gloria was a modest little restaurant," says Luise. "Nothing special, but convenient. Then you guys came along. I remember the notices George

100

put up : progress reports on the construction, information about himself, the architects, all very personal and friendly. When you opened, I was so thrilled, I felt like dancing.''

Luise's visits are erratic. She may come once a week or every few months. She's never missed New Year's Eve, except once. George was so concerned when she didn't show up that he called to find out if she was all right. Luise apologized : she had an unexpected houseguest who was an invalid. George promptly dispatched a waiter with ''New Years Eve dinner to go.'' Luise still talks about it.

Do we extend special treatment to old-time customers ? Of course we do. When they call for a last-minute reservation, we'll do our best to squeeze them in. If at all possible, we reserve their favorite table. The chef might send them a tray with *amuse-gueules*, the French name for cocktail snacks. Time permitting, George or I might sit at their table, share a glass of wine, or enjoy an after-dinner drink with them. We know about their children or their parents, what trips they have taken, and what restaurants they have been to. We gossip. Above all, we take good care of them.

I wish we could take good care of everybody, always. In this business, it seems impossible. There are too many factors that can throw things off balance : upstairs, there may be a private party, and the downstairs dining room may be fully booked. Due to traffic conditions and whatever other factors, almost everybody shows up late. Parties of four turn into six : ''We hope you don't mind.'' A party of five whose name we do not have on the list insists they made a reservation.

While we become furniture movers, rearranging tables to accommodate everybody, the kitchen is busy putting out the thirty appetizers for the upstairs party, which means no other order can be filled for the moment. The waiters, anxious to appease their hungry customers, appear, armed with orders. It is usual at this moment that the dishwasher breaks down, leaving the bar without glasses and the dining room short on silverware ; or a runner, with a tray full of hot soup, bumps into an incoming waiter ; or a cook, coming out of the walk-in, hits a waiter with the heavy metal door.

One time a bird flew into the kitchen, entering through the exhaust system. To kill the animal was unthinkable ; to have the bird fly into the dining room was equally inconceivable. Moises, our grill cook, finally managed to catch the frightened bird. Meanwhile, steaks and fillets burned in the oven, and braised endive turned charcoal brown.

"Communicate. Communicate with your customers," we urge the staff. Most clients are extremely understanding when told the reason for a delay.

What is a reasonable time for diners to wait for a dish?

As a rule, ten to fifteen minutes for appetizers once the order has been placed, another fifteen minutes for entrées after the appetizers have been removed. To remove dishes while one member of the party is still eating is rude. So, in my mind, is a waiter's solicitous inquiry: "How did you like your food?"

It's a loaded question, we tell our waiters. Far better to attend to every detail, maintain eye contact with each customer in case he or she has a request.

To avoid mutual grief and misunderstanding, I would like to propose two codes of conduct: one for the eating public, the other for restaurants.

THE RESTAURANT'S PLEDGE
or the diner's bill of rights

1. We shall receive each client as a welcome guest.

2. We shall seat clients without undue delay, at a table away from swinging doors and safely out of traffic.

3. We shall furnish a tranquil and comfortable environment.

4. We shall provide libation and fresh bread as soon as possible.

5. We shall provide good food and wine at reasonable cost.

6. We shall assign courteous, competent servers to the table.

7. We shall inform clients ahead of time in case the kitchen has run out of a dish and mention the prices together with the specials.

8. We shall endeavor to serve dishes within a reasonable time and give an honest appraisal in case of delay.

9. We shall serve the appropriate dish to each diner without having to ask questions.

10. We shall properly look after diners throughout the meal.

or the restaurant's bill of rights

1. I shall honor my reservation.

2. I shall give the correct number of people in my party.

3. I shall be forthright about my party's smoking habits.

4. I shall come on time or call in case of undue delay.

5. I shall appear in appropriate dress and, if at all, wear a discreet scent.

6. I shall graciously accept my assigned table (in accordance with my rights).

7. I shall be aware of a restaurant's cuisine and shall respect the chef's effort.

8. I shall be civil to the staff.

9. I shall keep the noise level low.

10. I will release my table at a reasonable time once the meal has terminated.

The wildly popular Tribeca Grill has the following notice posted next to the hostess stand: "Tables will have to be released after two and a half hours of reservation." In other words, for a seven o'clock reservation, the clock starts ticking at 7:00 P.M. At 9:30 that table has been rebooked and will be reclaimed.

I find that a bit harsh and not in keeping with the nature of a restaurant, which, after all, is a service business. However, I well understand these measures; it is the only way to maximize a restaurant's potential.

It all starts with the reservations book. This essential timetable serves two purposes: it helps the maître d' to assign his tables and have them set up accordingly; it informs the kitchen how many people to expect and when.

Our reservation sheet looks like this:

We have twenty-seven tables with a combined seating capacity of seventy, plus the upstairs Napoleon Room. On weekends, the demand for tables far exceeds our capacity. In order to take advantage of this, each table should be turned over twice. The way to do this is to take bookings for either a six o'clock or a nine o'clock seating. Most people, however, want to eat around 8:30. Only a restaurant of Le Cirque's stature can afford this luxury. People who want to dine at Le Cirque rarely change their minds. People who eat at less exalted places frequently engage in restaurant shopping. They will make reservations at two or three restaurants and, depending on their mood, or the consensus of the dinner party, will honor one of those reservations without bothering to cancel the others. If they cancel at the last minute, the harm is done. Honoring their reservation, we most likely turned three parties away.

That's one reason that people who call at the last moment for a table often have a better chance of getting a table than people who called that morning. Since George and I seldom can make advance plans for going out for dinner, I often ask for a reservation that very same day.

"We have a table at six o'clock and at ten-thirty," I am usually told.

"Good show," I want to say. Instead I give them our name and phone number. "If you get a cancellation, call us."

It rarely fails.

8

Promoting the Restaurant: Reviews and the Media

$\mathcal{O}ne$ star, two stars, three stars, no star, toques, and kisses—the symbols of restaurant reviews. We have received them all. In the seventeen years of La Colombe d'Or's existence, we have been featured in every medium and have been reviewed innumerable times by major and minor publications. The walls of our restaurant are covered with framed testimonials to our successes. The unfavorable notices are hidden in the files, reminders of the lows we had to overcome in this precarious business.

A few reviews almost buried us; two catapulted us to dizzying heights. Some reviews seemed grossly unfair and hurt us personally; others pleased us immensely because the reviewer understood and responded to what we are trying to do. Putting all the reviews together, there is only one review that counts: the one in the *New York Times*.

"The conventional wisdom now is that each star is worth half a million bucks. If the *New York Times* awards a restaurant an extra star, that's half a million more in revenue; if they take it away, it's the reverse." That was the appraisal of a New York restaurant consulting firm.

Revenues at La Colombe d'Or have never been in the multimillions. We are a small and relatively modest place. But within the framework of our operation, that observation was true.

In August 1988, La Colombe d'Or did a fair but by no means banner business. Wayne Nish was our chef. We averaged about forty people for lunch, fifty for weeknight dinner, and up to seventy on weekends. Check average for lunch was $25; dinner slightly higher. Starting on September 16, we doubled that volume. We could easily have tripled it if we had gone crazy and tried to squeeze in all the reservations. What had happened was every restaurateur's dream: Bryan Miller, the restaurant critic of the *New York Times*, had reviewed the restaurant and awarded it three stars. (In all of New York, with its thousands of restaurants, there were only twelve establishments with that rating.)

In a glowing review, Miller paid tribute to our "vibrant food, good service and engaging setting." He exclaimed his surprise at having found such a jewel in this "snug Provençal-style French restaurant that for 12 years has been an unassuming neighborhood spot in the Gramercy Park area with a hot-and-cold reputation."

That review made us so hot, people called from Dallas, Chicago, and

Miami, reserving tables weeks in advance. People, including friends, who had never set foot in the restaurant because it was out of their neighborhood pleaded for tables. To keep up with the increased volume, we redesigned the kitchen serving station, added more refrigeration, installed new sinks and shelving. We also retiled the walls and the kitchen floor. All told, we spent more than $50,000 on the improvement. It was well worth it; the kitchen became a model of efficiency; it looked new and sparkled.

Increased volume, highly individualized dishes, and picture-perfect presentation also meant putting on more help. We hired two additional prep cooks and two line cooks, plus—a real luxury for us—a full-time pastry chef.

We rode on the crest of this review for almost two years, after which two things happened: in May 1990, Wayne left, and the economy had changed. We were in the middle of a recession. Many restaurants, including well-established ones, went out of business. Thousands of people, among them people in publishing and advertising, who formed the bulk of our lunch business, were laid off. By January 1991 our sales were down by 40 percent; expenses were as high as before. We started to lose about $10,000 a month. We needed to become the focus of attention again; become a hot destination. We needed Bryan Miller.

In May 1991 he came. As is Miller's custom, he came on three separate evenings, in the company of three fellow diners, including his wife. Although he made the reservation under another name, we recognized him.

People frequently ask us what we do when a restaurant critic arrives on the scene. Very little. The food either does or does not stand on its own merit. We can do nothing to alter it at that point. The only thing we may be able to affect is service. We selected Miller's table with care and assigned our best team to him. We told the waiters to be natural and not to hover. Mark May, Wayne's successor, felt his future was at stake. He concentrated so hard on each of the dishes ordered at Miller's table that he neglected orders from other tables. George and I stayed in the background, reasoning that Miller would want to judge our performance on his own terms.

And judge he did. His review appeared on May 30, 1991. "La Colombe d'Or presents a troublesome rating dilemma," Miller wrote. "While much of the food floats in the three-star range, its substandard service attenuates the pleasure of dining here. Until that shapes up, two stars is a more accurate assessment."

Mark was crushed; George and I were bewildered. The service! What had gone wrong with the service! According to Miller, "the dining room team made a trip downtown to the Department of Motor Vehicles look speedy.... The lack of professionalism even extended to attire; one evening our waiter's rumpled white shirt looked as if he had been rolled on the way to work."

The review all but knocked the bottom out of our operation. I woke up every morning feeling sick and struggled with that feeling for most of the day. For the first time in our turbulent history, I lost heart. George, the proverbial Rock of Gibraltar, felt trapped. He would have liked to sell the business, the buildings, or both. But properties went begging and busted restaurants could be picked up for a song.

In the long run, however, Miller did us a favor. Instead of moping, we needed to come off our three-star horse and get real. That meant reduce the kitchen staff to what it had been in the pre–three-star period and operate with a realistic food cost. It was obvious that our needs did not coincide with Mark's, who had every reason to believe that, one day soon, he would make his mark as a celebrity chef. It was the beginning of summer. Nothing much was happening. Mark stayed on; we were loathe to make the inevitable move.

The day our accountant confirmed that the restaurant had lost $100,000, we snapped out of our inertia and went into action. George told Mark it was time to part. The next step was to reduce the kitchen staff. Hal Kennedy and Joyce Wong, our gifted sous-chef and pastry chef, had to go—also one prep and one line cook.

Mark, who together with his wife, Nini, had been looking for a suitable location to open their own restaurant, was relieved. He needed that decisive push. George put his customary to-the-point ad in the *New York Times*. Among the many applicants, five stood out. After our standard screening technique, Naj Zougari emerged as the number-one candidate. Working side by side with Mark for two weeks, Naj took over the kitchen in July 1991. One month later, Mark had found his own place on the fashionable Upper East Side, which he named *May We*.

Jonathan, our manager-cum-son, realized that we could no longer afford his service. He was eager to return to his beloved Oregon. As in the beginning, George took on the work of manager. With Nini, who had been hostess during Mark's tenure, gone, I took charge of the dining room. Once we had ceased to be a high-profile and chic place, many of our waiters left. We hired new ones and changed the structure of dining room hierarchy: there had been too many chiefs. We decided to have one bartender for lunch and one at dinner. George would supervise lunch, I the dinner shift. After about a month, Benoit, one of our new waiters, emerged as an obvious candidate for maître d', while another newly hired waiter displayed such strong organizational talents that George made him his assistant in the office.

With Naj Zougari in the kitchen, food again appeared on the table at a comfortable speed. We initiated a $24.50 prix fixe, in addition to our regular menu, which now included some old-time bistro favorites. Clients liked the food, telling us it was "better than ever."

Arthur Schwartz, restaurant critic of the *New York Daily News*, was the first to report on the change: "La Colombe d'Or has settled back into its old charming substantial self.... Chef Naj Zougari ... has brought the kitchen back to full flavor with his simultaneously earthy and sophisticated French Provençal food."

The review was extremely gratifying. Alas, in terms of business, it carried little weight. Reviews in papers other than the *New York Times* simply don't have the same impact. While any constructive critique is of value to us, it is of no great consequence to the people likely to visit our restaurant. Of course, any positive review is good for morale. It might even prompt some food editors or free-lance writers to feature the restaurant in a story or mention it in a roundup article.

Even *New York* magazine seems to have lost some of its clout. When Florence Fabricant, then the magazine's restaurant critic, "discovered" us in 1977, she put our restaurant on the map. When *New York* magazine's food writer Barbara Costikyan wrote that our Napoleon Room was a great place for private parties, we booked that room for six months straight. But when a few years later Barbara Costikyan featured our Bistro-to-Go in her "Best Bets" column, that mention resulted in a total sale of four orders, leaving us with one thousand aluminum containers that George, anticipating major sales, had driven to Hunt's Point to buy.

Again, we thought we hit the jackpot when *New York* magazine's "Insatiable Critic," Gael Greene, at the height of the 1991 winter recession, came to La Colombe d'Or, finding a "warren of small rooms, cozy and romantic." What's more, she waxed enthusiastic over chef Mark May, calling him "Gold Fingers." Anticipating a tremendous turnout, "Gold Fingers" Mark went to town. We assigned an extra person on phone duty and doubled the wait staff. On Monday, the day the magazine hit the newsstand, the phones remained quiet. We reasoned that because *New York* is a weekly publication, people read it at their leisure. The fact was that the write-up did not cause a stampede. Perhaps it was Gael Greene's aside that "the hostess should not spray-clean bare wooden tabletops while people are eating. The lemon scent is numbing."

That remark had us so puzzled—George and I thought Gael Greene had mixed up her restaurants. George abhors anything that is scented. In fact, since he is allergic to many chemicals, including perfume, if he could have it his way, he would bar people who use perfume from entering the restaurant.

Fortunately, Gael Greene included La Colombe d'Or in her "Ultimate Restaurant Guide," a roundup that appeared in *New York* magazine at the year's end. "A glaring game of musical chefs might paralyze some restaurants, but owners George and Helen Studley long ago composed the score played out in this cozy warren of small rooms," she wrote, this time calling attention to our Provençal dishes.

The immediate effect of the review was hard to gauge because December is the month of back-to-back parties and cannot be used as a yardstick. However, the review meant a lot to George and me. It was a confirmation that we had reestablished confidence and were on the right track.

But it was Bryan Miller's radio broadcast on WQXR, in which he mentioned La Colombe d'Or as one of the good choices for New Year's Eve, that had people reach for the phone, asking "Can we get a table?"

Occasionally, we too fall for media hype. That happened with Sheree Bykofsky's *The Best Places to Kiss In and Around New York City*, a book that appeared shortly before Valentine's Day 1992. Awarding La Colombe d'Or four kisses, Bykofsky's enthusiastic report of "this hidden treasure" prompted *Glamour* magazine to hail La Colombe d'Or as the "Most Romantic Restaurant in New York."

We were besieged with phone calls. Three weeks before Valentine's Day, we were completely booked. We put fifty couples on the wait list and turned at least two hundred away.

At six o'clock on Valentine's Day, sixty bottles of champagne were cooling; one hundred and twenty heart-shaped rolls had been delivered; the violinist, hired for the occasion, tuned his instrument; kitchen and dining room staff stood by.

It never happened. Certainly not the way we had anticipated. Although the phones kept ringing with last-minute pleas for a table, we ended up with fifty-two no-shows, a record high for us.

Some reviewers move in mysterious ways. Mimi Sheraton failed to include us in her early *New York Times Guide to New York Restaurants*, even though she had given La Colombe d'Or two stars during her reviewing stint at the *Times*. Ms. Sheraton, who now publishes her own restaurant newsletter and guide, continues to ignore us. Seymour Britchky, who publishes a monthly restaurant newsletter that forms the basis of his annual *Restaurants of New York*, once started his review with the observation that "the hostess on duty is a lady whose apparent preparation for this job was twenty years as warden of a school for delinquent girls." Apparently delighted with this idea, Britchky elaborated on the theme at length before getting around to our food, which he seemed to approve of. Given the style of Mr. Britchky's prose, it was hard to say. That review appeared unaltered in Britchky's subsequent annual guides, not taking into account that his bête noire, our all-time-favorite employee, the intensely missed Leila, had quit her job and moved to New Jersey.

The publication we cherish is *Gourmet*. Without creating the flutter and hysterics generated by a *New York Times* review, a *Gourmet* review has a cumulative effect; it's like an annuity. People hold on to their copies of *Gourmet*. They follow the magazine's endorsement at their leisure— sometimes months later. Out of towners, who before may have never heard of us, check us out on their next visit. They are seldom disappointed. Having been properly briefed and advised, they know what to expect.

"Fourteen years is quite a long time in this city for a restaurant not only to stay in business, but also to retain its charm and popularity," started Andy Birsh's April 1990 review of La Colombe d'Or. Next, Mr. Birsh described our dining rooms in great detail, giving the reader a picture of the exposed brick walls, the stamped-tin ceilings, terra-cotta-tile floor, rustic-looking chairs and benches with Provençal fabric. He mentioned the bleached old doors, bought at a flea market, with which we paneled our bar, and my collection of Léger scarves that we had framed and hung throughout the restaurant, gallery style. "Given it to do all over again, the Studley's probably wouldn't change a thing," he wrote before talking about our chef and the mouth-watering dishes he created.

Mr. Birsh knows fully well that chefs come and go, but that we will prevail. By lauding our commitment and good taste, this review gives the reader a sense of what we are all about. Even the fickle New York public pays heed to such an endorsement. Retrieving their coats from the coat-checking station, they catch a glimpse of the framed review. They nudge their husbands: "See, I told you *Gourmet* said this was a good place."

"It certainly was" agree the husbands. They turn to me: "Excellent food."

In general, men seem to pay less attention to reviews than women do. The one possible exception is *Forbes* magazine. A good rating from *Forbes* is like having won the approval of an all-male club.

There are a number of fairly reliable guide books to New York restaurants. Among them are the Zagat *New York Restaurant Survey*, John Mariani and Peter Meltzer's *Passport to New York Restaurants*, and Gault Millau's *The Best of New York*.

The Zagat survey is tabulated from an impressive number of its voluntary "Sunday" reviewers. Restaurants are rated on a scale from 0 to 30, according to food, decor, service, and price. The pocket-size guide carries considerable weight, particularly with out of towners.

"How did you come to choose our restaurant?" I inquire of three young women from Baton Rouge, Louisiana, who tell me this is their first visit to New York.

"Zagat said your restaurant was charming, intimate, and romantic, with delicious French food," they say.

La Colombe d'Or has always ranked high in *Passport,* based on the views of its editors, both of whom are genuinely fond of our food and of us. Gault Millau seems to mean more to French tourists seeking New York restaurants than to the New York public. When they recently gave us a promotion in the form of their symbol—a toque—our French friends called from Paris, while New Yorkers seemed unaware.

We don't know how to evaluate *Fodor's Pocket New York City: The Best of Manhattan.* We were not even aware of the guide's existence till one of our clients brought it to our attention.

"You should read it," she said. "You'll love it."

We did indeed: "Pots of geraniums by the front door, lace curtains at the windows...set a cozy bistro atmosphere, carried out by friendly, unfawning service. The food, however, goes well beyond standard bistro fare...."

George and I have devised our own rating of restaurant reviews. We give them stars for their immediate impact on business, crowns for most meaningful reporting, and dollar signs for lasting effect. Using these symbols, the list is as follows:

IMMEDIATE IMPACT ON BUSINESS	0 – ★★★★	stars	
MOST MEANINGFUL REPORTING	o – oooo	crowns	
LASTING EFFECT	0 – $$$$	long-term investment	

Fodor	★	oo	0
Forbes	★★★	o	$$
Gault Millau	★	oooo	0
Gourmet	★★	oooo	$$$
Mobil Travel Guide	★	o	0
New York Daily News	★	ooo	0
New York magazine	★★	ooo	$
New York Observer	★	ooo	0
New York Times	★★★★	ooo	$$$
Newsday	★★	ooo	$
Passport	★	ooo	0
Zagat survey	★★★	oo	$$$

Being a fair critic is not easy. George and I constantly vacillate between being too critical and not being critical enough. We are aware of the smallest detail that catches our eye: a dirty glass, a missing spoon, a napkin on the floor, sloppy plating, skimpy portions, a weak espresso, clients waiting unduly for their check.

We sit down to eat. My quail, straddling a mound of fava beans, is overcooked. I don't feel like making a fuss; I want to have a pleasant evening. I'll discuss the quail tomorrow.

The next day, George has quail for lunch. It is cooked to perfection.

Most of the professional critics visit a restaurant three times before forming an opinion. Like clients, they pay for their meals. Then there are the pseudo-reviewers who promise a favorable mention in exchange for free meals or similar favors. A restaurant gains nothing from such an evaluation; nor does the public.

We had been open fewer than three weeks when George received a phone call from Merv Griffin's office. The proposal was: Griffin plus a party of eleven would come and have dinner at our restaurant in exchange for a mention on "Merv Griffin Show."

I was excited. "Imagine. Merv Griffin!"

"A freebie for Merv Griffin and party of twelve for us," said George. "That's not my idea of business."

No free lunch, we decided.

About a week later, we had dinner at Passy (now the Post House). We had barely been seated, when Merv Griffin made a grand entrance, accompanied by an entourage of thirteen. Customers whispered and stared. The management made a big fuss.

"This place won't last long," said George. "Mark my words."

A few months later Passy closed.

There are few publications that appear under the guise of having chosen their restaurant listings solely on a restaurant's merit, but that, nevertheless, exact a certain price from the restaurant itself. When we were approached by *Epicurean Rendezvous Award & Restaurant Guide* to be included in their yearly guide, it seemed a great honor. We agreed to buy hundreds of copies from them and were proud to display these at a visible spot in our restaurant. However, when the following year we were told that we had to buy one thousand copies and favor their advertisers' products, we declined and consequently were deleted from the next issue.

"Mistake," said Calvin, who was our public relations man at that time. Calvin's fee was $1,500 a month—a bargain considering that the top public relations firms charge as much as $5,000. Many restaurants—among them the Rainbow Room, the Russian Tea Room, Tavern on the Green, all of the Restaurant Associates restaurants, and those of the Alan Stillman group—have their own in-house public relations department. Highly ambitious chefs often hire their own publicists.

Over the years, we have engaged the services of four different publicists. Each had his or her connections—the ear of this or that food editor or writer. All showed enormous enthusiasm and good results in the beginning. After about a year, that dwindled. Like overly prolonged psychoanalysis, their involvement inevitably became routine. Also, since all of them had other clients, there was just so much that they could do for us.

That's why we do our own PR. We don't go about it as diligently as we would like to, but we do the best we can. George and I discuss possible topics. We work on a release and send it to the press. To whom we send it depends on the nature of the release. The arrival of a new chef goes to the food editors and restaurant reviewer of every important newspaper, as well as to editors of food-oriented magazines, trade publications, and freelance food writers.

The annual fall return of cassoulet is sent only to local food editors who do roundups on New York's restaurant happenings, while news of a new herb-infused dessert might also be mailed to the food writers at large.

At best, it's a matter of hit or miss. Of the ten releases we send a year, one or two may actually get printed. Most magazines work with a nine-month lead, which means we'd have to tell them about our spring menu by Thanksgiving.

The jury is still out as to the effectiveness of advertising. A one-and-a-half-by-one-inch column in the *New York Times* costs between $3,000 and $4,000, depending on the placement. In our case, that means we have to sell three hundred extra covers to recoup that investment. Sometimes we place small ads in various publications, including the *New York Times*. If clients appear at the restaurant, ad in hand, we know that ad made an impact.

116

That was the case with the cassoulet and bouillabaisse advertisements we ran in the *New York Observer*. Modeled after a copy we had seen in an English gastronomical journal of the 1930s, both ads graphically depicted the ingredients of the respective dishes. Effective, yes. Meanwhile, the artwork alone for the ads cost $700.

"That's a lot of bouillabaisse," said George.

Granted, ads may have a subliminal effect. To us, running an ad is a bit of an ego trip. It feels good to see our name in the *New Yorker*, the *Observer*, or the *New York Times*. It reminds the readers we're still there.

The restaurant business has changed. Up to a few years ago, it was sufficient to offer good food in amiable surroundings. Today, that is not enough. At least not in New York City. Now, a restaurateur also has to show his muscle as a marketing expert. The big ones employ marketing consultants; the lesser ones devise their own schemes.

We have been very successful with our newsletter. When we started it, it was a one-page photocopied sheet in which I talked about happenings at La Colombe d'Or. Our first mailing was one hundred; now that list has grown to four thousand and the newsletter to four pages. I continue to write the newsletter; George edits it; a mailing house prints it and sends it out. Clients can't wait for the next edition. They share the newsletter with friends, sent it to relatives in Omaha or Manchester.

We produce four newsletters a year, corresponding to the seasons. In each instance we'll feature a special event at the restaurant to which we invite our readers. Events may range from cooking seminars to champagne tasting. Held in the late afternoon, these events draw a good crowd.

"So nice to meet you," people will say. "Makes us feel as if we are part of your family."

Will the *New York Times* come back? And how soon? Will they respond to the changes? How will they judge our food?

Their verdict is momentous and far-reaching. But with all the upheavals, past and present, I wonder if it's crucial for survival. There are our clients—from first-timers to steady customers. "We love this place," they say.

Our faith rests with them. They are our best critics.

9

Special Events

$O\kern-2pt wning$ a restaurant isn't as glamorous as many people imagine. Most days are ordinary, filled with menial details and humdrum routines. It's hard to sustain enthusiasm in this sea of dailiness. Fortunately there is the other side of owning a restaurant: celebrating festive occasions, staging special events, and giving private dinner parties are among my favorites. To me, these events are unabashed ego trips that let me sit back and enjoy myself while showing off the restaurant.

NEW YEAR'S EVE

New Year's Eve is our biggest night. It is a glorious affair without being boisterous. We usually have a 7:00 P.M. and a 10:30 P.M. sitting. The first sitting enables guests to get home before midnight; the second lets them greet the new year surrounded by a congenial crowd. Although we supply party hats, confetti, and noisemakers, the emphasis is on food shared in the company of friends and extended family. The menu is elaborate. Champagne flows. Viewing the size of the Pol Roger Nebuchadnezzar that we order for the occasion, I always envision Sarah Bernhardt taking one of her legendary champagne baths. A Nebuchadnezzar holds fifteen liters of bubbly—the equivalent of one hundred and twenty six glasses of champagne. For about a month, we display the bottle at the bar.

In anticipation of good tips, every waiter wants to work New Year's Eve; few volunteer to pop the champagne cork, which seems a formidable task. Actually, the cork is surprisingly small. But muscle and skill are required to lift the monster bottle and pour the first round of champagne without making a mess.

That's what prompted George to come up with a champagne harness, based on his own design. Converting liters into pounds, and adding the estimated weight of the bottle, George determined that the weight of the filled Nebuchadnezzar was sixty-five pounds. He bought yards of black nylon webbing, plus two big metal hooks from a marine supply store. Design in hand, George commissioned the shoemaker around the corner from the restaurant to furnish the harness. The shoemaker came to take

119

measurements. Two days later, he returned with the harness. He stayed to watch as George and the bartender, after much probing and knocking, located the beam in the ceiling over the bar, into which they secured the hooks. It took four people to lift the bottle and hoist it into the harness, in which it was cradled for the next four weeks.

Our maître d', however, had so little confidence in the scheme that he wedged stacks of books under the suspended bottle every night after service. The harness withstood the test of time. Two days before New Year's, the bottle was eased out of its harness and put into the walk-in to chill. Shortly before New Year's Eve dinner service was to begin, two waiters ceremoniously carried the bottle back to its rightful place. With the bottle safely in place, George climbed up the ladder, popped the cork, and, tilting the swinging Nebuchadnezzar ever so lightly, poured the first glass of the champagne. From that lofty height, he acknowledged the round of applause from his audience below with a toast.

On December 31, 1977, George and I were homeward-bound on a flight from Rio. Our visit to Brazil had been so enjoyable that we had postponed the return until the last possible day. Unexpectedly, the plane stopped in Miami; we had to deplane. Due to a bomb scare, our flight could not continue. Every flight from Miami to New York was fully booked; hundreds of passengers were stranded. Upgrading our ticket to first-class, agreeing to a standby—and never mind our checked luggage—we managed to get two seats on a seven o'clock flight. We arrived at Kennedy airport shortly before 10:00 P.M. George found a limo that whisked us to the restaurant in time to catch up with at least part of our second annual gala dinner.

Our first New Year's Eve at the restaurant was anything but a gala affair. Unknown as we were, only one party of four showed up. George, myself, and our then-teenage children sat opposite them in the otherwise empty dining room wondering why we had thought that running a restaurant would be fun. Among the various courses, Kai had prepared lobster à l'américaine, a dish of Provençal origin characterized by shallots, garlic, herbs, and tomatoes. The children opted for duck; George and I ordered lobster, which was meticulously cooked and succulent. I've never ordered lobster à l'américaine since. Partly in deference to Kai; partly because the memory of that first New Year's Eve dinner still depresses me.

Our most elegant New Year's dinner took place in 1989–1990, when we were at the height of restaurant fame. The $70 prix fixe dinner, exclusive of wine, prepared by star chef Wayne Nish, was sold out weeks in advance. Guests appeared in evening dress. Their attire did justice to a dinner marked by luxurious food and elegant service.

In a prophetic way, that dinner was the swan song of the carefree 1980s. Shortly thereafter, political and economic worries resulted in massive downscaling.

People's ability to spend lavishly may change; romance never does. Valentine's Day is a banner occasion at the restaurant. Weeks before the event, George and I mull over the menu. It should be romantic without being gimmicky. It should appeal equally to men and women. It should be festive, yet light. We tend to think in terms of visual and symbolic appeal: red—red snapper with red wine sauce, pomegranate, and raspberries; hearts of palm; chocolate truffles and coeur à la crème.

Our rolls, baked for the occasion by our bread supplier, come in the shape of hearts.

We hire a musician—a violinist, an accordion player, or a guitarist—to stroll around the dining room, troubadour fashion, and serenade individual couples. George buys long-stemmed red roses, which we hand to every diner after the meal. Our Valentine's dinner is so popular, we turn many people away. George is always willing to give up our table, but I say "No way; it's our restaurant. We are entitled." Besides, I know that George is a big romantic at heart. A few years ago he pulled off the ultimate surprise: our waiter presented me with the appetizer—a puff pastry supposedly filled with seafood salad. Not having ordered the dish, I wanted to send it back. But George said not to make a fuss. Reluctantly, I removed the pastry lid. Instead of the seafood salad, the shell contained a pearl necklace, which I retrieved with a fork to the applause of the initiated waiters.

The ages of our Valentine couples range from teenagers to septuagenarians. Some are in the throes of first love; others commemorate their third marriage.

Almost all Valentine clients have a story connected with La Colombe d'Or and feel compelled to share it with us.

"It was here, on our third date, that I made up my mind to marry Marge."

"When I saw Betty dig into your cassoulet, I knew she was my kind of woman."

"Fred proposed to me here."

"We think this is one of the most romantic restaurants in New York."

Newspaper articles have attested to that. Sheree Bykofsky's *The Best Places to Kiss In and Around New York City* confirmed it. And that was before we added Le Grand Amour to the menu. The almond-apricot liqueur is aptly named; its pastel-colored label depicts two swans, gliding in a lily pond at Fontainebleau, where Napoleon used to walk.

Napoleon did not earn his medal as the world's greatest lover, but he is the focus of our third big event: Napoleon's Birthday Dinner. We opened the Napoleon Room as a private dining room shortly after we opened the restaurant. Located on the second floor of the restaurant, the room originally held only six people and exhibited just two sketches of Napoleon. Since then the room has been greatly enlarged, the beautiful old brick and arches have been exposed, and many more *objets* have been added: prints of Napoleon's battles, marble busts of the emperor, vintage sketches of Josephine, original plates from Malmaison, a copy of David's famous painting, and a blowup of the actor Albert Dieudonné as he appeared in Abel Gance's 1927 epic film.

With its high ceiling, draped windows, and gilded mirrors, the room has a stately presence. It can accommodate up to thirty people at a single long table that stretches from one end of the room to the other. Set with starched linen, white china, silverware, and clusters of wine glasses, it is a formidable sight—perfect for festive celebrations.

The Napoleon event happened quite accidentally. Since August is the slowest month in the restaurant business, we were looking for an occasion to lift it out of the summer doldrums. That's how I discovered that Napoleon was born on August 15.

"That's it," said George. "Couldn't be better."

Choosing an appropriate menu posed a problem. Napoleon was an indifferent eater, known to have gulped down meals at record speed. Never knowing when the Emperor would want to eat, his cook prepared a roasted chicken every twenty minutes, just in case. Napoleon left the art of stately dining in the hands of his minister, Talleyrand, a born aristocrat, who mounted opulent banquets that reflected neither Napoleon's preference of eating nor our style of cooking.

"Corsica," said George, referring to Napoleon's birthplace. "Like Nice, it was Italian before it became French. There must be similarities."

Easier said than done. We could not find a single Corsican cookbook. Food and Wines from France, the organization that promotes French products in the States, was of no help. In fact, the French, we discovered, are embarrassed by Corsica and would just as soon return it to the Italians. Fortunately, a friend of ours who was about to leave for France volunteered to bring back as many Corsican cookbooks as he could find.

We studied the Corsican cuisine based on the two books our friend found. The cuisine is robust and earthy, relying heavily on game and game birds, lamb, and mutton. Fish and vegetables are plentiful. With a nod to Italy, there are many pasta and polenta preparations, with the polenta being made with chestnut flour. *Herbes du maquis* is the predominant flavoring agent. Wild herbs grow in profusion in Corsica's maquis; intensely fragrant, they have an aroma that permeates the entire island.

"I could find Corsica blindfolded by the smell of the maquis," Napoleon said.

Feeling a bit blinded ourselves, we created our version of the maquis by adding dried myrtle to the usual bouquet of *herbes de Provence*.

Our very first Napoleon celebration was sold out because Florence Fabricant, informed by our release, mentioned the event in her column in the *New York Times*. Since we suggested that people wear festive dress or decorations, that first party resembled a Hollywood spectacular: Men arrived covered with medals. Women wore Empire-style gowns and tiaras. Our waiters looked smart in tricolor hats.

We celebrated Napoleon's two hundred and sixteenth birthday with the following menu:

We served white and red Corsican wines throughout dinner. The food was robust and succulent; the wines were dreadful.

Wines aside, the dinner was an unqualified success. When chef Rick Steffann appeared in the dining room—hand in his chef's coat, wearing a tricolor hat—he received a rousing ovation.

Among the guests was a board member of the New York Public Library who contacted us a few days later, suggesting we host a Napoleon dinner for the benefit of the library as part of its annual Tables of Content dinners.

Tailored and refined, the dinner—together with one hundred other dinners given throughout Greater New York—took place in December 1985. Participating guests paid $250 per person to attend, of which $150

127

was a donation to the library. With the guests arriving in limousines, dressed to the hilt, the evening took on the form of a court function. We distributed fans to the ladies, clay pipes and cigars to the men.

An artist friend had made me a Napoleon pin that combined a portrait of the emperor—surrounded by fleur-de-lis—with a stone-studded crown, fake diamond cameo, tussles, and pearl drops in an artful arrangement. The piece of jewelry stole the show.

Our 1988 Napoleon dinner was of particular significance because it served as the culinary coming-out party of the recently hired Wayne Nish.

By the time we celebrated Napoleon's two hundred and twenty-first birthday, the event had become so popular that we held it on two successive evenings.

Not all our plans for special events work. We bombed out with one event that we thought would be a sure winner. We had contacted Steven Jenkins, the *maître fromagier-affineur* of Dean & DeLuca, to orchestrate a French cheese tasting to initiate the 1991 fall season. The tasting would consist of a series of cheese trays, to be presented in order of their potency, each one accompanied by a matching wine.

We announced the event in our newsletter and informed the press. The newsletter was delayed at the printer and did not go out in time; the press remained silent. We hoped that by spreading the event by word of mouth, we would generate sufficient interest among our regular clients and therefore did not cancel the affair.

On the scheduled day Steven arrived with three hundred dollars' worth of France's stellar cheese. So far, nobody had signed up. George and I figured we'd call a few friends, sit down with Steven, and have a cheese orgy. It was a Tuesday night in late September. We had so few reservations on the book that we sent two waiters home. Steven went to the Napoleon Room to arrange his bounty.

George and I never made it upstairs till after ten o'clock, by which time Steven had left in a huff, leaving his cheeses to fend for themselves. We had served more than one hundred dinners—unforeseen and unexpected, a record for this time of year. Later we learned that an important auction had taken place in a nearby gallery.

At 10:30 George and I went up to the Napoleon Room, where the aroma of thirty pounds of cheeses at their prime awaited us. We uncorked a bottle of Châteauneuf-du-Pape '86, Beaucastel, and throwing cholesterol precautions to the wind, orchestrated our own cheese extravaganza.

For the next few days, we offered the cheeses as a special. We sold the Gruyère-type cheese, the Brie de Meaux, and most of the Roquefort. The goat cheeses, however, would not move.

"What a pity," I said.

George was way ahead of me. "Can you bake me a goat-cheese cake?" he asked the chef.

Naj, who has yet to question anything George suggests, said, "Sure, why not?"

The first cake was tasty, but the texture was too dense. Naj whipped some ricotta cheese into the second batch. Flavor and texture were great, but the cake looked plain. We thought of serving it with a bitter orange marmalade and finally settled on a sour-cherry *coulis*. The result was such a knockout we put the goat-cheese cake on the menu.

Steven Jenkins, to whom we sent a cake with our apologies, congratulated us on the cake and suggested the three of us get together for a quiet dinner.

CHARITY EVENTS

George and I give a yearly fund-raising party for God's Love We Deliver, an organization that delivers hot meals to homebound people with AIDS. We ask our guests to donate $100 to God's Love We Deliver. George and I contribute the dinner. A few days before we held the first benefit, our friend Michael Weisberg, from whom we had learned about the organization, died of AIDS.

We went ahead with the dinner, which took place in March 1990. Jacques Pépin was our guest of honor.

"I leave everything to your chef," Jacques had said.

"I have a pretty good idea of what Jacques likes," said Wayne Nish.

Jacques seemed embarrassed to be the center of attention. He was unassuming and charming. Everyone was thrilled to meet him. We had our baker bake a gigantic bread for Jacques. The round loaf was twenty inches in diameter, decorated with sheaves of wheat.

"I think I'll lacquer it and hang it as a wall sculpture," said Jacques.

"I think we'll eat it," said his wife, Gloria.

There was no argument about the meal; Jacques declared it superb, and everybody seconded this. The event raised $3,000 for God's Love We Deliver.

—

For our next God's Love We Deliver benefit, we asked Craig Claiborne to be our guest of honor. Craig had been to our restaurant a number of times. Hearing what the event was about, he agreed immediately. Florence Fabricant put a note about the event in her powerful column in the *New York Times*. It drew a substantial crowd. Guests came with volumes of Craig's cookbooks for him to autograph.

We fashioned the meal after one of Craig's favorite French menus, published in his book *Memorable Meals*. Craig was delighted. What pleased him even more was to find artist and cookbook author Ed Giobbi and his wife, Ellie, among the guests. A longtime friend of Craig, Ed had done most of the illustrations for Craig's book.

The evening started with champagne and hors d'oeuvres and then settled down to serious eating. Craig ate heartily. After the meal he made a brief speech: "I want you to know, La Colombe d'Or is one of my favorite restaurants," he said. He then went from table to table, thanking everyone for having come and thus helping the God's Love cause.

The money generated by the evening bought meals for six hundred people.

The success of each party depends greatly on the chef's ability to rise to the occasion. None did better than chef Rick Steffann at our Festival of Portuguese Food and Wine, held in April 1986 with the cooperation of Maria de Lourdes Modesto. Ms. Modesto, a well-known cookbook author and radio and TV personality in Portugal, supervised the preparation of the dishes, leaving the rest in Rick's expert hands.

The festival began with a press party organized by the Portuguese tourist office. Prominent American food writers, Portuguese food and wine distributors, and lovers of Portuguese food crowded into our dining room to meet Portugal's equivalent of Julia Child and sample the food. The dinner was served buffet style. Our cooks, looking smart in their starched toques, manned the various stations.

The Portuguese Trade Commission was so impressed with our performance, they invited us to the inaugural dinner of the New York chapter of the Portuguese Wine Society, where, in the company of other worthy recipients, we were knighted into the society.

Festivals with less exalted consequences have featured sausages, spring lamb, and soft-shell crabs. Our *Semaine du Poulet*, Chicken Week, offered eleven French regional chicken specials. We have given dinner parties for our purveyors and for the construction workers who renovated George's office, enlarged the cellar, and helped build the Napoleon Room. In addition there have been many parties for various food and wine associations, among them the Confrérie de la Chaîne des Rôtisseurs, Les Amis du Vin, Les Dames d'Escoffier, and Food and Wines from France.

We celebrated leap year in the French fashion. Bissextile du 29 Février 1988 featured *grand aïoli,* the great classic Provençal dish, relatively unknown in this country. *Grand aïoli* is composed of a variety of ingredients, such as boiled cod, snails, fennel, onions, carrots, beans, artichokes, potatoes, hard-boiled eggs, and chicken. Essentially, anything at hand— there is no set rule.

In our case, the chef took the word *grand* literally, preparing a feast of gigantic proportions, adding octopus and fowl to the already opulent

fare. The dish was presented on one huge platter and served, family style, with the guests helping themselves to whatever they fancied. The main point, of course, was to add dollops of *aïoli*, the garlic-infused Provençal mayonnaise that leaves one's breath unfit for anything but fire fighting.

Bean-inspired cassoulet is classic winter fare. Its appearance heralds the coming of the cold weather, an occasion that merits an annual party, which has become as traditional as the Napoleon dinner. But while the Napoleon dinner is a public event, the cassoulet dinner is a private affair to which we invite members of the press, colleagues, and friends.

No matter what the mix, the chemistry always works. Of course, the food is the big icebreaker. The dinner is a Rabelaisian feast that turns the most diet-conscious eaters into trenchermen.

Every food maven knows there are three different types of cassoulet, relating to three towns located in the Languedoc area of southeastern France—Carcassonne, Castelnaudary, and Toulouse. Each town has a version, claiming that its cassoulet is the best. What distinguishes one cassoulet from the other is whether the cassoulet contains only pork, or pork and lamb, *confit* of duck or goose, and an occasional partridge. Basically, a cassoulet need contain only two ingredients to be authentic—beans and sausages.

''What version is your cassoulet?'' people sometimes ask.

''Ours,'' says George, knowing full well that even within a given season ingredients may vary. Sometimes our cassoulet includes rabbit, garlic, and lamb sausages, in addition to the *confit* of duck. And then again, when one of the sausages is too dry, the chef may substitute pork or double up on lamb.

Whatever the. ingredients, cassoulet must be simmered very slowly, since it takes time for the beans to absorb all the flavors. At the height of the season, we prepare three big batches a week. Each batch is divided and ladled into individual twenty-two-ounce white flameproof crocks. This enables the chef to be sure that each portion contains the same number of sausages, *confit*, and the rest of the meats.

The cassoulet feast begins; the wines are poured. Waiters bring baskets with country bread, crocks of butter and tapenade. The appetizers arrive. Mindful of the gargantuan portion of the cassoulet, we keep the appetizers light: fish soup, house-smoked skate, or ratatouille. Within mi-

nutes the atmosphere changes from that of a formal banquet to a country fair. Everybody is talking and having a good time. I look past the long row of people that separates me from George and catch his eye. George winks at me. I smile.

"Yeah," I want to say. "Look at us now. We've really done it." I feel extremely fortunate. I'm also mighty proud.

While everyone is enjoying the first course, waiters and runners are bringing the cassoulet up from the kitchen, depositing it at the serving station. As soon as the appetizer plates have been cleared, the waiters come swooping down with cassoulet—thirty steaming hot crocks, exuding tantalizing aromas.

The scene reminds me of the cruise-ship days, when waiters, in a grand finale, would march into the dining room, balancing flaming baked Alaska on their trays. Dramatic effect notwithstanding, everybody digs in, and soon a strange noise comes over the room—it is the sound of thirty people concentrating on cassoulet.

The cassoulet dinner elicits fan letters from participants.

"Your cassoulet feast makes the thought of winter bearable."

"Toulouse, Carcassonne, and Castelnaudary, what do I care? I like your cassoulet the most."

"Our idea of what food is all about."

FAMILY EVENTS

Without a doubt, the most memorable parties are our family celebrations: the birthday dinners for Jonathan and Alexandra, my sister's fiftieth wedding anniversary, George's brother's engagement party, a family reunion, a surprise party for George's mother, the nautical dinner I gave for George's fifty-seventh birthday.

George, a passionate sailor, had recently completed a yearlong project of restoring and outfitting our vintage sailboat, *Avanti*. George agreed to my giving him a party and not asking any further questions. I decided on the nautical theme and invited George's sailing buddies, among them a

New York dentist whose boat docks next to ours; Alfi, who comes from Liverpool and has crossed the Atlantic with his twenty-six-foot sloop; Jeff, who had done the carpentry work on *Avanti;* the owner of the boatyard; the harbormaster; plus a few of our friends who had gone sailing with us.

Our waiters had seldom dealt with such a jolly bunch. The jolly bunch, in turn, had rarely encountered such food. Digging into the paella, they swapped stories of food experiences at sea: horror tales of grills falling overboard, tins exploding, perishables rotting, and biscuits drowning. Their most fondly remembered meals ran toward the bizarre: frankfurter soup, dried shrimp and boiled potatoes, chocolate-chip sandwiches.

I silently renewed my vow never to go for more than an overnight sail. Meanwhile, everyone had such a good time, I thought they might stay overnight.

Once, George decided to hold a dinner party at which he, accompanied by a friend, would give a concert. Although George is a good violinist, I was skeptical.

"People will feel awkward; they may be too embarrassed to come."

"Want to bet?" said George.

We invited friends. Concert or no concert, few turned us down. As could be expected, the dinner was superb. After dessert, George, his friend and fellow violinist Norman Pickering, and a harpsichord player engaged for the occasion took their positions. They tuned their instruments. Our guests sat respectfully, facing the musicians. I tried to imagine what went through their minds. George nodded to Norman. They raised their bows, and the first strains of Vivaldi's Concerto for Two Violins and Continuo echoed through the Napoleon Room.

The expression on everyone's face changed from that of politeness to utter amazement and delight. I felt so moved I broke into tears.

There was another celebration that touched a special chord: my first birthday in our newly opened restaurant. In those days, George and I worked together in the evening: George acted as bartender and cashier, and I worked as hostess. As usual, before closing, George and I sat at table fifteen, the one next to the kitchen. Instead of bringing the menu, the waiter presented me with an envelope. *Consommé Hélène,* it said—announcing the first course. The entire four-course dinner proceeded in this fashion. Every dish was heralded by an envelope, and every dish was named after me. When it came to the famous *poire belle Hélène,* chef Kai joined us at the table.

_"Surprised?" he asked.

I felt like a kid.

The idea of giving a midsummer night's party most definitely went back to a childhood fantasy. George, whose maternal family came from St. Petersburg, in Russia, improved on it.

"White nights," he said, thereby giving us the theme for the meal: Russian. We asked the guests to dress in white. They responded to a person, appearing in everything from tennis shorts to a wedding dress. Our surgeon friend, Ira Barash, wore a bed sheet that he had artfully draped around his ample girth, toga style. Staying within the color scheme, we served white wine throughout the meal, which included a yogurt-and-barley soup, beef Stroganoff, rice pilaf, and blini with sour cream. The Napoleon Room was lit by white candles.

"Very Ingmar Bergman, no?" I whispered to George.

"Looks more like Buñuel to me," said George.

But it was the toga-clad Ira who put the festivity in proper perspective. Glass in hand, he made a sweeping gesture around the room. "Napoleon met his nemesis in Russia," Ira said. "The Studleys made it their triumph."

For one reason or another we have as yet to celebrate Bastille Day. We will, though. Two years from now. That's when Baruch College, which bought the two factory buildings adjacent to the restaurant, will tear down the scaffolding, the wire fences, and barricades; remove the cement trucks, the dumpsters, and other vehicles that block off half of our street; and unveil their new library.

Come that July 14, we hope to join forces with our corner neighboring restaurants—Ray's Pizza Place, Abu Sido's Mid Eastern Cuisine, Abby's Irish Tavern, and Deno's Greek Tavern. We will close the street to traffic, hang lanterns and streamers from every lamppost. There will be an unending procession of food; wine will flow out of barrels. Of course there will be a *bal musette.* Neighbors and passersby, strangers and friends, young and old, everybody will dance in the street until the wee hours of the morning.

10

When We Eat Out

$\mathcal{George}$ and I eat out about once a week, to see what's going on in other restaurants. The places we choose fall into two categories: those that are similar in food or concept to La Colombe d'Or and those that serve ethnic food, of which both of us are fond. In between, we might go to a newly opened place with a prominent chef.

I imagine we are tough customers. The standards we have set at La Colombe d'Or have become second nature. We notice everything: a napkin on the floor two tables away from ours, a guest in need of a soupspoon, a table that ought to be cleared. The temptation is to call it to the waiter's attention or, worse yet, to get up and take care of it.

The restaurants we like all have two things in common: we feel comfortable there, and we get our money's worth. The restaurant may be a modest place, like Chaplin's in Charleston, South Carolina, where our pizza was so much better than the food we had tasted in Charleston's more exalted restaurants that we went there daily for the duration of our visit. The bill averaged $22 and included salad, two glasses of house red, and a darn good espresso. The place was clean and functional. Blowups of Charlie Chaplin gave it a touch of frivolity. Our waitress was a young woman from Iran, pretty and very apologetic about her limited knowledge of English. She was so pleasant, we offered her a job at our restaurant should she ever consider coming to New York.

On the other end of the scale was a dinner at Louis XV, Alain Ducasse's three-star restaurant in Monte Carlo, which costs a fortune, but for us was worth it. We sat in the gilded dining room, surrounded by cameos of Madame de Pompadour, feeling every bit like royalty ourselves. We started the meal with *légumes de printemps*, which were baby carrots, artichokes, celery, leeks, fava beans, and tomatoes in a truffle-perfumed light vinaigrette. This was followed by a warm salad of *coquillages*, mere mouthfuls of shrimps, mussels, and oysters on a bed of *mesclun*. Next came turbot and *daurade*. The turbot was roasted and served in a cocotte, together with fennel, onions, and capers. The *daurade* was braised in beef stock and fresh herbs and laced with a faintly spiked orange sauce. Next came a simply roasted *poulet de Bresse*, followed by a cheese tray. Although we were ready to pass it up, the waiter persuaded us to try the fresh mountain cheese. Served with coarse sea salt, fresh pepper, and an exceptionally delicate Italian olive oil, it was so sensational I had a second helping. A lineup of sorbets arrived in dome-covered silver pots, looking like Turkish rooftops. We sampled a semibitter chocolate tart with wild strawberry sabayon. wh.

Following the sommelier's suggestion, we drank a lively Châteauneuf-du-Pape Blanc and then a beautifully balanced Margaux Château d'Issan.

In spite of the many courses, we felt remarkably light. If money were no object, we would gladly return time and again. Not just for the food, but because the evening was enhanced by enthusiastic service from the charming staff.

Of course, although we had crossed an ocean to eat at Louis XV, we had not taken much of a risk: the restaurant's reputation for fine food and service was legendary. The search for a good restaurant can become difficult when seeking an honest meal in lesser-known establishments.

Over the years George and I have developed a formula that helps us detect whether or not a restaurant is likely to live up to our expectations. The formula may be called How-to-Spot-a-Good-Restaurant-Before-the-Food-Arrives. Essentially, we have reduced it to six points.

It starts with the impression just beyond the door. Being pounced on with "Do you have reservations?" is not our idea of gracious hospitality. Chances are we have a reservation. In the rare instances when we do not, there are only two possible courteous responses: either the restaurant can accommodate us, or it cannot. If the restaurant cannot accommodate us and communicates that politely, we will most likely return another time.

The next point is honesty about the wait. If we are told we will be seated in ten minutes and then have to wait for half an hour, we know we are in for trouble. Waiting at a crowded bar, nursing one or two drinks, kills our mood and appetite, and, by the time we are seated, we will probably not do justice to the meal.

Now, as for table location: as restaurateurs we understand the difficulty of satisfying clients with seating arrangements. An entire thesis could be written on the topic. Between clients' requests for tables in smoking and nonsmoking sections, tables in a certain waiter's station, spacious tables, intimate tables, tables in full view of the action, secluded tables, window tables, tables upstairs, tables downstairs, a maître d' can lose his mind. Not every request can be honored; not every customer arrives or departs when anticipated. But if a table assignment becomes a power play, if we are relegated to a remote table next to a swinging door while other tables are held for favorite clients, we cringe. This practice, most frequently encountered in restaurants with snob appeal, shows a lack of respect and makes us uncomfortable.

A restaurant's biggest telltale sign is the appearance of its menu. This may be scribbled, typed, printed, or engraved; the paper may be plain or sumptuous, stapled together or bound in leather—it doesn't matter as long as the menu is clean. A grease-stained menu signals sloppy management and makes us wonder how the kitchen handles the food. Cleanliness of glasses falls in the same category.

George is so attuned to how the serving staff handles glasses that he carries the following drawing with him.

When he suspects that a server is about to stick his fingers into the glasses, he flashes the drawing in front of me.

"Mazeltov," I want to say. But I agree; fingers do not belong in glasses. Nor do unsightly bandages belong on waiters' fingers.

Next is the food selection. I have been known to agonize endlessly over a menu where one dish sounds more tempting than another. However, when faced wtih a situation in which the kitchen is out of the very dishes I wanted to eat, and none of the remaining dishes appeals to me, I wonder why I am there.

147

Beyond that, I am a firm believer in "As the bread goes, so goes the meal." The sight of fresh bread is a fair promise of things to come. Stale bread, which George can spot before it even hits the table, either indicates penny-pinching or a what-the-hell attitude.

Occasionally something quite unexpected happens during the course of a meal that can turn a sense of pleasure into one of dismay. A few years ago George and I were lunch guests of three wine merchants in Bordeaux. The restaurant our hosts had chosen was one of the oldest and most respected eating establishments in Bordeaux. Captains and waiters hovered attentively around our table, decanting rare Bordeaux and placing more silverware in front of us than I could imagine needing for a day's worth of meals. Enjoying my salad of *carottes râpées*, I suddenly felt a strange object in my mouth. The object turned out to be a thumbtack. I whispered the fact to George, who asked our hosts if it would be all right for him to bring the matter to the captain's attention. "Absolutely," they agreed.

George signaled the captain and, showing him the thumbtack, explained in French that there was a nail in the lady's salad. The captain examined the thumbtack and disdainfully placed it on George's butter plate. "Monsieur," said the captain, "you are wrong. This is not a nail; this is a thumbtack." George had made the mistake of referring to the thumbtack as *clou*, while the correct word for "thumbtack" is *punaise*.

Another disastrous dining experience actually helped break the ice between us and a haughty waiter. George and I were having lunch at Oustaù de Baumanière, perhaps one of the most beautiful spots in France, legendary for its fine food and service. We were eating outdoors on a terra-cotta–tiled terrace, surrounded by bougainvillea and cypress and olive trees. The entire setting exuded a charm and delight that, unfortunately, wasn't echoed by the waiter's aloof attitude. Our rack of lamb arrived, ceremoniously rolled to the table on an ornate silver cart. Cutlery poised, the waiter was about to begin carving, when the lamb—which smelled divinely of rosemary-infused oil—slipped off the board and landed on the floor. Without missing a beat, the waiter scooped the lamb up from the floor, returned it to the cart, and, looking imploringly at George, began to carve our meat.

We understood the look. It meant "If I return this perfectly cooked, expensive piece of meat to the kitchen, I am through.'' We also reasoned that considering food cost, chances were that any frugal French chef would wipe off the roast and send it back to our table. The floor at Beaumanière was polished to the *n*th degree. We smiled at the waiter, who became, if not our friend for life, our enthusiastic ally.

Occasionally, there is nothing wrong with the restaurant, the service, the table, or the menu; it's George or I who are out of sorts.

Chez Garin, in Paris, was a restaurant where, no matter how exquisite the food and polished the service, George and I always ended up fighting. One evening, we fought so bitterly—I have forgotten over what—we left in the middle of dinner, divorce on our minds. Fortunately, George was able to figure it out: Monsieur Garin bore an uncanny resemblance to George's father. Unwittingly, George expected signs of paternal care. Instead, Monsieur Garin was too busy cooking in the middle of the dining room to even acknowledge George's existence. Being treated like a stranger upset George, made him anxious.

It became clear: either George would have to go through extensive analysis, or we would forget about Chez Garin. Not much of a hardship, considering the choices of good restaurants in Paris.

Aside from establishments like Allard, Pharamond, La Coupole, Fouquet, plus a variety of obscure little restaurants in unfashionable neighborhoods—places that have changed dramatically over the years—Paris has never been our favorite eating city in France. We much prefer the provincial restaurants that offer good regional cooking in a convivial atmosphere. High on the list is Auberge des Seigneurs in Vence. The proprietor, Monsieur Rodi, has turned gray and walks stooped. But the brass and copper pots in the dining room are as polished as ever, and the anemones as fresh as morning dew. As of old, the reception is boisterous. When it comes to Rodi's spit-roasted chicken, infused with pistachio nuts and doused with Armagnac, there simply is no equal.

Tétou, in Golfe-Juan, has remained another favorite, despite the fact that our last bouillabaisse was $60 per person—without lobster. Deceptively simple and unpretentious, looking like a diner run by Cartier, Tétou is a constant inspiration. I could come here twice a week to eat their *Salade niçoise.* But it's Tetou's bouillabaisse and their *loup de mer* that bring us from across the ocean. The *loup,* a Mediterranean fish, poorly translated as "wolffish," is grilled over fennel branches and presented whole. To watch the waiters bone our fish with two soupspoons while amicably chatting with us always strikes me as the height of understated showmanship.

Hiély, in Avignon, now sold, was a restaurant for which we had tremendous admiration. Sitting in the airy dining room at Hiély, amid solid French middle-class burghers, always gave us a reassuring feeling. The service was so smooth, the rhythm so fine-tuned, and people so well behaved, we felt all was right with the world. The food was not always consistent, but it was never less than good and occasionally superb.

Michel, in Marseille, has remained a bastion of the Provençal spirit that attracted us to this part of France in the first place. The *aïoli* that accompanies the bouillabaisse at Michel, near the old port in Marseille, is as seductive as it was when we tasted it two decades ago, prompting us to change our travel plans and stay an additional day in Marseille, so that we could sample that garlic mayonnaise once again.

Among all the magnificent towns in Italy, Bologna is our favorite. We like its manageable size and its historic treasures. Above all, we love Bologna's food. We'll be barely unpacked when we rush to Diana, an old-fashioned establishment whose *bollito misto* alone is worth a special detour. In Verona, another one of our favorite Italian towns, we like the atmosphere and the robust food of the 12 Apostoli, although it's difficult to coordinate our visit with their operating days. In Venice, one meal at La Colomba, our Italian namesake, is a must, more for the sentiment than from conviction about its food. For that, the risotto at Harry's Bar is hard to beat.

London to us means the Savoy Grill. Our first meal at the Grill came about by accident. We had made reservations at a highly touted restaurant near Covent Garden. The noise level of the place was excruciating, the crowd alarmingly dense, and the maître d' out of control. We fled. There was no taxi in sight. The wind blew fiercely. It began to rain. Lost in unknown territory, I thought about Jack the Ripper, when, suddenly, the Savoy Hotel rose out of the fog. Looking like drowned rats, we appeared at the Grill, asking for a table. The welcome we received was a testament to the British sense of civility. We enjoyed a superb supper of a simple salad, followed by a seafood platter, lemon tart, and house Chablis.

When we returned to the Savoy Grill the next evening—this time with a reservation—we were greeted by name and ushered to "our" table. The waiter remembered every detail of our meal, including the mineral water we preferred. We felt so much at home that we stayed till closing time and watched the staff count the silver before locking it up for the night.

Tradition is hard to maintain for restaurants in New York. Many of our favorite eating establishments have vanished. Among them is Café Chauveron, where George and I would lunch on Saturdays, years before we opened La Colombe d'Or. But Chauveron's chocolate cake, a dark, dense confection of sinful richness, was reborn as *gâteau victoire* at La Colombe d'Or.

Our favorite Italian restaurant was Ballato, on East Houston Street. Ballato had eleven tables. Signor Ballato, the portly proprietor, took the orders and made his recommendations. He introduced me to what was to become one of my favorite appetizers: spinach spiked with garlic, served at room temperature with strong Sicilian olive oil. George inevitably started wtih a half portion of green noodles, served in a thick cream sauce. It was at Ballato that I learned to appreciate osso buco, "better than in Rome," according to Ballato, who was not given to false modesty. Occasionally, he would join us at the table, entertaining us with tales of his Sicilian past.

For authentic Spanish food, we went to Fornos on West 52nd Street, now occupied by Victor's Café. Men with pinched faces, wearing Basque caps, lined the Fornos bar, where they rolled dice out of leather cups. It was at Fornos that I tasted my first *caldo gallego,* a soup made with potatoes, white beans, ham, garlicky sausage, and sharp greens. George ate *picadillo,* the beef dish served with fried bananas and a mound of rice. For dessert we had creamy flan and espresso so strong it kept me up half of the night.

One of the reasons these places felt so genuine, especially in the 1950s and early 1960s, was the transatlantic liners that crowded the New York harbor. Each ship carried between a five-hundred- and one-thousand-man crew, who all flocked to their favorite home-away-from-home New York hangout. Just as the foreign sailors lent authenticity and character to the waterfront restaurants, many of the ocean liners' chefs eventually stayed in New York and opened their own restaurants.

La Rôtisserie, on East 52nd Street, now the site of Citicorp, was our hangout for Sunday dinner. Here, the burly Breton Jean Claude roasted our favorite *poulet rôti*. The dish came with mountains of *frites* and generous portions of creamed spinach.

Jean Claude's prices were ridiculously low even for the 1960s. A meal averaged $8 per person. Our only gripe at La Rôtisserie was the wines, which ranged from poor to undrinkable. We kidded Jean Claude about the wines. But we never told him about the rancid butter that accompanied the decent bread. The butter, served in earthen crocks, had obviously been assembled from leftovers from the entire week. We figured it was Jean Claude's way of improving his food cost.

The children's favorite place was Micha Fu, a Chinese restaurant on Broadway and 125th Street. Sunday lunch at Micha's usually included George's parents. Micha, the proprietor, spoke fluent Russian, which he had learned when working at the Russian embassy in Berlin. It seemed Micha was just waiting for us in order to practice his Russian on George's Russian-speaking family. Taking it for Chinese, the other customers were impressed. The children, in turn, were impressed by the fact that the people around us were impressed. For my part, I was impressed by the variety of Micha's dumplings—the first I ever tasted.

For a while, Warner Leroy's madcap Maxwell's Plum, on 1st Avenue and 64th Street, became our restaurant away from restaurant. The menu was as eclectic as the decor, a helter-skelter collection of faux-Tiffany lamps, glass ceiling, gilded mirrors, ornate columns, carousel horses, ceramic animals, statuary, fountains, hanging plants, and balloons. Maxwell's was a genuine brasserie with a menu that ranged from potato skins to wild boar. My favorite dish was their warm chicken salad, quite a novelty in those days.

Maxwell's was so popular, throngs of people waited patiently for a table. The crush at the bar—a big singles scene—resembled that of the Fire Island Ferry on a Friday night. Luckily, Van, the maître d', was a friend of our chef, Kai. Spotting us among the crowd, Van would whisk us to a table, either at the casual café or the more formal back-room restaurant.

In the 1980s dining out became complicated; so many new restaurants opened that it was difficult to keep track. Many were backed by celebrities

—actors, designers, prizefighters—who poured millions of dollars into the ventures, making them dazzling showcases. Most of the restaurants were located in renovated warehouses in the SoHo and TriBeCa areas. All were designed by renowned architects and heralded as much for their high-fashion style as for their food. Attracting all the right people, many were so instantly successful that it was a triumph to get in.

To see what we were up against, we visited many of them. Alexandra, a sophisticated teenager, by now, knew her way around: Odeon, La Coupole, Batons, Indochine, and Mr. Chow. Between the frenetic scene at the door, the noise level, the aisle blocking, and the table-hopping, it was difficult to concentrate on the food. But we had to admit, in terms of design, they were worth the visit. Glass doors by Lalique, lamps by Giacometti, ice buckets from the *Normandie*—the details alone at Mr. Chow took my breath away.

There were other places: Texarkana, El International, One Fifth Avenue, Joanna, Café Seiyoken. El International was a wacky, kitsch-laden establishment that served tapas together with good Spanish bread and wine. The crowd was as eccentric as the decor. Café Seiyoken was more serious—at least to us, because we came primarily for the food. Seiyoken offered Japanese fare and French dishes, prepared with an Oriental twist. One could get French rolls and decent wine—items that are important to us. The place was packed with beautiful people, all so thin, I wondered if they ate at all.

Looking back, it seems that one minute one could barely get a table in these places, the next minute they were gone. El International is now El Teddy's; Café Seiyoken became Prix Fixe, Terrance Brennan's "now" place; and the formerly chic One Fifth Avenue enjoys a reincarnation as a top fish restaurant.

Fortunately, while many highly touted places opened and went under, a number of high-caliber restaurants opened and then went on to become important fixtures on the New York restaurant scene. Among them, Montrachet, in TriBeCa, has remained one of our favorites. The setting is understated and tranquil, playing second fiddle to the food. And what food! I want everything. The food is consistently superb; the wines are carefully chosen and well priced. But it's Drew Nieporent, the affable owner, whose attentiveness and attention to detail gives Montrachet its singular style.

While we admire everything Drew does, Drew, in turn, credits us with being his role model. We obviously enjoy each other's act.

It's Drew's touch again that makes the cavernous Tribeca Grill, co-owned by Robert De Niro, run so smoothly. Madly popular, it is crammed with stargazers and handsome people dressed in black; we nevertheless enjoy our visits. The menu is straightforward, the dishes well prepared. The help is so pleasant that we wonder where Drew gets them from.

It's not the help, which can be snotty at times, that draws us to Gotham Bar & Grill on East 12th Street. It's the food and the concept. Big, airy, relaxed, Gotham is like a sophisticated brasserie with consistently good food. If I had to name my favorite dish in all of New York, I'd pick Alfred Portale's seafood salad, a gravity-defying spire of squid, lobster, scallops, octopus, and mussels tossed in a lemony vinaigrette. Sautéed quail over shiitake mushrooms runs a close second.

Alison on Dominick Street ranks high on our Sunday dinner outings. Their family-style prix fixe menu features the kind of honest home-style French fare we like: a crock of *brandade,* garlic soup, roast chicken, and a warm apple tart, each dish meticulously cooked and flavored. A few years ago, we almost hired chef Tom Valenti. But George could not get in touch with Valenti's previous employer and finally gave up trying.

We liked Jean-Georges Vongerichten's cooking at Lafayette, but found the place overly stiff and formal. That changed when Jean-Georges opened Jo-Jo. The menu may be limited, but Jean-Georges' flavor combinations are exciting, and his seasoning masterful. The ambience of casual elegance is just the sort of thing we like.

I must confess we receive special treatment: Jean-Georges is a dear and familiar colleague. He sends *amuse-gueules,* those savory little snacks meant to stimulate one's appetite. My appetite doesn't flag throughout the meal; I can barely do justice to the desserts Jean-Georges insists we try. We would be fools not to admit that such attention does have its effect. In fact, we sometimes wonder how restaurant reviewers can keep their heads.

In some instances George and I are harsher critics than the pros. The Four Seasons had been a favorite from the moment Paul Kovi and Tom Margittai took it over in 1973. We had celebrated so many special occasions here that it had become our ceremonial stomping ground. The food, which never pretended to be extraordinary, had always been immaculately prepared. The service was so attentive and the atmosphere so refined we had considered it a privilege to join the civilized people who gathered here and dined either in the formal Pool Room or in the more casual Grill. Anticipating another pleasant meal, George and I were shocked on our last visit. We had come with Alexandra for a late supper. The Grill Room was surprisingly empty. Waiters and busboys were so busy talking that it was hard to get their attention. The rolls—once the pride of its bakery—were stale. We waited for Alexandra's appetizer. Upon George's request, the waiter went into the kitchen to inquire and returned with the news that the kitchen had run out of it. After that, it hardly mattered that the entrées were disappointing, all of them.

"I'll have to tell Tom," said George. "He is obviously not aware of what's going on." George called Tom Margittai the next morning. Tom sounded peeved. "If it weren't for friends like you, we would go down the drain and not even know it," he said.

We know the feeling. Who knows how we would have reacted under similar circumstances?

Shortly after our meal at the Four Seasons, Bryan Miller gave the restaurant a devastating review. Taking one star away from it, Miller lamented the fact that much of the crispness and spunk of the place was gone.

Luckily Tom Margittai and his partners responded to the review with professional aplomb. Instituting dramatic changes in the Grill Room and rejuvenating the concept of the lavish Pool Room, the Four Seasons soon returned to its position as New York's uncontested showplace for elegant dining.

Much as we have tried, we have yet to understand what the fuss about Union Square Café is all about. Danny Meyer runs a pleasant, user-friendly establishment. We admire him for having initiated a nonsmoking policy throughout the restaurant. We appreciate his innovative wine list. But the food? We find it rather dull. To accord it the same rating as Aureole, Montrachet, and Gotham is doing those fine chefs an injustice.

Going out is a very subjective experience. Our fondness for certain places is sometimes hard to justify.

That is the case with Tony May's San Domenico on Central Park South. We arrive late. We don't have a reservation. The maître d' can't bear turning us away. He'll find us a table; he'll also find a jacket for George, who is casually dressed. George is size forty-six. The maître d' brings a jacket a third that size.

"Perfect fit," he says, beaming.

It reminds us of a similar experience in Naples.

We relish the flamboyance and glitz here, the haute-and-demimonde, the air of intrigue. There is a noblesse oblige quality about the place that makes us tolerate the grossly overpriced wines and be indulgent with the much-harassed waiter.

Come spring, we make an appearance at the Oyster Bar, in Grand Central Station, to indulge in the annual Dutch fresh herring blowout. We eat those fatty herrings and drink Dutch gin and talk to the Cuban waiter and wonder why are we doing this, only to return the following year.

When we want to sneak away on a hot summer day, we cross the East River and have an aperitif at the River Café in Brooklyn. Sitting on the terrace and looking at the distant skyscrapers, freighters, pleasure boats, and the Brooklyn Bridge give us the illusion of being on a holiday. We never ate here, not even during David Burke's reign. Ironically, the minute David Burke crossed the river and opened Park Avenue Café, we raced to the restaurant. I was so bowled over by the finesse of Burke's creation of tuna and salmon tartare with caviar and the barbecued squab atop a corn cake with sautéed foie gras, that I begged George to return as soon as possible. A week later George called me from our restaurant: "How about meeting me at Park Avenue Café at 7:30 P.M.?"

We started with the tuna and salmon tartare. It was so good, I wanted to nominate it for a culinary Oscar. We have been back twice since then, a record in our eating-out history. And if, as they did, the critics object to the Ralph Lauren/Martha Stewart–like decor and find some of Burke's food combinations too "gimmicky," we don't mind. Park Avenue Café does not pretend to be a temple of gastronomy. By featuring assertive American food in a casual, countrified setting, it strikes us as being very much a restaurant of the 1990s.

When we want to have a bite in our neighborhood on the Upper East

Side, we head for Elio's. There is a homey, family atmosphere here that is most gratifying. The waiters appear a bit rough at times, but they are pros —always a plus with us. George satisfies his pasta craving, and I my eternal infatuation with *insalata di mare*. The bread is good, and the wines affordable. Three minutes after the meal we are back home.

George, more than I, is a devotee of Asian food. We've done the whole Japanese circuit: Benihana of Tokyo, Hatsuhana, and an unsung little place near Lincoln Center that served delectable sea urchin and eel until its untimely closing.

George loves Chinese food. If he could have his way, he'd feast on dim sum seven days a week. When his favorite place in Chinatown, the Golden Unicorn, became overly popular, he felt seriously deprived. But now that George's brother, Julian, has married a Chinese lady, all is well. Jane, our sister-in-law, is an extremely gifted cook. She adores George and will prepare twelve to fifteen different dishes for him on short notice.

We thought we were onto something when we discovered Jaiya-Thai, a Thai restaurant in an obscure neighborhood in Elmhurst, Queens. We were so enamored of their duck soup with preserved lemon, raw shrimp salad, and taro-root custard that, much against our firmly established habit, we used to queue up for a table, together with the local Thai families. Then Jaiya-Thai opened a branch practically around the corner from La Colombe d'Or. Ultraslick, it lost much of its former appeal; even the flavors seem to have suffered in transfer.

Lately we have discovered Korean cuisine, which we sample at Woo Con, a two-story establishment on West 36th Street in Manhattan. Instructed by my Korean manicurist, we order octopus in red sauce; buckwheat noodles and puffer-fish soup; *pa ju,* a seafood and scallion pancake; and any one of their barbecued dishes, which we help prepare at a gas grill at the table.

I have a weakness for everything Indian. In a way, I have never gotten over my visit to that magnificent and confusing country and long to recapture some of those experiences. As it happens, La Colombe d'Or is in a neighborhood that is a regular Indian enclave, populated with sari boutiques, Indian spice shops, and Indian fast-food places and restaurants. Alas, although the sound of Indian music and the smell of Indian spices waft through the rooms, the food is mediocre and does not compare with the dishes I tasted in Delhi, Madras, and Cochin, nor in the kitchen of our friend, cookbook author Julie Sahni.

Next to La Colombe d'Or is an unassuming pizza place that tries to be all things to all people. In the back, an Egyptian cook prepares Middle Eastern fare. Among the dishes is a dynamic chicken sandwich: chunks of moist chicken, shredded lettuce, and slices of tomatoes are embedded in a mountain of tahini and stuffed into pita bread. The price is $3.75. That sandwich sends my taste buds back to Damascus, Beirut, and Cairo, places I was fortunate to visit and where I shared many meals with the people in the street and, contrary to all predictions, was never the worse for it. One chicken sandwich plus an order of eggplant from the pizza place makes a satisfying supper for two. We eat it at home while watching a rented movie —a rare and altogether delicious treat.

Whenever possible, we spend weekends in Sag Harbor. During the off-season, we catch a movie and afterward head across the street to the American Hotel—a haven of gentility and charm. Our dining routine is pretty set: We'll sit at a table close to the fire and start with Belon oysters and a glass of champagne. George has steak; I'll have roasted squab. Owner Ted Conklin, a white carnation in his meticulously tailored English suit, recommends a Bordeaux from his wine list, which is one of the best in the country. Moving to the lobby, we settle into one of the Victorian sofas. George chooses a cigar from Ted's humidor and orders a B and B. I'll have a chilled muscat. We may play backgammon or chess and feel fortunate to be here.

We seldom "go out for dinner" at our own restaurant. We simply don't find it very relaxing. There are too many distractions: George disapproves of a new garnish; I notice a napkin on the floor and a small spot on the waiter's shirt; clients stop to chat; George is wanted on the phone. Once in a while, however, the miracle happens. We have stayed to eat. We are relaxed and in a good mood. We look around and feel really proud. Seventeen years and half a million meals later—this is some terrific place!

Restaurants are the last bastions of individualism. La Colombe d'Or allowed us to do our thing with a minimum of compromising—we are particularly grateful for that.

recipes

11

From Our Kitchen
to Yours

As a child I liked to play grocery store. I never dreamed that one day I would own a restaurant where three hundred staples are kept in-house on any given day, at any time. Inventory of these staples is noted daily on a master checklist that runs from fresh figs to cornstarch. The staples are stored in various places, the most important of which is our main refrigerator, the walk-in.

The walk-in, seven by thirteen feet, is bigger than my office; six people could easily occupy it. Built flush into the wall of our prep kitchen, adjacent to the kitchen, the contents of that walk-in provide the lifeblood of our kitchen operation. Stored according to kind are most of the prepped and perishable items needed for the next two to three days of service. Within easy reach, resting on movable wire racks, are flat metal trays, called hotel pans, with roasted tomatoes, deep-fried beets, julienne leeks, trimmed artichokes, shredded cabbage, minced onions, and peeled potatoes. Underneath are milk crates with apples, pears, lemons, oranges, limes. Boxes hold shipments of *mesclun* and mushrooms; fresh herbs are kept in square plastic containers.

Next to the vegetable station are the fish, kept over ice: loins of tuna, fillets of monkfish, salmon steaks, sea and bay scallops, shrimps, buckets with mussels and clams covered with seaweed, prepped crabmeat and squid, live lobsters. Farther down are the meats: slabs of liver, racks of lamb, tenderloin steaks, sausages, and veal chops. Next to the meat are butchered duck, boned chicken breasts, trussed guinea hens, tiny quail, an occasional capon or turkey.

A wheel of Parmesan cheese is stored in a big round plastic container. Next to it are the goat-cheese logs and containers with fresh goat curds. Looking like something out of a pharmacy is a lineup of plastic bottles, each filled with a different-colored liquid. These are the flavored oils, vinaigrettes, and vegetable juices, the latest "must have" flavoring agents for many of our dishes.

A battery of twenty-five-gallon stockpots sits on the stone floor. Each pot contains one particular type of stock in a finished or semi-finished state.

Smaller stockpots hold duck legs curing in rock salt and black pepper—on their way to becoming *confit*.

Every nook and cranny is filled to capacity. There are brown bags containing leftover breads on their way to becoming bread cubes and bread crumbs. Tins hold bread cubes and bread crumbs in their flavored and unflavored states.

Naj loves to show me his provisions in the walk-in. The place looks neat enough to be a display window at Bloomingdale's. Meanwhile the temperature in the walk-in is forty degrees, that in the kitchen close to one hundred. During the course of one serving, the chef and cooks go in and out of that walk-in at least twenty times. It's a wonder they stay healthy.

Some staples are kept in two small refrigerators in the kitchen. Stacked under the cold station, where all cold orders are assembled, is the line refrigerator with the necessary supply of cleaned salad greens, minced parsley, chives, dill, prepped tarragon, thyme, rosemary, and mint sprigs needed for lunch or dinner service. Next to it is the dessert refrigerator, crammed with freshly made *gâteau Victoire*, apple *feuilleté*, lemon sabayon, walnut tarts, grapefruit slices in a gin-and-grapefruit-juice marinade, raspberry *coulis*, dishes with ginger custards, ramekins with bread puddings, and containers with heavy cream, bowls, and wire whisks, ready to beat into whipped cream.

Above the line and dessert refrigerators are metal containers filled with the day's *mis en place*: ratatouille, baby artichokes, roasted peppers, julienne of turnips and carrots, sliced carrots, diced potatoes, diced tomatoes, rounds of goat cheese, chilled tomato or cucumber soup. Close to the dining room, underneath the bread station, is the counter refrigerator. Here we keep one service supply of tapenade, butter, rouille, and *aïoli*, plus chunks of Parmesan, which the waiters will offer to grate over pasta dishes.

All dry staples are kept in storage places in the basement. Standing in one corner are bins with flour, rice, legumes, and sugar. Shelves hold bags of coffees and teas, containers of salt, canned juices, and an occasional item that has long outlived its usefulness. Wire racks support gallon-size bottles of peanut and canola oils and smaller-size bottles of extra virgin olive and walnut oils. Next to these are the vinegars: red wine, champagne, aged sherry, and balsamic. Buckets are filled with twenty-five pounds of Kalamata olives; Dijon and grainy mustards come in ten-pound crocks. One wall is lined with jars of capers, green olives, and cocktail onions and tins of anchovies, sardines, and snails.

Baking goods have their own space, most of it taken over with chocolates: eleven-pound Callebaut bars, said to be Belgium's finest; Valrhona chocolate from France; Dutch Cacao Barry chocolate; white chocolate; Hershey's cocoa; almond paste; almond powder; almond extract. Also sacks of walnuts, confectioners' sugar, brown and cubed sugar. Boxes and bowls hold vanilla beans, vanilla sugar, cinnamon sticks, and crystallized violets.

Perishable staples—primarily butter, cream, milk, and eggs—are kept in the basement refrigerators. The freezer—small compared with the refrigerators—is bare except for labeled bags of frozen bones and carcasses, collected for future stocks. Kept under lock and key are the white truffle oils from Urbani, the tinned black truffles from Périgord, truffle shavings from the Vaucluse, metal boxes containing precious saffron threads from Spain, and a couple of tins of foie gras, "just in case."

Taken all together, this battery of staples forms the backbone of our kitchen. Always available, properly stored, they are a chef's security blanket. Over the years, many of these staples have changed, reflecting different eating habits and styles. Gone are the days of terrines and rillettes, pastry-encrusted roasts, beurre blanc, soufflé potatoes, *sauce nantua*, and *gratinées*. While stockpots continue to simmer on our back burners, there is a whole battery of new staples to fulfill today's quest for dishes that are light in texture and low in fat content.

Leading the list is *jus de poulet*, a concentrated chicken jelly similar to a meat extract. *Jus de poulet* came into vogue in the late 1980's, around the same time Mark May joined La Colombe d'Or. Mark, who learned about *jus de poulet* from France's innovative chef Alain Ducasse in Monte Carlo, was so enamored of the potential of this magic potion our cooks called him Mr. Jus de Poulet.

We use large quantities of *jus de poulet*. To prepare the base is a two-day process, involving slow roasting of bones and carcasses, simmering, straining, skimming, cooling, reducing, storing, re-straining, and refining. It is a labor-intensive job. Naj, who followed Mark as chef, calls it his kitchen gold, which equally applies to the *jus de canard* and the *jus d'agneau*, both of which follow the same prep method as *jus de poulet* and are part of the kitchen staples.

Confit of garlic, achieved by slow-cooking garlic cloves in oil, is another relative newcomer in our kitchen. Because it is milder than minced garlic, we use the *confit* whenever we want to create a suggestion rather than a pronounced statement of garlic.

Various vegetable compotes, purées, *coulis*, and condiments are always on hand. Some are part of our regular menu; others appear according to the season or a chef's personal preference. Presently we use eggplant compote for sea scallops, zucchini chutney for lamb, tomato *concassé* for monkfish, and caramelized onions for liver. But then again, we may dress sea scallops with braised endives and yellow-orange butter, lamb with goat-cheese gnocchi, monkfish with lima beans and red peppers, and liver with a carrot purée.

Flavored oils are a must in our current *mis en place*. Among these oils, the most widely used is a basil-mint combination, which goes over our seared tuna dish. Other flavored oils include cumin, curry, and red pepper oils. Called upon to lend depth to duck or veal stock, these oils offer a refreshing newness to a vinaigrette, and, when used in plating, add a painter's touch to dishes that vary from braised cod to *confit* of duck.

We store small amounts of these oils in plastic squeeze bottles, a simple device that enables the chef to squirt just the right amount of oil over or around a dish.

Different dishes call for different vinaigrettes. These, too, tend to change. A few years ago, we made a classic French vinaigrette, composed of red wine vinegar and French olive oil. Then balsamic vinegar, the Italian elixir from Modena, achieved such popularity that it went into everything. Next, fruit-flavored vinaigrette came into vogue. Today, we achieve new subtleties by combining different vinegars—sherry with balsamic, champagne with tarragon, or any of the above with the occasional addition of a vegetable juice.

Credit for utilizing vegetable juice as a flavoring agent goes to Jean-Georges Vongerichten, the former four-star wunderkind at New York's posh Lafayette restaurant, now chef-owner of Jo-Jo and author of *Simple*

Cuisine. While our Hobart juicer may not be quite as active as that of its great champion, house-made fennel, carrot, or leek juices are always at hand to be incorporated into a vinaigrette, give zip to a purée, or blend into a fish sauce.

Garnishes change with the season. Winter's truffled mashed potatoes become herb-infused roasted potatoes; baked kale and broccoli rabe turn into eggplant compote and zucchini cream. Carrot and lima bean purées might retire in favor of fava beans and summer squash. *Brunoise,* the term for raw, small-diced vegetables, is one of our summer garnishes, consisting of cucumbers, carrots, yellow squash, zucchini, red peppers, Spanish onions, and celery. Kept in a marinade of capers, anchovies, garlic, red wine vinegar, oil, salt, and pepper, *brunoise* is used to dress our house-smoked salmon or skate. During the winter, that garnish changes to braised red cabbage and mustard greens dressed in a mustard vinaigrette.

Sausage-making is a technique that has never gone out of style in our kitchen. In the winter, the chef is busy making the lamb and garlic sausages that go into cassoulet, one of the most popular cold-weather dishes on our menu.

Aïoli and rouille, served with bouillabaise and fish soup, have been standbys from the beginning of our restaurant. We continuously prepare fresh batches, particularly of rouille—which is George's personal preference.

And, of course, there is tapenade, a trademark at La Colombe d'Or. We serve this authentic Provençal peasant black-olive spread together with bread and butter. Once or twice we tried to take it off the menu. However, that created such furor among clients that we immediately put the tapenade back on.

Pitting olives, roasting bones and carcasses, deglazing stock, butchering meat, dressing fish, and cleaning greens and vegetables are part of the daily morning prep. However, some chopping, slicing, and whisking goes on all day, sometimes way into the evening. Chefs often lend a hand. In fact, most chefs thrive on prepping, finding it particularly soothing.

Each chef finds his own particular therapy.

Joe M. said whipping egg whites cooled his temper. Rick Steffann used to start peeling potatoes when the going got particularly rough.

Wayne Nish received a Zen-like satisfaction from stemming fresh tarragon and thyme leaves. Wrapping spiderlike caul fat over monkfish always put Mark May in a good mood. Naj grinds spices or pits olives.

Whatever is done, is done meticulously. While staples may change, the concept behind each one of them does not. Prepping, cooking, and plating follow the same exacting standards set by the legendary chefs of haute cuisine several centuries ago. According to these priests of culinary perfection, a dish is only as good as the least visible of its ingredients.

Our line cooks—American, Mexican, Peruvian—may never have heard of Escoffier, but by the way they handle food, the pride they take in doing their job, there is a bit of Escoffier in all of them.

ABOUT EQUIPMENT

As much as I envy our chef for all that wonderful equipment at the restaurant, at home I have neither the space nor the need for even a fraction of it. Having a typical New York City kitchen, I'm forced to keep my *batterie de cuisine* to a minimum. Even in the country, where George and I cook on weekends, I operate with limited equipment, having permanently retired an army of copper pots that, in the days of reckless spending before we had a restaurant, I bought at Dehillerin every time we went to Paris.

My *batterie de cuisine* consists of a roasting pan, an eight-inch and a twelve-inch skillet, a two-quart saucepan with a lid, a six-quart saucepan with a lid, a twelve-quart stockpot with a lid. All of these are made of heavy stainless steel. The skillets have stainless steel handles so they can go into the oven, a practice I picked up from the restaurant kitchen where almost all sautéed and grilled dishes are finished in this fashion.

For braising and slow cooking, I prefer to use a four-quart or an eight-quart enameled cast-iron casserole, because it can go directly from the stove onto the dining room table.

My baking equipment consists of one heavy-duty cookie sheet, one nine-inch tart pan with a removable bottom, one ten-inch round cake pan, plus one wire rack.

I keep four sizes of knives made of high-carbon stainless steel with a ground, sharp cutting edge. They are a paring knife with a four-inch blade, a boning knife with a six-inch blade, an all-purpose utility knife with a seven-inch blade, and a large chef's knife with a ten-inch blade. Jacques Pépin suggests that the length of the blade of a chef's knife should be determined by the width of the hand of the person using it.

That would present a problem in our household because the width of George's hand is almost twice that of mine. Fortunately, it doesn't matter because I prefer to work with a cleaver, a skill I learned from the Chinese cookbook author Florence Lin, a longtime friend.

Although the knives are considered dishwasher-safe, I clean them by hand. To avoid having anybody, including myself, grab one of the knives to cut kitchen twine, stems of flowers, and whatnot, I store the knives wrapped in kitchen towels, capping their points with a cork to avoid accidents.

Knives must be kept in top condition. A sharpening tool performs that function up to a point. After the knives have been used a lot, it's best to have them sharpened professionally. I use a polyethylene chopping board instead of a wooden one because the plastic board protects the knives from turning prematurely dull and doesn't hold odors.

My electric appliances include a blender, a six-cup food processor, and a miniature electric grinder, called a Quick Mill. Actually, I rarely use that Quick Mill. I much prefer to crush garlic the old-fashioned way in my cherished marble mortar, and to grind spices in a food mill that I picked up in a flea market ages ago.

In the country, I have a microwave oven that I use primarily to reheat or quickly thaw one or two dishes from the freezer. This is a godsend when we arrive late from the city, starved for a hot meal and too tired to cook. In the country we have an outside gas grill; in the city I use a cast-iron stove-top grill, which sears meat quickly and makes those desirable grill marks. Testing the recipes for the deep-fried vegetables (artichokes, beets, carrots, leeks), I discovered that in order to achieve the effect we get at the restaurant, I needed a deep-fry thermometer. This small investment turned out to be so useful that I wonder how I ever cooked without one.

Among the gadgets I am particularly fond of are the one-cup plastic squeeze bottles for my flavored oils. Following the restaurant's practice of storing prepped garnishes, I keep a set of round plastic containers with lids, holding from one to four cups.

The one luxury gadget I haven't used in at least three years, but wouldn't give up because you never know, is the truffle slicer I bought in Milan the last time truffles were affordable.

ABOUT THE RECIPES

All of these recipes originated at the restaurant. To do them justice in this book, I went into the kitchen and cooked alongside the chefs. The first thing I learned: there are no shortcuts; every step, from mincing fresh herbs to finishing a sauce, receives the same minute attention. Work surfaces are kept meticulously clean, knives razor sharp. Every ingredient, bowl, and utensil receives a sniff before using it, making sure that a cream hasn't turned or a container hasn't picked up the odor from a previous dish. Every pan, pot, and casserole is brought up to required temperature; oils must be sizzling hot; an onion compote must stew ever so slowly. Even at the height of service, nothing is rushed.

What impresses me most about the kitchen crew is their respect for food, a respect that borders on reverence.

To Moises, our grill cook, every meat and fish order is a call for sensory perception: he looks and touches and senses when a dish is ready. Moises works with great calm and takes as much care with his tenth order as he does with his first. Carlos, who taught me how to make the deep-fried dishes, crepes, galettes, *socca* roulade, and ginger custard, talks about ingredients as if they have a soul.

"Galettes like speed."

"Watch out, or the beets will start bleeding."

Greg, tattoos on his biceps, smooths out the mixture for the walnut tart with a tenderness befitting a lady's lace handkerchief.

Naj Zougari orchestrated and supervised most of my efforts.

"You're late," he said when once I showed up fifteen minutes after the agreed time. He was only half joking. A restaurant kitchen is not a kindergarten. Step by step I followed as Naj made cassoulet, bouillabaisse, *jus de poulet, confit* of duck, and Paris-Brest—recipes I had imagined as tough, all "easy," according to him.

After each stint in the restaurant kitchen, I streamlined the recipes to serve four, occasionally six to ten, people and prepared the recipes at home. The only major adjustment here was timing, because the temperature of professional ovens and stoves is much higher than that of ordinary home appliances. (In general, since time in cooking is not a precise science, I depend largely on sight and touch to gauge when a dish has been cooked to my liking.) Much as I tried, I discovered that there is no decent substitute for *jus de poulet;* also, not every recipe was "easy," and, of course, I had to wash my own dishes.

In organizing the recipes I have followed the kitchen's sacred practice of separating the preparation of a dish into prep, cooking, and presentation. In many instances the prep can be done well in advance; in some instances prep and cooking must be done in one fluid operation. The way I have written the recipes is as follows: When something can be done well in advance, even if it requires cooking, I call it prep. All staples and the basic garnishes fall into this category. When a recipe needs to be done entirely *à la minute,* even if there is preparatory work, I call the whole process "cooking." When a certain amount of prep can be done prior to the actual cooking, I divide the recipe accordingly.

This way of organizing a recipe may seem odd, but I wanted to express how we create our meals at the restaurant. What's more, having switched to this method, I can assure you that it works as well in the home kitchen as it does in the restaurant. It's always a good idea—here as in every cookbook—to read the recipe through before you start to cook.

If prep, or *mis en place,* is a chef's best friend, it is the home cook's salvation. Having frequently needed staples and garnishes on hand—stored in containers, labeled, and dated—makes it easier to be a confident cook. Since some of the staples may be kept for one year, while others will have to be used within a few days, identifying and dating each staple is important.

I have given each recipe an appropriate garnish. To me, having a file full of recipes without knowing how to pull each one together is like having a closet full of little black dresses and no jewelry, shoes, or scarves. Garnishes can be mixed or interchanged. One single garnish can successfully dress five different dishes. Two or three garnishes together make a light meal.

The last step in each recipe is presentation. I'm still in awe watching a chef send out a plate. That goes for every one of our chefs, past and present. They may have been bullies, macho guys, or culinary princelings, but when it came to plating, all behaved the same way: tucking a stray mint into place, straightening out a crooked scallop, wiping away a mere droplet of sauce; they acted like mothers making sure their fledglings went out into the world looking their best.

One final word. In our restaurant the preparation and presentation of each dish remains the same—day in, day out—until we decide to change it. Expecting their favorite dish to be exactly as they had it last time, clients often get upset over minute deviations.

That's not likely to occur at home. The main thing is to understand the fundamentals of a recipe. The rest is open to improvisation. That, after all, is the fun in cooking: it brings out the artist in us.

The recipes chosen for this collection have earned their place because they have been enthusiastically accepted and are greatly cared for by our discerning clients. Since La Colombe d'Or specializes in the cuisine of southern France, the recipes represent a healthy collection of Provençal and Mediterranean-inspired dishes: food that relies on good olive oil, fresh produce, garlic, herbs, and spices to achieve its lusty character. Most recipes can be turned out by anyone with a penchant for cooking. Some offer a bit of a challenge; two or three require the skill of an accomplished cook.

All of the recipes, I hope, will appeal to food lovers who get pleasure out of reading recipes without even wanting to cook. Recipes have a magic of their own: they conjure up visions of gastronomic possibilities. Perhaps they will transport you to La Colombe d'Or, where I wish I could invite each and every one of you to come and enjoy a pleasant meal.

12

Recipes from La Colombe d'Or

STAPLES	GARNISHES
tapenade	red pepper coulis
.....	.....
ooo	ooo
rouille	beet frites
.....	.....
ooo	ooo
aïoli	brunoise
.....	.....
ooo	ooo
garlic confit and garlic purée	fried leeks
.....	.....
ooo	ooo
house vinaigrette	tomato concassé
.....	.....
ooo	ooo
jus de poulet	roasted tomatoes
.....	.....
ooo	ooo
duck stock	zucchini chutney
.....	.....
ooo	ooo
herb-flavored oils	lima bean purée
.....	.....
ooo	ooo
croutons	basil pistou
.....	.....
ooo	ooo
herbes de provence	onion compote
.....	.....
ooo	ooo
	braised red cabbage
	.....
	ooo

carrot purée
· · · · ·
o o o

almond pralines
· · · · ·
o o o

PARTY SNACKS

anchoïade
· · · · ·
o o o

pissaladière
· · · · ·
o o o

COLD SALADS

and appetizers

braised baby artichokes
with tomato and coriander
· · · · ·
o o o

salad of baby zucchini with
grilled portobello mushrooms
and sea scallops
· · · · ·
o o o

house-cured salmon
· · · · ·
o o o

HOT APPETIZERS

ratatouille
· · · · ·
o o o

socca roulade with ratatouille
and goat cheese
· · · · ·
o o o

goat-cheese gnocchi with
white truffles
· · · · ·
o o o

poached shrimps with
zucchini cream and
basil pistou
· · · · ·
o o o

mushrooms provençal
· · · · ·
o o o

garlic sausage with lentils
· · · · ·
o o o

galettes of vegetables and herbs
· · · · ·
o o o

brandade de morue
· · · · ·
o o o

SOUPS COLD

cucumber soup with salmon
· · · · ·
ooo

chilled tomato soup with
crabmeat and chives
· · · · ·
ooo

SOUPS HOT

leek-and-potato soup
· · · · ·
ooo

lentil soup
· · · · ·
ooo

PASTA

fettuccini with
wild mushrooms and
rabbit sausage
· · · · ·
ooo

FISH

bouillabaisse colombe d'or
· · · · ·
ooo

cod with provençal blend
of white beans and
roasted tomatoes
· · · · ·
ooo

sea scallops with
orange-braised endives and
broccoli rabe
· · · · ·
ooo

grilled salmon with braised red
cabbage and carrot curls
· · · · ·
ooo

seared tuna steak with
basil-mint oil, yellow squash,
and beet frites
· · · · ·
ooo

lotte à la marseillaise
· · · · ·
ooo

monkfish scallops on a
bed of lima bean purée with
basil pistou
· · · · ·
ooo

monkfish in tomato marinade with
fried baby artichokes

ooo

monkfish roast with herbs,
potato–fava bean purée,
and red pepper coulis

ooo

CHICKEN, DUCK,

and other fowl

chicken with roasted shallots and
truffled mashed potatoes

ooo

poached chicken roulade with aïoli
and haricots verts

ooo

poulet maison

ooo

duck: grilled breast and
thigh confit with sweet and
aromatic spices

ooo

braised squab with
turnip-pear purée and black figs
in honey-thyme vinaigrette

ooo

MEAT

grilled spring lamb chops with
zucchini chutney and
rosemary potatoes

ooo

gigot d'agneau with
chestnut polenta and raisin-
pine nut spinach

ooo

rabbit with polenta

ooo

cassoulet

ooo

grilled calf's liver with
carrot purée and
grilled onions

ooo

boudin noir with
caramelized apples,
mashed potatoes, and
fried leeks

ooo

DESSERTS

gâteau Victoire
. . . . .
o o o

paris-brest
. . . . .
o o o

ginger custard
. . . . .
o o o

walnut tart
. . . . .
o o o

lemon sabayon tart
. . . . .
o o o

grapefruit sections with
fresh raspberries
and sorbet
. . . . .
o o o

apple tart
. . . . .
o o o

bread pudding with pear coulis
and chocolate sauce
. . . . .
o o o

goat-cheese cake with
black currant coulis
. . . . .
o o o

TAPENADE

makes about 2 cups

Tapenade is a typical Provençal peasant spread. It is a trademark at La Colombe d'Or, where we serve it along with bread and butter. While tapenade is not your average kitchen staple, it is a helpful condiment to have on hand. When spread on crackers, it is a zesty cocktail nibble; served with tuna carpaccio, it spikes the delicate fish; stirred into yogurt, mayonnaise, or *crème fraîche*, it zips up dishes from steamed vegetables to leftover stews.

2 CUPS KALAMATA OLIVES, PITTED (ABOUT 1 POUND UNPITTED)

4 TABLESPOONS DRAINED CAPERS

8 ANCHOVY FILLETS, RINSED AND DRIED

4 TABLESPOONS BITTER ORANGE OR FIG MARMALADE

3 TEASPOONS DIJON MUSTARD

2 TEASPOONS WHITE WINE VINEGAR

PREP

1. Place all the ingredients in a food processor. Blend for a few seconds. (The mixture should remain fairly coarse.) Adjust the seasoning.

2. Store in a tightly covered jar.

NOTE: Refrigerated, tapenade will keep for 2 weeks.

makes 1½ cups

Fiery garlic-scented rouille is the crowning touch of bouillabaisse and classic *soupe de poissons*. Floating on rounds of grilled bread or stirred directly into the heady broth, rouille, or its cousin *aïoli*, adds authenticity to these two most Provençal dishes. Preference for one or the other is a matter of personal choice.

To remember the difference between *aïoli* and rouille, it helps to know that "rouille" comes from the French word for "rust," the color of this mayonnaise, achieved by the addition of saffron and cayenne pepper. When making rouille, always have all the ingredients and equipment at room temperature.

6 LARGE GARLIC CLOVES, PEELED

PINCH OF SALT

2 EGG YOLKS, AT ROOM TEMPERATURE

¾ CUP PEANUT OIL

¼ CUP EXTRA VIRGIN OLIVE OIL

⅛ TEASPOON SAFFRON

1 TEASPOON CAYENNE PEPPER

PREP

1. Place the garlic in a mortar. Add a pinch of salt and mash evenly with a pestle to form a paste.

2. Add 1 egg yolk. Stir, pressing slowly and evenly with the pestle. Add the second egg yolk and repeat the stirring process until well blended.

3. Begin to slowly work in the oil, drop by drop. After you have added a few drops of oil, add the saffron and the cayenne pepper. Gradually, whisk in the remaining oil until the sauce is thickened to a mayonnaise like consistency. (If the mayonnaise becomes too thick, add a few drops of hot water.)

4. Taste for seasoning, adding more cayenne pepper and salt if desired. Rouille should always be served tepid. If it has been refrigerated, warm the desired amount over warm water.

NOTE: If making rouille in a blender, crush the garlic with the salt as instructed above. Blend the egg yolks, covered, at high speed for half a minute. Add the garlic paste. Cover and blend for about 1 minute. Then start pouring in the oil, a few drops at a time. Gradually add the rest of the oil, always waiting until the oil has been completely absorbed by the eggs. (Adding the oil too quickly will break the texture.) When the sauce is smooth and firm, blend in the saffron and the cayenne pepper. Check and adjust the seasoning.

181

AÏOLI

We use *aïoli* to garnish our Poached Chicken Roulade with Haricots Verts, a popular summer dish. *Aïoli* and cod are a perfect match; a dollop of this bold garlicky mayonnaise is frequently added to our cod dish.

You can make *aïoli* by simply leaving out the saffron and cayenne pepper from the recipe for rouille and adding a few drops of fresh lemon juice and additional salt and pepper. But I like to make *aïoli* with the addition of a boiled potato, which gives the mixture a denser texture.

When making *aïoli*, always have all the ingredients and equipment at room temperature.

1 LARGE IDAHO POTATO, BOILED AND PUT THROUGH RICER

3 EGG YOLKS, AT ROOM TEMPERATURE

5 LARGE GARLIC CLOVES, PEELED AND CRUSHED IN MORTAR

SALT AND A GENEROUS PINCH OF FRESHLY GROUND WHITE PEPPER

JUICE OF ¼ LEMON, STRAINED

1¼ CUPS EXTRA VIRGIN OLIVE OIL

PREP

. . . . . .

1. Put the potato in the blender. Beat in the egg yolks, one at a time.

2. Add the garlic paste, salt, pepper, and lemon juice. Blend until the mixture is thoroughly combined and smooth.

3. Begin adding the oil, a few drops at a time. Gradually add the rest of the oil, always waiting until the oil has been completely absorbed by the eggs. Add a little lukewarm water if the mixture becomes too thick or separates. Adjust the seasoning to taste. Like rouille, *aïoli* will keep in the refrigerator for 2 weeks.

GARLIC CONFIT AND
GARLIC PURÉE

Since garlic *confit* is more subtle than raw garlic, we use the *confit* in many dishes that call for just a hint of garlic. Garlic *confit* emulsifies vinaigrette and innumerable sauces, marinates fowl and game, and enhances many meats as a spread before cooking. It goes on top of roasted tomatoes, into *pistou* and ratatouille, while the *confit's* cousin, garlic purée, quietly slips into yellow-pear-tomato sauce and zucchini cream.

Garlic *confit* is one of the most reassuring staples to have on hand. It's there when you need it and leaves no lingering odor on your hands.

25 GARLIC CLOVES, PEELED

EXTRA VIRGIN OLIVE OIL TO COVER

PREP

(Our cooks easily prep 100 garlic cloves a week. An easy way to separate the garlic cloves from the bulb is to whack the whole garlic with the flat side of a cleaver. Immersing the cloves in lukewarm water for 25 minutes loosens the skin and makes peeling easier.)

1. Place the peeled cloves of garlic in a heavy saucepan and cover with the oil. Cook over the lowest possible heat until soft. (This may take up to an hour.)

2. Remove the mixture from the heat and let it cool. Store in a 6-ounce mason jar with a tight lid. If desired, cover with additional oil.

3. To make garlic purée, place the desired amount of garlic *confit* in a blender and blend until smooth.

NOTE: Stored in a tight container, refrigerated garlic *confit* will keep almost indefinitely. The garlic-infused oil is a wonderful flavoring agent by itself. It should be replenished every so often.

A WORD ABOUT
garlic ←

Garlic is the essence of Provençal cooking. Sometimes pungent, sometimes subtle, it is the leitmotiv that runs through almost every dish of France's Mediterranean region. It is therefore not surprising that practically every second recipe in my book calls for garlic, often in the form of garlic *confit*. Garlic *confit* is foremost a convenient way of always having this vital ingredient on hand. If that's not your case, use good, fresh garlic. Since fresh garlic is considerably stronger than the *confit*, use half the amount indicated in a recipe. Also, realize that a finely minced clove of garlic is infinitely more pungent than a clove of crushed garlic. As always, it helps to experiment.

HOUSE VINAGRETTE

makes 2 cups
½ cup will dress a salad for 4

At the restaurant, we prepare 1 quart of vinaigrette every other day. We keep the vinaigrette in glass bottles, which are stored at room temperature. The basic vinaigrette, which dresses our mixed salad, is just the beginning. One or 2 tablespoons of vegetable juice, cooking liquids, meat or poultry pan drippings, or a touch of honey is frequently added to the vinaigrette and used to dress anything from steamed vegetables to sautéed squab. Of late I have discovered the beauty of hazelnut oil, a unique elixir with a subtle nutty flavor that I use primarily to dress especially delicate greens, such as Italian *frisée*. It is so frightfully expensive that I tried to make my own, a task that took all afternoon and left me with an inferior product. Store-bought, I realized, often makes a lot of sense. Besides, a few drops of hazelnut oil go a long way. Since hazelnut oil is more potent in flavor than walnut oil, the proportions would be 2 tablespoons hazelnut oil to 1½ cups plus 2 tablespoons extra virgin olive oil.

To dress our seafood salad, we substitute lemon juice for the red wine vinegar and add chopped shallots.

2 TABLESPOONS BALSAMIC VINEGAR

¼ CUP AGED SHERRY VINEGAR

¼ CUP RED WINE VINEGAR

SALT TO TASTE

¼ CUP WALNUT OIL

1¼ CUPS EXTRA VIRGIN OLIVE OIL (WE USE PUROLIVE FROM MASEILLE)

¼ CUP PEANUT OIL

FRESHLY GROUND BLACK PEPPER

PREP

In a bowl, whisk together the vinegars and the salt. Add the oils in a thin stream, whisking until well blended. Season with pepper.

NOTE: Kept in a tightly covered jar, vinaigrette will keep for 2 weeks. If it has thickened too much, correct with 1 or 2 tablespoons of warm water.

The lemon-shallot vinaigrette should be used within a day.

JUS DE POULET

makes 2 cups

Jus de poulet, a highly concentrated form of chicken jelly, is one of the most vital staples in our kitchen. Low in calories and high in protein, *jus de poulet*—a modern version of *glace de viande*—has become the favorite binding agent for most of our sauces and dressings.

Preparing *jus de poulet* takes time. But it's worth the effort, since a mere dollop of that precious *jus* will transform the most ordinary dish into a respectable *plat*.

Actually, preparing *jus* is not at all that complicated. Think of it as making basic stock, with some additional steps. Properly stored and reheated once a week, refrigerated *jus de poulet* will keep in the refrigerator up to a month. I freeze a batch of it in ice-cube trays and then transfer the cubes into individual freezer bags—like having flavor assets in a bank.

20 POUNDS CHICKEN BONES, CARCASSES, AND NECKS

3 LARGE GARLIC HEADS, UNPEELED, HALVED

BOUQUET GARNI: 5 BLACK PEPPERCORNS, 3 CLOVES STAR ANISE, 2 BAY LEAVES TIED IN CHEESECLOTH

PREP

Preheat the oven to 350 degrees.

1. Place the chicken pieces on a roasting sheet. Roast in the preheated oven for 1½ to 2 hours until well browned.

2. Transfer the browned chicken parts to a large stockpot; add the garlic and bouquet garni. Cover with cold water, and bring the mixture to a boil. Lower the heat and let the chicken simmer, uncovered, to reduce, for 2 to 3 hours, occasionally skimming the scum that rises to the surface.

3. Strain through a *chinois* or a cheesecloth-lined colander. When the liquid has sufficiently cooled, cover and refrigerate overnight.

4. The next day, skim off the thick fat layer on top, leaving the thin layer of pale yellow fat. Cook the liquid over medium heat to reduce it by half, about 2 hours. Let it cool and store as in step 3.

5. When the liquid has set, skim off the new layer of fat and simmer the stock until it reaches a thick, almost gelatinous consistency. Let it cool. The base is now ready to be used as directed in individual recipes.

NOTE: Since 20 pounds of bones will render only 2 cups of *jus*, it barely pays to make *jus* in smaller quantities. Most of the necessary chicken parts can be collected over a period of time by butchering whole chickens instead of buying ready-made cuts and faithfully saving bones, back, and necks in freezer bags. For the rest, ask your butcher to save you some cuts.

185

DUCK STOCK

· ·

makes 2 cups

Let's face it, most cooks can live without duck stock. However, since duck stock is an essential ingredient in the duck recipe, I have included it. Flavored with aromatic spices, this duck stock goes far: it raises ordinary braised red cabbage to a noble dish and does the same for anything from mushrooms to pasta.

stock
· · · ·

5 POUNDS DUCK BONES AND CARCASSES

2 LEEKS, CUT IN HALF AND WASHED THOROUGHLY

1 ONION, HALVED

2 TEASPOONS BLACK PEPPERCORNS

1 BAY LEAF

4 QUARTS COLD WATER

aromatics
· · · ·

1 CINNAMON STICK

2 TABLESPOONS WHOLE CORIANDER

1 TEASPOON WHOLE MACE

1 SMALL PIECE GINGER (ABOUT 1/2 INCH), PEELED

PREP
· · · · · ·

Preheat the oven to 350 degrees.

1. For the stock, bake the duck bones and carcasses in a roasting pan in the preheated oven until golden brown, about 2 hours. Transfer to a stockpot; add the leeks, onion, black peppercorns, and bay leaf. Cover with the water, and bring the stock to a boil. Lower the heat and let the stock simmer, uncovered, to reduce by half, about 2 hours. Skim off any foam that rises to the top.

2. Strain the stock and discard all the solids. Return the strained stock to the fire and continue to cook until reduced again by half. (You can hold the duck stock in the refrigerator for a few days at this point, then proceed with the final reduction.)

3. Add the aromatics. Continue to cook to reduce down to about 2 cups. Remove the stock from the heat and strain through a *chinois* or a cheesecloth-lined colander.
Refrigerate till ready to use.

NOTE: Stored in a closed container, refrigerated duck stock will keep for 1 week. To keep the stock longer, reboil it, let it cool, and replace in refrigerator.

CILANTRO OIL

makes 1 cup

1 BUNCH CILANTRO, WASHED BUT NOT STEMMED

1 CUP GRAPE-SEED OR CANOLA OIL

PREP

1. Blanch the cilantro in boiling water for 20 seconds. Shock under cold water. Drain and dry well.

2. Put the cilantro into the blender with the oil. Blend at medium speed for 5 minutes. Store in a closed jar. Refrigerate for 1 day, until the herbs have settled. Then filter the oil through a paper coffee filter.

NOTE: Stored in a closed jar, flavored oils will keep in the refrigerator for 1 week.

HERB-FLAVORED *oils* ⬅

Flavored oils are the culinary wizards of the 1990s. They are used in place of butter, binding and enhancing sauces and purées. They are extremely effective drizzled over grilled meats, fish, or vegetables and add the finishing touch to a dish.

For flavored oils, we prefer to use grape-seed or canola oil because they are low in saturated fat and have no particular flavor of their own.

The basic recipe below is also used when flavoring oil with other fresh herbs, such as:

Parsley	*Mint*
Chervil	*Basil*

At the restaurant, we use a combination of basil and mint oils for our seared tuna dish.

At home, I've adopted the restaurant's practice of keeping flavored oils in plastic dispenser bottles, extremely useful gadgets that enable me to finish my dishes like a pro. Thanks to the dispenser bottles, no other utensil is required. An obvious advantage for any cook.

CROUTONS

Spread with rouille or *aïoli*, croutons are a vital component of fish soup and bouillabaisse. Croutons accompany *anchoïade* and *brandade de morue*. Rubbed with garlic cloves, brushed with olive oil, and sprinkled with Parmesan cheese, croutons become a quick cocktail snack.

1 LOAF STALE FRENCH BREAD

PREP

Preheat the oven to 350 degrees.

1. Cut the bread on the bias into ¼-inch-thick slices.

2. Arrange the slices on a baking sheet and toast in the preheated oven for 3 to 4 minutes, or until golden brown on one side. Turn and brown lightly on the other side, approximately 2 to 3 minutes. (Check the croutons while toasting since they burn easily.)

NOTE: Stored in a tightly covered plastic or metal container, croutons will keep for at least a month.

HERBES DE PROVENCE

Herbes de Provence are an assortment of herbs most commonly used in southern French cooking: among them rosemary, thyme, marjoram, sage, basil, and mint. While gardening is not my forte, I've discovered that herbs practically grow by themselves. My *herbes de Provence* do as nicely in the country as they do on the windowsill of my city apartment.

At the end of the season, I clip the plants and hang the branches upside down. Once the herbs have dried, I fashion my own mixture, which I put into individual sachets made from cheesecloth. These I store in a glass jar, next to the salt and peppercorns.

"You should package them in little clay pots, cover them with Provençal fabric, and sell them at the restaurant," advise my friends.

I tell them I am neither that good a gardener nor an entrepreneur. Besides, there are plenty of stores that do just that.

RED PEPPER COULIS

makes 1 cup

Red pepper *coulis* is a cook's best friend. Easy to prepare, it adds color and zest to anything from crudités to pasta. At the restaurant we serve monkfish garnished with potato-fava bean purée, topped with red pepper *coulis*.

4 LARGE RED PEPPERS

⅓ CUP PLUS 1 TABLESPOON OLIVE OIL

SALT AND FRESHLY GROUND BLACK PEPPER

PINCH OF SUGAR

PREP
. . . . . .
Preheat the oven to 300 degrees.

1. Rub the peppers with 1 tablespoon of the olive oil. Bake them in the preheated oven for 30 minutes.

2. Transfer the peppers to a metal bowl. Seal with plastic wrap and set aside for 10 minutes. When they are cool enough to handle, remove the skins and seeds from the peppers.

3. Purée the peppers in a blender, together with the oil. Strain through a sieve to remove any impurities. Season with salt, pepper, and a pinch of sugar.

NOTE: Stored in a closed glass jar, red pepper *coulis* will keep for at least a month. I have never managed to keep the *coulis* for that length of time because, before I know it, I've depleted my stock.

189

BEET FRITES

Making beet *frites* is messy business because the beets leave incredible red stains. In addition, the job has to be done with record speed, lest the beets lose their color and turn soft.

The reason I decided to include the recipe just the same is simple: our clients are crazy about them, including those who say they have never touched beets before. And, messy or not, they are worth a try.

Beet *frites* are our standard garnish for Seared Tuna Steak and frequently garnish other fish dishes. We also offer beet *frites* at the bar, where they are appreciated by diners who may have to wait for their table. In fact, the beet *frites* are so popular, we offer them as a side dish.

1 QUART PEANUT OIL

6 LARGE RED BEETS (ABOUT 2 POUNDS)

CORNSTARCH

SALT

PREP

Preheat the oil to 350 degrees, using a deep-fry thermometer.

1. Peel the beets, and slice them on a mandoline. Put the sliced beets in a metal mixing bowl, rubbing them with your hands to make sure they are separated.

2. Sprinkle the beets with cornstarch to lightly coat them, mixing them with your hands. (They should have the color of a young Burgundy.) Throw a handful of beets at a time into the hot fat, gently pushing them down with a wire-mesh spoon.

3. As soon as the beets come to the surface, after about 1½ minutes, they are ready. Remove them with a wire-mesh spoon. Spread them on a paper towel to drain off the oil. Sprinkle them lightly with salt and place another layer of paper towel on top.

NOTE: Layered in a plastic or metal pan and covered with plastic wrap, beet *frites* will keep for 5 days. They should be kept in a cool spot. Do not refrigerate or reheat.

FRIED LEEKS

makes 4 garnishes

In my mind, the leek is one of the best and worst vegetables around. The best, because it has such a pronounced taste and can be used in many ways; the worst, because there is more sand in one stalk of leek than in a pound of spinach. That sand has to go; for no matter how well executed a leek dish is, it will be ruined by a mere grain of sand.

Paper-thin fried leeks are part of our *boudin noir* garnish; at other times, the leeks may garnish a monkfish dish or a pork chop preparation.

"Best fried grass I've ever tasted," said one of our clients after having finished the leek garnish before even touching her dish. We brought her seconds.

2–3 LARGE LEEKS

1–1½ QUARTS PEANUT OR GRAPE- SEED OIL

SALT

PREP

1. Remove and discard the leeks' outer and tough green leaves. Cut the leeks into even julienne. Wash them thoroughly, and keep them in cold water. When ready to use, rinse and pat them dry.

2. Heat the oil to 350 degrees in a 4- to 6-inch-deep saucepan, using a deep-fry thermometer. Toss in the leeks a few handfuls at a time. Deep-fry until golden, about 2 minutes. Remove them with a wire-mesh spoon. Place the leeks on paper towels to remove the excess oil. Sprinkle them generously with salt.

NOTE: Fried leeks will stay crisp for 3 hours.

> **A WORD ABOUT**
> *deep-frying* ←

At the restaurant we use a heat-controlled electric deep fryer. At home I use an adjustable clip-on deep-fry thermometer that also works as a candy/jelly thermometer. For deep-frying, we use peanut, sunflower, or grape-seed oils because they are light in texture and have a pleasant nutty flavor.

191

TOMATO CONCASSÉ

Much like a supporting actor or actress, tomato *concassé* has played a minor yet vital role in garnishing dishes from sea scallops and monkfish to chicken. The name comes from the French verb *concasser*, "to chop or crush."

2¼ POUNDS RIPE TOMATOES

1 TABLESPOON OLIVE OIL

3 SHALLOTS, PEELED AND FINELY CHOPPED

BOUQUET GARNI: 3 SPRIGS FRESH THYME, 3 SPRIGS ITALIAN PARSLEY, 1 GARLIC CLOVE, PEELED AND CRUSHED, TIED IN CHEESECLOTH

SALT AND PEPPER

PINCH OF SUGAR

PREP

1. Blanch the tomatoes in boiling water for a few seconds, then drain and plunge them into ice water; drain again. Peel the tomatoes, cut them in half, remove the seeds, and dice into small pieces. Pour off any excess liquid.

2. Heat the olive oil in a skillet. Add the shallots and sweat them slowly till they give off their moisture, about 4 minutes. Add the tomatoes and the bouquet garni. Season with salt, pepper, and the pinch of sugar.

3. Reduce the heat as low as possible. Let the mixture simmer, uncovered, for 30 to 45 minutes. The slower you cook the *concassé*, the better its flavor.

4. Remove the bouquet garni. Adjust the seasonings. Let the *concassé* cool.

NOTE: Stored in a tightly covered glass jar and refrigerated, tomato *concassé* will keep for 2 to 3 days, after which it tends to turn slightly bitter.

192

ROASTED TOMATOES

makes 30 pieces

We use roasted tomatoes to garnish dishes all year round. During the summer we buy local beefsteak tomatoes; for the rest of the year we get hand-picked Florida tomatoes. If neither is available, small plum tomatoes will do the job.

4 OR 5 BEEFSTEAK TOMATOES, OR 15 PLUM TOMATOES (ABOUT 2 POUNDS)

2 TABLESPOONS GARLIC CONFIT (SEE PAGE 888)

2 TABLESPOONS EXTRA VIRGIN OLIVE OIL

SALT AND PEPPER

5 SPRIGS FRESH THYME, PLUCKED

PREP

1. Trim the top and bottom of the tomatoes, then trim off a thin slice on each side to give each tomato two flat sides. Cut the beefsteak tomatoes crosswise into ½-inch slices; cut the plum tomatoes crosswise in half.

2. Arrange the tomato slices on a lightly oiled baking sheet. Spread a dollop of garlic *confit* on each slice; dribble olive oil over it. (Unseasoned and covered with plastic wrap, the prepped tomatoes can sit for 1 hour. Once they have been seasoned, they need to be cooked immediately to prevent the salt from drawing out their juices.)

COOKING

Preheat the oven to 250 degrees.

Sprinkle the tomato slices with salt, pepper, and thyme. Bake in the preheated oven for 45 minutes to 1 hour.

NOTE: Covered with plastic wrap, roasted tomatoes can wait for a few hours before serving.

ZUCCHINI CHUTNEY

makes 8 garnishes

This is a favored summer garnish for our Grilled Spring Lamb Chops. Served cold, it also makes a refreshing little lunch dish.

½ SPANISH ONION

3 SMALL YELLOW SQUASH (ABOUT 1 POUND)

3 SMALL ZUCCHINI (ABOUT 1 POUND)

SALT AND PEPPER

1 SMALL PIECE GINGER (ABOUT ½ INCH), PEELED

¾–1 CUP FRESH SQUEEZED ORANGE JUICE

ZEST OF ½ ORANGE

1 TABLESPOON HONEY, OR TO TASTE

PREP

1. Peel the onion and slice it crosswise into thin slices.

2. Peel the squash and zucchini. Cut in half, lengthwise, then in half again, also lengthwise. Cut into small triangles.

3. Heat the oil in a saucepan. Sweat the onion in the oil until translucent, about 5 minutes. Add the squash, zucchini, salt, pepper, and ginger. Sauté to coat. Cover with the orange juice and bring the mixture to a boil.

4. Reduce the heat. Let the chutney simmer, for 25 to 35 minutes, or until soft.

5. Remove from the heat and whisk in the orange zest and honey. Adjust the seasonings.

NOTE: Properly stored and refrigerated, zucchini chutney will keep for 1 week. In fact, the true flavor of this condiment only emerges once the dish has completely cooled down. The chutney will taste even better 1 or 2 days after it has been made.

LIMA BEAN PURÉE

makes 4 to 6 garnishes

Lima bean purée is frequently a garnish for monkfish, cod, or shrimp dishes. Served in combination with either moss-green basil *pistou*, fire engine-red peppers, or pale roasted shallots, lima bean purée is one of the most attractive and useful staples to have on hand.

At the restaurant we prepare the dish with fresh lima beans. At home I use frozen ones. I find that, like tiny frozen peas, frozen lima beans are of exceptional quality. Less work, too. I always keep a pack in the freezer.

1 BUNCH ROSEMARY

1 BUNCH SAGE

1 BUNCH PARSLEY

2 10-OUNCE PACKAGES FROZEN BABY LIMA BEANS

2 TABLESPOONS BUTTER, SOFTENED

3 TABLESPOONS EXTRA VIRGIN OLIVE OIL

4 TEASPOONS SHERRY VINEGAR

1 TABLESPOON CHOPPED PARSLEY

1 TABLESPOON CHOPPED CHERVIL

SALT AND PEPPER

SNIPPED CHIVES (OPTIONAL)

PREP

1. Tie the bunches of herbs into a bundle with butcher's twine. Put them in a pot with water to cover. Bring to a boil; add the lima beans. Reduce the heat and cook, covered, as per package instructions.

2. Drain the beans, reserving some of the cooking liquid. Discard the herb bundles. Purée the beans and the butter in a food processor. Gradually add the oil and vinegar and as much of the reserved cooking liquid as needed to form a medium-thick purée.

3. Blend in the chopped parsley and chervil. Season with salt and pepper to taste, and sprinkle the top with snipped chives if desired.

NOTE: Properly stored, lima bean purée will keep in the refrigerator for 3 days; in the freezer for 3 months.

BASIL PISTOU

makes ¾ cup

This basil *pistou* is a fairly thick mixture that packs a powerful wallop. Moss green, with a crunchy texture, it offers an intriguing contrast to smooth lima bean purée or gentle zucchini cream.

I like to put a dollop of basil *pistou* over fresh tomatoes; basil *pistou* also earns double points when added to hot pasta.

1¼ CUPS BASIL LEAVES, TIGHTLY PACKED

¼ CUP EXTRA VIRGIN OLIVE OIL

¼ CUP FRESHLY GRATED PARMESAN (ABOUT 2 OUNCES)

¼ CUP SHELLED WALNUTS (ABOUT ¼ POUND)

1 TABLESPOON GARLIC CONFIT (ABOUT 4 CLOVES); (SEE PAGE ███)

2 TABLESPOONS WATER, IF NEEDED

SALT

PREP

Wash the basil leaves and pat them dry. Purée the next 4 ingredients in a blender. Add the basil and finish puréeing. If the mixture is too thick, add water. Adjust the seasonings.

NOTE: Refrigerated in a covered plastic container, basil *pistou* will keep for 1 week.

BRUNOISE

makes 2 to 2½ cups

Brunoise is a classic example of *mis en place*. The kitchen always has two batches of *brunoise* on hand: a blanched version and a marinated version. Blanched *brunoise*, quickly sautéed, flavors soups, pasta, or sauces; marinated *brunoise*, dressed with capers, anchovies, garlic, red wine vinegar, oil, and salt and pepper, garnishes anything from house smoked salmon to grilled lobster.

Because it's so useful to have on hand, I put small portions of blanched *brunoise* in plastic bags and keep them in the freezer.

ANY 3 OF THE FOLLOWING:

1 LARGE CARROT

1 YELLOW SQUASH OR YELLOW
PEPPER

1 ZUCCHINI OR CUCUMBER

1 RED PEPPER

1 SPANISH ONION

2 CELERY RIBS

PREP
......
Peel and dice any 3 of the vegetables. (The easiest way to prep *brunoise* is with a mandoline.) Blanch them briefly in boiling water. Strain and store in a covered container.

ONION COMPOTE

makes 4 garnishes

Onion compote is a favorite winter garnish for our Grilled Calf's Liver. So many customers asked if they could have the compote as a side dish that we now have put it on the menu.

1 TABLESPOON PEANUT OIL

1¼ POUNDS SPANISH ONIONS,
PEELED AND THINLY SLICED
(ABOUT 2 CUPS)

2 TABLESPOONS HONEY

¼ CUP RED WINE VINEGAR

¼ CUP WATER OR CHICKEN
STOCK

2 TABLESPOONS BUTTER

SALT AND BLACK PEPPER

PREP
......
1. Heat the oil in a saucepan. Add the onions and honey. Sauté over medium heat for 15 to 25 minutes, or until the onions begin to turn golden brown.

2. Deglaze the pan with the vinegar. Continue cooking until the vinegar evaporates. Add the water or stock. Cook the mixture over low heat, uncovered, for 30 minutes, or until the liquid has been completely absorbed and the onions have melted together. Remove from heat.

3. Whisk in the butter. Season with salt and pepper. Let cool and store in a mason jar.

NOTE: Stored in the refrigerator, onion compote will keep for 2 weeks.

BRAISED RED CABBAGE

makes 4 to 6 garnishes

When I was a child, red cabbage was the only winter vegetable thought fit to accompany roasts, venison, duck, and the ubiquitous Sunday goose. Seeing red cabbage served with salmon makes me realize how far both of us have come.

2 POUNDS RED CABBAGE

6 OUNCES *PANCETTA*, SLICED 1 INCH THICK

3 TABLESPOONS OLIVE OIL OR DUCK FAT (SEE PAGE 000)

1 SPANISH ONION, PEELED AND CHOPPED

¼ CUP RED WINE

SALT AND FRESHLY GROUND WHITE PEPPER

1 TEASPOON CARAWAY SEEDS (OPTIONAL)

PREP

1. Quarter the cabbage, remove the core, and shred fine.

2. Cut the *pancetta* into small cubes.

3. Sauté the *pancetta* in a heavy skillet till slightly crisp, about 5 minutes. Pour off the rendered fat.

4. Heat the oil or the duck fat in the same skillet. (At the restaurant we use duck fat instead of oil.) Add the onion and sauté till translucent. Add the cabbage and wine. Lower the heat and braise the cabbage, covered, for 45 to 50 minutes, or until soft.

5. Season with salt and pepper. Add the caraway seeds, if desired.

NOTE: Covered with plastic wrap, the cabbage will keep in the refrigerator for a few days. If made with duck fat, it will keep for 1 week.

CARROT PURÉE

makes 4 garnishes

The intriguing flavor of this dish comes from the browned butter, which gives the carrots a wonderful nutty taste. Carrot purée is a frequent garnish for our Grilled Calf's Liver. I like it equally well with lamb or pork chops.

3 TABLESPOONS BUTTER

2 POUNDS CARROTS, PEELED AND CUT INTO BIG CHUNKS

SALT AND FRESHLY GROUND BLACK PEPPER

PREP

Preheat the oven to 400 degrees.

1. Heat a small, heavy saucepan. Add 2 tablespoons of the butter and warm it over medium heat, shaking the pan from time to time until the butter turns a deep golden brown. Do not let it burn or get too dark.

2. Line the bottom of an ovenproof saucepan with aluminum foil. Pour on the browned butter and a splash of hot water to start a little steam action. Add the carrots. Season with salt and pepper. Seal the dish with foil.

3. Put the carrots in the preheated oven and roast for 1 hour, or until cooked.

4. Purée the carrots, together with the collected cooking liquid and remaining tablespoon of butter, in a blender. Adjust the seasonings.

NOTE: Properly stored, carrot purée will keep in the refrigerator for 1 week; in the freezer for 3 months.

ALMOND PRALINES

I never realized how much I needed almond pralines in my pantry until I found myself with 2 cups of almond pralines—the result of my test cooking. In addition to being part of various dessert recipes in this book, almond pralines give a lift to store-bought ice cream, enhance fresh berries, and make a decent dessert out of yogurt and bananas.

Moreover, making almond pralines is fun, which, quite frankly, cannot be said for all work.

1 CUP SLICED BLANCHED
ALMONDS

¾ CUP SUGAR

1¼ TABLESPOONS WATER

PREP
. . . . . .
Preheat the oven to 300 degrees.

1. Spread the almonds on a cookie sheet and toast them in the preheated oven till slightly browned, about 8 to 10 minutes.

2. Put the sugar in a heavy casserole over medium heat, mixing it with a wooden spatula to melt. When the sugar has melted, dissolve it with the water, stirring with a wooden spatula until caramelized, about 6 minutes. Add the toasted almonds and continue stirring until the praline has evenly browned, about 15 minutes.

3. Spread out the praline on a large sheet pan to harden. When it has cooled, crush the pieces with a rolling pin, then blend in a food processor. (I blend 2 separate batches: one very fine for cakes and tarts; the other fairly coarse, for ice cream and poached fruit.)

NOTE: Stored in a tightly sealed plastic bag, almond pralines will keep practically forever.

200

PISSALADIÈRE

serves 6 to 8

This popular pizzalike Provençal onion tart got its name from the original *pissala* topping. which is a purée of fermented and salted anchovies, still a popular spread in Collioure. the ancient French anchovy port near the Spanish border. If you plan to serve pissaladière to a large crowd. you may ask your neighborhood pizza place to sell you a sheet of baked pizza dough.

dough

1 PACKAGE DRY YEAST

1 CUP LUKEWARM WATER

2 CUPS PLUS 2 TABLESPOONS ALL-PURPOSE FLOUR

1 TABLESPOON CANOLA OR OLIVE OIL

PINCH OF SALT

onions

4 TABLESPOONS EXTRA VIRGIN OLIVE OIL

2 POUNDS YELLOW ONIONS, PEELED AND FINELY CHOPPED

1 SPRIG THYME

12 ANCHOVY FILLETS, RINSED AND DRIED

12 BLACK OLIVES, PITTED

PREP DOUGH

1. In a small bowl, dissolve the yeast in the warm water. Stir and let it sit for 15 minutes.

2. Place the flour in a mound on a pastry board or kitchen table. Make a well and add the dissolved yeast, oil, and salt. With a fork, work the inside of the well into the liquid. When the mixture becomes solid enough, work in the rest of the flour with your hands, using a folding motion.

3. Place the dough in a bowl, cover it with a damp cloth towel, and let it rest in a warm spot until double in size (about 1 hour).

4. Punch down the dough and reshape it into a ball. Cover it with a damp cloth and set it in a warm place to rise for another 30 to 45 minutes.

PREP ONIONS

1. While the dough is rising, prep the onion topping. Heat 3 tablespoons of the oil in a large skillet over medium heat. Add the onions and thyme. Sauté until tender, stirring occasionally, for about 40 minutes.

2. Remove the thyme. Set the onions aside till ready to use, up to 2 hours at room temperature.

COOKING

Preheat the oven to 375 degrees.

1. Stretch or roll the dough evenly on a lightly oiled sheet pan. Spread the onion mixture evenly over the dough. Arrange the anchovy fillets on top in a lattice pattern. Sprinkle lightly with the remaining olive oil.

2. Bake it in the preheated oven until the crust is crisp, approximately 25 minutes.

PRESENTATION

Dot the top with olives. Cut the *pissaladière* into 2-inch triangles. Serve warm.

NOTE: Covered with plastic wrap, *pissaladière* will keep in a warm place for 1 hour. It can also be reheated in a 350-degree oven for about 5 minutes.

SUGGESTED WINES

A Minervois or a Fitou.

ANCHOÏADE

. . . .

serves 6 to 8

Combine anchovies with oil, add garlic, herbs, and some spicing, and, voilà, you've made *anchoïade*. Spread on toast, it is a popular Provençal snack. *Anchoïade* is frequently requested at private dinner parties; it is "le must" at our annual Napoleon dinner.

6 OUNCES ANCHOVY FILLETS

2 GARLIC CLOVES, PEELED AND CRUSHED

2 TABLESPOONS RED WINE VINEGAR

1 TABLESPOON DIJON MUSTARD

1 TEASPOON FRESH THYME

FRESHLY GROUND BLACK PEPPER

3 TABLESPOONS OLIVE OIL, PLUS MORE IF NEEDED

LEMON JUICE TO TASTE, IF DESIRED

12 SLICES FRENCH BREAD

EXTRA VIRGIN OLIVE OIL

PREP
. . . . . .

Thoroughly rinse the anchovies and pat them dry. Put in a blender together with the crushed garlic, vinegar, mustard, thyme, and pepper. Purée to a paste while slowly adding the oil. Season to taste with a few drops of lemon juice.

COOKING
. . . .

When ready to serve, sprinkle the slices of bread with olive oil, place on a baking sheet, and toast under the broiler for 2 to 3 minutes, or until crisp. Cut each slice into 4 triangles. Spread with the *anchoïade*.

PRESENTATION
. . . .

Sprinkle the *anchoïade* with a hard-boiled egg passed through a sieve, and small black olives from Nice.

NOTE: Stored in the refrigerator, *anchoïade* will keep for one week. Should it dry out, whisk in some additional oil.

SUGGESTED WINES

A chilled Lillet or St. Raphael.

BRAISED BABY ARTICHOKES WITH TOMATO AND CORIANDER

· ·

serves 4 to 6

When we first put this salad on the menu, I was so taken with the dish I ordered it for 2 weeks straight. It's still one of my favorite salads, particulary when I am in the mood for a light and refreshing dish.

The recipe requires a lot of work. But once it's cooked, it can wait. In fact the salad's lovely flavor will intensify when kept in the refrigerator for a few hours before serving.

2 CARROTS, PEELED AND THINLY SLICED ON THE BIAS

2 POUNDS BABY ARTICHOKES

1 LEMON, HALVED

JUICE OF 2 LEMONS

4 TABLESPOONS EXTRA VIRGIN OLIVE OIL

1 SPANISH ONION, PEELED AND COARSELY CHOPPED

1 CARROT, PEELED AND COARSELY CHOPPED

SALT AND PEPPER

¼ CUP WHITE WINE

BOUQUET GARNI: 5 CORIANDER SEEDS, SEVERAL PARSLEY STEMS, 2 BAY LEAVES, 3 SPRIGS THYME TIED IN CHEESECLOTH

SALT AND FRESHLY GROUND WHITE PEPPER

1 TABLESPOON BALSAMIC VINEGAR

4 SHALLOTS, PEELED AND FINELY CHOPPED

2 RIPE BEEFSTEAK TOMATOES, PEELED, SEEDED AND DICED

SMALL BUNCH ITALIAN PARSLEY, CHOPPED

COOKING
. . . .
1. Blanch the 2 thinly sliced carrots, and set them aside.

2. With a sharp knife, cut off approximately half of the top leaves of the artichokes. Remove the stems, peel away the tough outer leaves, and trim the bottoms to form a small heart. Put the artichokes in a bowl of cold water with the lemon halves and the lemon juice. (This is one of the instances when the prep cannot be done in advance: the artichokes are held in the lemon water for a short time to prevent them from turning brown. If you leave the artichokes too long in the lemon bath, they become waterlogged.)

3. Heat 1 tablespoon of the olive oil in a large skillet. Add the onion and sweat over high heat. When the onion is translucent, add the 1 coarsely chopped carrot. Sauté the mixture for about 4 minutes.

4. Drain the artichokes and lemon halves. Pat them dry. Add the artichokes and lemon halves to the skillet. Sauté until the artichokes turn slightly brown, about 10 minutes. Season with salt and pepper.

5. Raise the heat; add the wine, bouquet garni, and water to cover. Bring to a boil, then reduce the heat. Let the mixture simmer, covered, for 35 to 45 minutes, or until the artichokes are tender.

6. Strain the cooked artichokes, reserving 2 tablespoons of the liquid. Discard the bouquet garni and the lemon halves. Let the artichokes cool to room temperature.

7. Prepare a vinaigrette by whisking together the salt, pepper, vinegar, the remaining 3 tablespoons of oil, and the reserved braising juice.

PRESENTATION
. . . .
Put the artichokes in a mixing bowl. Add the chopped shallots, diced tomatoes, blanched carrots, and chopped parsley. Toss the vegetables with the vinaigrette. Adjust the seasoning.

NOTE: Tightly covered, the dressed salad will keep in the refrigerator for 3 days. Check seasonings before serving.

SUGGESTED WINE

A white, fruity Côtes de Provence such as Domaine Gavoty.

205

SALAD OF BABY ZUCCHINI WITH GRILLED PORTOBELLO MUSHROOMS AND SEA SCALLOPS

serves 4

This dish fairly explodes with textures and flavors: there are crunchy baby zucchini dressed in a lemon vinaigrette; delicate scallops, barely cooked; and macho mushrooms, full of spunk and character. The salad could easily serve as a main dish.

zucchini salad

- 1½ TABLESPOONS BALSAMIC VINEGAR
- ½ TABLESPOON FRESH LEMON JUICE
- ⅓ CUP EXTRA VIRGIN OLIVE OIL
- SALT AND FRESHLY GROUND BLACK PEPPER
- 1 POUND MIXED GREEN AND YELLOW BABY ZUCCHINI

mushrooms and scallops

- 3 MEDIUM PORTOBELLO MUSHROOMS (ABOUT 1 POUND)
- 2 TABLESPOONS EXTRA VIRGIN OLIVE OIL
- SALT AND FRESHLY GROUND BLACK PEPPER
- ½ TEASPOON FRESH THYME LEAVES
- 12 OUNCES SEA SCALLOPS, PATTED DRY
- SALT AND PEPPER

PREP ZUCCHINI SALAD

Mix all the vinaigrette ingredients together.

1. Wash the zucchini. Blanch them in boiling salted water for 2 to 3 minutes.

2. Drain the zucchini and refresh them under cold running water. Pat them dry and cut them in half lengthwise. Toss the zucchini in the vinaigrette. Set aside till ready to use.

PREP MUSHROOMS AND SCALLOPS

Separate the mushroom caps from the stems. (Reserve the stems for future use.) Clean the caps with a damp cloth. Cut each in half.

COOKING

Preheat a grill.

1. Preheat the oven to 350 degrees. Brush the mushrooms with olive oil, using about 1 tablespoon. Season with salt and pepper. Place the mushrooms on a preheated grill and grill for 8 to 10 minutes, turning frequently (use tongs) to prevent the mushrooms from burning. Remove the mushrooms to a baking sheet or ovenproof

skillet. Brush with the remaining olive oil and sprinkle with the thyme. Finish cooking in a preheated oven for 5 to 7 minutes, or until cooked through. Remove from the oven and let sit for 2 minutes before cutting the mushrooms into 1-inch diamond shapes.

2. Heat a nonstick pan to hot. Pan sear the scallops for 30 seconds per side. Season with salt and pepper.

PRESENTATION

On each of 4 serving plates, arrange the zucchini to form a triangle. Spoon the mushrooms within this triangle. Top with scallops. Drizzle with remaining vinaigrette. Serve at room temperature.

HOUSE-CURED SALMON

serves 4

A winner at the restaurant, where we serve it over *mesclun* greens and lightly pickled cucumber slices, or with a marinated vegetable *brunoise*, tossed in sherry-based vinaigrette.

This dish is the perfect summer appetizer: it requires no cooking, has to be made in advance, and is light and refreshing. Extra portions will enhance Cucumber Soup, another summer crowd pleaser.

¼ CUP CORIANDER SEEDS

¼ CUP BLACK PEPPERCORNS

2¼ CUPS KOSHER SALT

4 6-OUNCE SALMON FILLETS, WITH BONES REMOVED

PREP

1. Place the coriander seeds and peppercorns in a food processor and run the machine for 1 minute to grind coarsely. Incorporate this mixture into the salt.

2. Place half of the seasoned salt on a nonreactive tray or in a glass dish. Place the salmon fillets on top and cover with the remaining salt-spice mixture. Cover with plastic wrap and refrigerate for 5 to 6 hours.

3. When it's ready to serve, remove the salmon and rinse under cold water. Blot dry and brush off any remaining coriander seeds or pepper corns.

PRESENTATION

Thinly slice the salmon fillets against the grain and arrange with the garnish of your choice.

NOTE: Well-wrapped, cured salmon will keep in the refrigerator up to 1 week.

RATATOUILLE

makes 10 to 12 appetizer portions

Ratatouille is commonly called a Provençal vegetable stew. To me, that's like describing Provence as a nice warm place. Regarding a plate of ratatouille, vibrant with red, aubergine, green, and yellow, is like looking at a field of wildflowers that grow in profusion in the Haute Provence.

At the restaurant, we pull out all the stops and fill *socca* roulade—another genuine Provençal item—with ratatouille, topping the dish with a thick slice of goat cheese.

As the French would say, *pas mal.*

2–3 SMALL EGGPLANTS (ABOUT 1 POUND)

3 MEDIUM YELLOW ONIONS (ABOUT 1 POUND)

2 GARLIC CLOVES

3 MEDIUM ZUCCHINI (ABOUT 1 POUND)

2 RED PEPPERS (ABOUT 1 POUND)

3–4 MEDIUM TOMATOES (ABOUT 1 POUND)

4 TABLESPOONS CANOLA OR EXTRA VIRGIN OLIVE OIL

1 TABLESPOON HERBES DE PROVENCE (SEE PAGE ███)

SALT AND FRESHLY GROUND BLACK PEPPER

5 CLOVES GARLIC CONFIT (SEE PAGE ███), OR 3 GARLIC CLOVES, COARSELY CHOPPED

PREP
......

1. Peel the eggplants and cut them into 1-inch cubes. Put the cubes in a colander, sprinkle with salt, and leave to drain for 30 minutes. Meanwhile, peel and coarsely chop the onions. Peel and mince the 2 garlic cloves.

2. Wash the zucchini and cut them into 1-inch cubes. Slice the peppers, remove the seeds, and cut the peppers into 1-inch strips. Quarter the tomatoes; squeeze them gently to extract excess juice and seeds.

3. Blot the eggplant with a paper towel.

COOKING
....

1. Heat 1 tablespoon of the oil in a large, heavy-bottomed sauté pan. Sweat the onions and minced garlic for 5 minutes till translucent. Remove them with a slotted spoon and set aside. (At the restaurant, the chef has 4 sauté pans going simultaneously to sauté the individual vegetables. Aside from not possessing 4 sauté pans at home, I simply can't handle 4 tasks at the same time, and therefore I sauté my vegetables one after the other.)

2. Sauté each vegetable, except the tomatoes, separately in 1 tablespoon oil for 10 minutes.

3. Wipe the sauté pan. Add the sautéed onions, garlic, eggplant, zucchini, and peppers. Heat through. Add the tomatoes, *herbes de Provence*, salt, and pepper.

4. Let the mixture simmer over medium heat, with the cover ajar, for 45 minutes.

5. Spoon the vegetables into a colander or *chinois* and collect the juices. Place the collected liquid into a saucepan and reduce the liquid over high heat until thick and syrupy.

6. At the restaurant we now blend the reduced liquid together with garlic *confit* in a blender. At home, I add the garlic *confit* or garlic cloves directly to the saucepan, together with the vegetables.

7. Adjust the seasoning.

PRESENTATION
....

At the restaurant we invert 1 cup of ratatouille in the center of individual serving plates and surround the ratatouille with a few raw carrot strips. At home I serve ratatouille warm or cold, family-style.

NOTE: I'd suggest you double or triple the ratatouille recipe, particularly during the summer when the vegetables are at their prime. Stored in a covered container, ratatouille will keep in the refrigerator for 2 weeks, in the freezer for 3 months.

SUGGESTED WINE

A cool, refreshing Côtes de Provence Rosé.

SOCCA ROULADE WITH
RATATOUILLE AND GOAT CHEESE

makes 6 to 8 socca roulades

Made with chick-pea flour, *socca* roulade, a typical crepe, used to be the most popular street food in the old quarter of Nice. People would stand in line and wait patiently for another batch of *socca* to come out of the stone oven. The *socca*, cut into wedges pizza-style, was served on a piece of paper. Alas, even old Nice has gone modern. It's up to nostalgic travelers like us to rescue *socca* from oblivion, giving it a new twist by filling it with ratatouille.

socca roulade

- 1 CUP GOOD-QUALITY CHICK-PEA FLOUR (THE BEST ONE TO USE IS TRIPLE LION, SUPERFINE, FROM ENGLAND)
- 1¼ CUPS WATER, MORE IF NEEDED
- ¼ CUP CANOLA OR OLIVE OIL
- SALT AND PEPPER
- ½ TEASPOON MINCED FRESH ROSEMARY LEAVES, OR ¼ TEASPOON DRIED ROSEMARY
- 3 TEASPOONS SNIPPED CHIVES
- ¾ CUP RATATOUILLE PER PERSON (SEE PAGE 000), AT ROOM TEMPERATURE
- 4 1-INCH SLICES GOAT CHEESE, AT ROOM TEMPERATURE

PREP SOCCA ROULADE

1. In a stainless-steel mixing bowl sift the chick-pea flour. Make a well. Whisk in just enough of the water to form a paste, eliminating small lumps.

2. Whisk in the remaining water, 1 tablespoon of the oil, salt, pepper, rosemary, and chives. (The batter should not be too thick.)

COOKING

1. Heat an 8-inch nonstick pan or iron skillet till very hot. Coat the pan with a scant teaspoon of oil. When the oil starts smoking, pour a 2-ounce ladle, or ¼ cup, of *socca* batter to cover the bottom evenly.

2. When the batter has completely set and browned, about 3 minutes, flip it over and cook the other side for about 1 minute. (The first side should be fairly brown, the second side yellow.)

3. Turn the crepe onto a plate. Repeat with the rest of the batter, stirring the batter occasionally to prevent the flour from settling at the bottom. You will need to add a fresh scant teaspoon of oil for each crepe.

PRESENTATION

Spoon 2 tablespoons of ratatouille on one side of each crepe. Fold the crepe over. Top with a slice of goat cheese. Serve warm.

NOTE: Leftover crepes can be refrigerated. Thinly sliced, they add a nice touch to clear soups or almost any salad.

SUGGESTED WINES

A Côtes de Provence Rosé or a red Sancerre, slightly chilled.

GARLIC SAUSAGE WITH LENTILS

serves 8 as an appetizer, or 4 as a main dish

This is French bistro fare at its best. I like the lentil salad so much, I know I need to prepare extra portions because I can't resist preservice noshing.

The garlic sausage, called *saucisson à l'ail* in French, is a large, semisoft sausage that must be cooked. Almost every region in France produces its own style of sausage, claiming it to be the best. At the restaurant we use *saucisson de Lyon*, available in specialty stores. The French green lentils called for here are young, small lentils that do not require soaking.

lentils
....

- 12 OUNCES FRENCH GREEN LENTILS (2 CUPS)
- 1 TABLESPOON BUTTER
- 1 TABLESPOON EXTRA VIRGIN OLIVE OIL

- ½ SPANISH ONION, PEELED AND CUT INTO CHUNKS
- 1 LARGE CARROT, PEELED AND DICED
- 1 PINT CHICKEN STOCK (2 CUPS), MORE IF NEEDED
- BOUQUET GARNI: 2 BAY LEAVES, 2 SPRIGS THYME, SEVERAL SPRIGS ITALIAN PARSLEY, TIED IN CHEESECLOTH
- SALT AND FRESHLY GROUND BLACK PEPPER
- ½ TEASPOON CHOPPED FRESH ROSEMARY

brunoise
....

- 1 CARROT, PEELED
- 2 CELERY RIBS
- ½ YELLOW PEPPER, SEEDS REMOVED
- 2 TEASPOONS BUTTER

211

Vinaigrette

SALT

1 TABLESPOON SHERRY
VINEGAR

3 SHALLOTS, MINCED

¼ CUP EXTRA VIRGIN OLIVE OIL

2 TABLESPOONS SNIPPED
CHIVES

FRESHLY GROUND BLACK
PEPPER

1¼ POUNDS GARLIC SAUSAGE

SPRIGS OF CURLY PARSLEY

DIJON MUSTARD (OPTIONAL)

PREP LENTILS

1. Wash the lentils under cold running water, picking out any small pebbles.

2. Heat the butter and the oil in a saucepan. Sauté the onion and the carrot till translucent, about 4 mintues. Add the lentils; sauté to coat them. Add half to the chicken stock and the bouquet garni. Stir well.

3. Reduce the heat. When the liquid has been absorbed, add the rest of the stock. Let it simmer for 1 hour, or until the lentils are soft. (Add more liquid if needed.)

4. Drain the lentils, reserving 2 tablespoons of the juices for the vinaigrette. Discard the bouquet garni. Season the lentils with salt, pepper, and rosemary. Cover and set aside.

PREP BRUNOISE AND VINAIGRETTE

1. For the *brunoise*, dice the vegetables as small as possible. Blanch in boiling water for 1 minute.

2. Heat the butter in a skillet. Sweat the blanched vegetables for 2 minutes. Set aside.

3. For the vinaigrette, mix the salt, vinegar, reserved lentil juice, and shallots together. Whisk in the olive oil.

COOKING

1. Place the garlic sausage in a heavy casserole. Cover with cold water; bring to a boil. Reduce the heat, and cook, covered, for 20 to 25 minutes.

2. Remove the sausage and drain on paper towels.

PRESENTATION

Toss the lentils and the *brunoise* with the vinaigrette. Add the chives and black pepper. Arrange the lentils in the center of a serving dish. Slice the garlic sausage in ¼-inch-thick slices and place on top of the lentils. Garnish with sprigs of curly parsley. Serve family-style with Dijon mustard if desired.

SUGGESTED WINES

A robust Côtes du Rhone-Villages such as Vacqueyras, or a sturdy Southern Rhône such as Gigondas.

MUSHROOMS PROVENÇAL

serves 4

This was a popular dish at the restaurant when we first opened. Then it went out of style. With bistro fare back in fashion, I wouldn't be surprised to see this toothsome appetizer reappear on our menu.

1½ POUNDS SMALL FRESH BUTTON MUSHROOMS

½ CUP EXTRA VIRGIN OLIVE OIL

2 LARGE GARLIC CLOVES, PEELED AND CRUSHED

½ TEASPOON FRESH THYME LEAVES

½ TEASPOON FRESH MARJORAM OR SAGE LEAVES, CHOPPED

1 TABLESPOON CHOPPED PARSLEY

2 TEASPOONS FRESH BREAD CRUMBS

SALT AND PEPPER

LEMON WEDGES, DIPPED IN CHOPPED PARSLEY

PREP

Remove the bottom part of the mushroom stems. Wipe the mushrooms with a damp cloth and cut them into quarters.

COOKING

1. Heat the oil in a large skillet. Add the mushrooms. Sauté over high heat till slightly brown, about 8 to 10 minutes, shaking the skillet back and forth.

2. Reduce the heat. Add the gralic and herbs and continue to sauté for 2 to 3 minutes. Mix in the bread crumbs. Season with salt and pepper.

PRESENTATION

Serve family-style on a platter, surrounded by the lemon wedges.

NOTE: If the mushrooms are not to be served immediately, let them cool before storing in the refrigerator. The mushrooms will keep for 1 day. Bring up to room temperature before serving.

SUGGESTED WINE

A lovely Côtes du Ventoux, such as La Vieille Ferme.

GOAT-CHEESE GNOCCHI WITH
WHITE TRUFFLES

makes 20 to 24 gnocchi

To me, there is nothing in the entire food repertoire that beats the aroma and flavor of white truffles, the pungent fungi from the Piedmont region of Italy. The price of this extremely limited seasonal item has reached astronomical heights—$62.50 per ounce, as of this writing. I remember when street vendors in Milan sold a good-size truffle for the equivalent of $10. Unfortunately, that was before we had the restaurant.

Actually, these delicate gnocchi stand nicely on their own, served with freshly ground pepper, grated Parmesan, and just a touch of truffle oil if you happen to have it on hand. Barring that, they still make a lovely dish, especially if accompanied by red pepper *coulis*.

16 OUNCES FRESH GOAT CHEESE

2 EGG YOLKS

⅓ CUP ALL-PURPOSE FLOUR

⅓ CUP SEMOLINA FLOUR

1 OUNCE FRESH WHITE TRUFFLES

PREP

1. Line a sheet pan with parchment paper or foil.

2. Combine the goat cheese and egg yolks in a mixing bowl. Beat with a wooden spoon until smooth. Incorporate the all-purpose flour and semolina flours. Continue beating until the mixture resembles cream cheese.

3. At the restaurant, we spoon the mixture into a pastry bag and pipe the mixture onto the parchment- or foil-lined sheet pan to form 2 or 3 long rolls. At home, I dispense with the pastry bag and form the rolls by hand. The result is not as pretty; but there definitely is less waste and less cleanup.

4. Chill in the refrigerator for at least 2 hours.

COOKING

1. Bring a large pot of salted water to a boil.

2. Form gnocchi by cutting the rolls into 1-inch pieces. Pass the back of a fork over the gnocchi to form ridges.

3. Toss the gnocchi into the boiling water in batches. When they start to float, reduce the heat and let them simmer for 2 minutes.

4. Remove the gnocchi with a wire-mesh spoon. Transfer them to a plate to prevent overcooking.

PRESENTATION
. . . .
Shave white truffles over the gnocchi just before serving.

SUGGESTED WINES

A light Northern Rhône, such as a young St.-Joseph, an elegant Chambolle-Musigny, or Champagne.

GALETTES OF VEGETABLES AND HERBS

serves 4 to 6

Bad news: galettes have to be cooked right after they have been prepped.

Good news: galettes can be made 1 to 2 hours ahead of serving time and then reheated.

At the restaurant, we serve the galettes as an appetizer with a reduction of duck stock. In a lighter vein, the galettes make a lovely lunch dish, topped with roasted tomatoes or garnished with tomato *concassé*.

2 GARLIC CLOVES, PEELED AND MINCED

1 TABLESPOON CHOPPED ITALIAN PARSLEY

1 CARROT, PEELED

1 SMALL YELLOW ONION, PEELED

2 MEDIUM ZUCCHINI

2 MEDIUM POTATOES, PEELED

2 EGGS

1 TABLESPOON ALL-PURPOSE FLOUR

SALT AND FRESHLY GROUND BLACK PEPPER

1 TEASPOON FRESH THYME LEAVES

¼ CUP PEANUT OIL

1 CUP DUCK STOCK (OPTIONAL, SEE PAGE ███)

1½ TABLESPOONS BUTTER

215

PREP

Preheat the oven to 450 degrees.

1. Place the minced garlic and parsley in a mixing bowl. Grate the carrot, onion, zucchini. and potatoes into the bowl. (At the restaurant we grate the vegetables by hand, because this way they release less liquid. Since I am not as speedy and also not as fussy as our cooks, I grate the vegetables in a food processor and drain them in a strainer. The important thing is that, regardless of how you grate your vegetables, once they are grated, the galettes have to be cooked immediately.)

2. Add the eggs, flour, salt, pepper, and thyme to the grated vegetables. Mix quickly.

COOKING

1. Heat a 5-inch iron or nonstick skillet to very hot. Pour 2 teaspoons of the oil into the skillet. When the oil is hot, fill the skillet with the vegetable mixture, using a 2-ounce ladle. Shake the pan from time to time.

2. Cook the mixture for about 2 minutes, just until set. Transfer the galette to an oiled baking sheet. Repeat with the rest of the mixture. (If you use a large pan, adjust the sauté and baking times accordingly. When ready to serve, cut the galettes in 4 quarters.)

3. Bake the galettes in the preheated oven for 10 minutes. Flip the galettes over and bake for an additional 10 minutes. Galettes should be crisp and golden brown when finished.

VARIATION: If you have duck stock and wish to sauce the galettes with it, bring the stock to a slow boil and let it thicken. Whisk in butter and adjust the seasonings. To serve, spoon 1 tablespoon of duck sauce over each galette.

NOTE: If the galettes are not being served immediately, leave them on the baking sheet and cover them with foil. When ready to serve, remove the foil, and reheat in a 350-degree oven for 5 minutes.

SUGGESTED WINES

A fresh and fruity Beaujolais-Villages, or a Brouilly.

216

BRANDADE DE MORUE

serves 10 to 12 as an appetizer

I tasted my first *brandade* in Arles at the magic hour of sunset. The rich gratin of salt codfish, garlic, cream, and oil came with rounds of bread, fried in butter and olive oil, and a side dish of tiny black olives from nearby Nyons. The food was part of *aperos*, Provençal appetizers. I ate so much, I skipped dinner. And although friends told me dinner was excellent, I didn't care, for I was convinced that I had encountered the soul of Provençal cuisine.

1¼ POUNDS BONED SKINLESS DRIED COD

2 IDAHO OR RUSSET POTATOES, PEELED AND BOILED

3 GARLIC CLOVES, PEELED AND MINCED

1 CUP HEAVY CREAM, AT ROOM TEMPERATURE

½ CUP EXTRA VIRGIN OLIVE OIL, AT ROOM TEMPERATURE

JUICE OF ½ LEMON

FRESHLY GROUND BLACK PEPPER

3 SLICES OF FRENCH BREAD, CUT INTO TRIANGLES AND TOASTED

BLACK OLIVES

SPRIGS OF ITALIAN PARSLEY

PREP

1. The day before you plan to serve the *brandade*, start soaking the cod in cold water. You will need to change the water 4 or 5 times.

2. Drain the cod. Remove and discard loose pieces. Cut the cod into chunks.

COOKING

1. Place the cod in a pan of cold water to cover and bring to a boil. Reduce the heat, let it simmer for 6 to 8 minutes, and drain.

2. Cut the potatoes in half. Place them in a mixer, together with the minced garlic. Start on low speed, and add the cod with ½ cup of the heavy cream. Continue on low speed and gradually pour in the rest of the cream, olive oil, and the lemon juice.

3. Season with black pepper. The mixture will be fluffy and white, with a pleasant hint of the cod's stringy fiber.

PRESENTATION

Place the *brandade* in a shallow dish, and surround it with toasted triangles of French bread. Garnish with black olives and sprigs of Italian parsley. Serve at room temperature.

NOTE: Properly stored and refrigerated, *brandade* will keep for 3 days. To serve, reheat over a low flame, stirring gently for 2 minutes, or until sufficiently warmed through.

SUGGESTED WINE

A ripe, meaty Languedoc red, such as Faugères, or, alternatively, a cool and slightly fruity Costeries de Nîmes.

POACHED SHRIMPS WITH ZUCCHINI CREAM AND BASIL PISTOU

serves 4

This dish looks like a garden in bloom: apple-green zucchini cream, moss-green *pistou*, and pale-pink shrimps. Since I like the contrast between the lukewarm zucchini-basil *pistou* and the hot shrimps, I don't bother to reheat anything, which means that the dish can be assembled within minutes.

zucchini cream

- 3 MEDIUM ZUCCHINI (ABOUT 1 POUND)
- 1 TABLESPOON FRESH THYME LEAVES
- 1 GARLIC CLOVE, PEELED AND MINCED
- 2 TABLESPOONS WATER
- SALT AND FRESHLY GROUND BLACK PEPPER
- ½ CUP EXTRA VIRGIN OLIVE OIL

shrimps

- 1 CUP KOSHER SALT, OR ½ CUP SEA SALT (SEE NOTE)
- 12 MEDIUM SHRIMPS, SHELLED
- 1 CUP BASIL PISTOU (SEE PAGE 888)

PREP ZUCCHINI CREAM

1. Trim the zucchini, quarter them lengthwise, and cut the quarters into ½-inch pieces.

2. Place the zucchini, thyme, garlic, water, salt, and pepper in a medium pot. Bring to a quick boil. Lower the heat, cover, and cook till the zucchini turn translucent, 12 to 15 minutes.

3. Place the zucchini in a blender. Add the oil. Purée for a few minutes. Adjust the seasonings. Set aside.

COOKING

1. Bring cold water to cover the shrimps to a vigorous boil. Add the salt. (The liquid should taste like seawater.) Add the shrimps.

2. The shrimps are done when pink and firm to the touch, after about 1 minute. Remove them with a slotted spoon. Spread them on a plate to prevent overcooking.

PRESENTATION

On each plate, make an open circle about 4 inches in diameter with the basil *pistou*. Fill the inside with zucchini cream. Place 3 shrimps on top.

NOTE: The idea behind the inordinate amount of salt here is to approximate the taste of seawater.

SUGGESTED WINES

A fruity Alsatian Riesling or Sancerre.

218

CHILLED TOMATO SOUP WITH CRABMEAT AND CHIVES

serves 4 to 6

This soup is so simple to prepare that a child could whip it up. The wonder is that it tastes as if a professional chef had toiled hours over it.

2 POUNDS RIPE PLUM TOMATOES

1 OR 2 CANS (12–14 OUNCES TOTAL) GOOD-QUALITY TOMATO JUICE

SALT AND FRESHLY GROUND BLACK PEPPER

PINCH OF SUGAR

2 TABLESPOONS CRABMEAT, PICKED OVER FOR CARTILAGE

2 TEASPOONS SNIPPED CHIVES

PREP

1. Core the tomatoes. Puree them in a food processor or blender, adding tomato juice to thin to a medium-thick consistency.

2. Season the soup with salt, pepper, and sugar. Refrigerate to chill.

PRESENTATION

Spoon the soup into individual soup plates. Float some crabmeat on top, and garnish with chives.

SUGGESTED WINES

A chilled Fino Sherry, or the wine you are serving with the first course.

CUCUMBER SOUP WITH SALMON

serves 4

A refreshing, attractive summer dish that can be made a day ahead of time. At La Colombe d'Or we use our house-smoked salmon. Since I don't have a smoker at home (and imagine that most people don't), I have made the soup with cured salmon.

3–4 CUCUMBERS (1¼ POUNDS)

KOSHER SALT

3 OUNCES SHELLED WALNUTS (¾ CUP)

¾ CUP SOUR CREAM

¾ CUP YOGURT

¼ CUP EXTRA VIRGIN OLIVE OIL

2 TEASPOONS WHITE WINE VINEGAR

2 TABLESPOONS SNIPPED CHIVES

1 TABLESPOON MINCED CHERVIL

FRESHLY GROUND WHITE PEPPER

6 OUNCES CURED SALMON (SEE PAGE 000), CUT INTO JULIENNE

MINT, CUT INTO JULIENNE

PREP

1. Peel, seed, and slice the cucumbers into ½-inch chunks. Spread them out on a tray, sprinkle them generously with the kosher salt, and let them sit for 30 minutes. Rinse and pat dry.

2. In a food processor or blender, purée the walnuts with the sour cream and yogurt. Slowly add the olive oil and vinegar. Remove the purée to a large mixing bowl and set aside.

3. Purée the cucumbers, using some of the nut–sour cream mixture to help liquefy them. Add the chives, chervil, and pepper. Incorporate the cucumber mixture into the nut–sour cream mixture. Stir well. Adjust seasonings. Refrigerate to chill.

PRESENTATION

Divide the soup into 4 individual soup bowls. Garnish with a julienne of salmon and mint.

LEEK-AND-POTATO SOUP

serves 4 to 6

This soup is simplicity itself. Restorative served hot on cold winter days, it is equally refreshing chilled during the summer. If served with the addition of black truffle shavings, the soup becomes a noble dish.

Actually, this is old-fashioned vichyssoise, parading under a new name. Created at the Ritz-Carlton Hotel in New York City by Louis Dial, a French chef who had grown up near Vichy, vichyssoise was all the rage in this country until well into the 1970s. The name change is one of the curious fates many dishes go through in their culinary career.

3 MEDIUM LEEKS

1 SPANISH ONION

4 IDAHO OR RUSSET POTATOES (ABOUT 1½ POUNDS)

2 TABLESPOONS BUTTER

1½ QUARTS CHICKEN STOCK

2 BAY LEAVES

1 CUP HEAVY CREAM

SALT AND FRESHLY GROUND WHITE PEPPER

2 TEASPOONS SNIPPED CHIVES

1 TEASPOON SNIPPED CHERVIL

2 TEASPOONS SHAVED BLACK TRUFFLES (OPTIONAL)

PREP

1. Trim the leeks at the roots, and split them lengthwise. Discard the dark-green and tough leaves. Chop the leeks coarsely. Wash and rinse them under cold water a number of times to remove all the sand, then drain.

2. Peel and chop the onion. Peel the potatoes and cut them into cubes. Keep in cold water until ready to use.

COOKING

1. Heat the butter in a saucepan. Add the leeks and the onion. Sweat them until they are translucent. Drain the potatoes and add them to the saucepan. Continue sautéing over low heat until potatoes have softened, about 4 minutes.

2. Add the stock and bay leaves. Cover and simmer for 25 minutes, or until the potatoes are cooked.

3. Remove the bay leaves. Purée the soup in a food processor, and return the purée to the saucepan. Bring the soup to a boil, lower the heat, add the cream, and warm through. (If the soup is to be served cold, whisk in the cream just before serving.) Season with salt and pepper.

NOTE: Properly stored, the chilled soup can be kept in the refrigerator for 2 days.

PRESENTATION

Ladle the soup into warmed soup plates. Sprinkle with the herbs and black truffles, if desired.

SUGGESTED WINE

A fleshy Côteaux du Languedoc.

LENTIL SOUP

serves 4 to 6

In contrast to champions of chicken soup, my cure-all food is lentil soup. I like mine thick, with chunks of smoked bacon or pork butt, and have this fantasy of consuming a big bowl of this potage—fortified with a jigger of *vin de pays*—for breakfast.

1 POUND FRENCH GREEN LENTILS

1 CARROT

1 ONION

1 CELERY RIB

1 GARLIC CLOVE

6 OUNCES SMOKED BACON, CUBED

1 TABLESPOON CANOLA OIL

1 SPRIG ROSEMARY

2 QUARTS CHICKEN STOCK
OR WATER

1 TEASPOON RED WINE VINEGAR

SALT AND FRESHLY GROUND
BLACK PEPPER

PREP

1. Wash the lentils in cold water, picking out all the small pebbles. Drain. Peel the carrot and onion, and remove any tough strings from the celery, and cut them into small dice. Mince the garlic.

COOKING

1. In a large saucepan heat the bacon to hot, but not smoking. Sweat the vegetables and garlic in the rendered bacon fat, about 4 minutes, stirring all the time to prevent the vegetables from burning. Add the oil and the lentils, and continue to cook for 5 minutes. Add the rosemary sprig.

2. Pour in the liquid, a little at a time. Bring to a boil, then lower the heat. Cover and simmer over low heat for 45 minutes, or until the lentils are cooked.

3. Remove the rosemary sprig, add the red wine vinegar. Season to taste. Serve hot in soup bowls.

SUGGESTED WINE

A Côtes du Rhône Vin de Pays.

223

FETTUCCINI WITH WILD
MUSHROOMS AND RABBIT SAUSAGE

serves 4

This dish recalls the first time George and I had dinner at Ed Giobbi's house. Ed served wild mushrooms that he had picked that morning. We were skeptical.

"I've been mushroom hunting since I was four," said Ed. "That was back in Italy; my father took me."

We finished the plate down to the last mushroom.

Ed also gave us a valuable tip: since cultivated mushrooms have no flavor and most store-bought wild mushrooms don't have that much taste either, adding a small amount of reconstituted dried porcini will give either mushroom the needed lift.

If rabbit sausages are not available or not to your liking, skip them. The dish will still be a success.

mushrooms

1 POUND FRESH WILD MUSHROOMS, SUCH AS SHIITAKE, MORELS, CEPES, OR CHANTERELLES

2 OUNCES DRIED PORCINI MUSHROOMS

½ CUP CHICKEN STOCK

2 GARLIC CLOVES, PEELED AND MINCED

2 SHALLOTS, PEELED AND MINCED

3 TABLESPOONS EXTRA VIRGIN OLIVE OIL

2 TABLESPOONS BUTTER

2 TEASPOONS CHOPPED PARSLEY

SALT AND FRESHLY GROUND BLACK PEPPER

4 RABBIT SAUSAGES (ABOUT 1 POUND)

1 POUND FRESH FETTUCCINI OR 1 POUND GOOD-QUALITY DRIED FETTUCCINI (PREFERABLY THE ITALIAN BRAND DESECCO)

SALT AND FRESHLY GROUND BLACK PEPPER

EXTRA VIRGIN OLIVE OIL

½ BUNCH CHIVES, SNIPPED

224

PREP MUSHROOMS

1. Wipe the mushrooms with a damp cloth. Remove the stems, trim, and chop coarsely. Cut the caps into quarters.

2. Soak the dried mushrooms in lukewarm water for 15 minutes. Drain, adding the mushroom juice to the chicken stock (you should have ⅓ cup mushroom juice).

3. Sauté the garlic and shallots in hot oil to brown, shaking the pan vigorously. Add the fresh mushrooms. Sauté briefly over high heat to brown, about 5 minutes, tossing the pan back and forth. Add the soaked dried mushrooms, the chicken stock, and the mushroom liquid; boil over high heat to reduce almost completely, about 10 to 15 minutes. Whisk in the butter and sprinkle with parsley. Season with salt and a generous portion of black pepper.

COOKING

Preheat the oven to 450 degrees.

1. Heat a pan over high flame. Add the rabbit sausages and brown for about 2 min

utes per side. Pour off the rendered fat and place the sausages in the preheated oven to finish, 5 to 6 minutes.

2. Toss the fettuccini in rapidly boiling water and cook for 2 minutes; if using dried fettuccini, adjust the cooking time accordingly. Pour into a colander. Shake to drain the excess water. Season with salt and pepper and squirt a little bit of extra virgin olive oil onto the pasta.

PRESENTATION

Place the fettuccini in a deep dish. Top with the mushrooms. Slice the rabbit sausage thick on the bias and arrange it over the mushrooms. Sprinkle the dish with chives. Serve family-style.

NOTE: In a gesture that never fails to impress me, chef Naj tosses the fettuccini high into the air while throwing a well-aimed measure of salt and pepper, plus a squirt of olive oil, at the pasta in midair.

SUGGESTED WINE

A rich and slightly heady Northern Rhône such as Cornas.

225

COD WITH PROVENÇAL BLEND OF WHITE BEANS AND ROASTED TOMATOES

serves 6

Cod is a winning dish for us: cost-effective and a cinch to get ready because the accompanying garnishes are part of our *mis en place*. The presentation of the dish always solicits an expression of delight, followed by applause after the first forkful.

white beans

. . . .

1 POUND GREAT NORTHERN BEANS (SIMILAR TO CANNELLINI BEANS)

½ SPANISH ONION, PEELED, HALVED, AND STUDDED WITH 2 CLOVES

1 CARROT, PEELED AND HALVED LENGTHWISE

1 BAY LEAF

2 SPRIGS THYME

½ GARLIC HEAD, UNPEELED, HALVED

SALT AND FRESHLY GROUND BLACK PEPPER

1 TABLESPOON EXTRA VIRGIN OLIVE OIL

6 ROASTED TOMATOES (SEE PAGE ■■■) SLICED INTO QUARTERS

1 TABLESPOON CHOPPED ITALIAN PARSLEY

cod

. . . .

2 POUNDS COD FILLETS, CUT INTO 6 PORTIONS

SALT AND FRESHLY GROUND BLACK PEPPER

3 TABLESPOONS EXTRA VIRGIN OLIVE OIL, MORE IF NEEDED

¼ CUP PARSLEY OIL (SEE PAGE ■■■)

PREP BEANS

1. Rinse the beans and pick them over for small pebbles. Fill a pot ¾ full with water. Add the onion, carrot, bay leaf, thyme, and garlic. Bring to a boil.

2. Lower the heat, and simmer, uncovered, till the beans are soft, about 1½ to 2 hours, occasionally skimming off the foam that may rise to the top.

3. Strain the stock and save the liquid. Discard the vegetables and seasonings. Season the beans with salt and pepper. Store in a sealed container till ready to use. (This could be prepped a few days in advance. When ready to serve, reheat the beans, moisten with the olive oil or the reserved stock.)

4. Mix the quartered roasted tomatoes into the beans together with the chopped parsley. Adjust the seasoning.

COOKING

Preheat the oven to 450 degrees.

1. Trim the fillets, and pat them dry. Season with salt and pepper.

2. In an ovenproof skillet heat 1 tablespoon of the oil to very hot. When the oil is almost smoking, add the first two portions of cod. (This is done so as not to crowd the pan.) Sauté for a few minutes till the cod becomes slightly crisp and brown. Turn the cod over, and put it into the preheated oven for 5 to 7 minutes, depending on thickness of the fish.

3. Repeat with the second and third batches, adding more oil.

PRESENTATION

Put a mound of beans in the center of individual serving dishes. Place the cod, crisp side up, on top. Squeeze a generous amount of parsley oil over the cod. Serve immediately.

NOTE: The method used here of sautéing the fish on one side and finishing it by baking the other side works particularly well with thick cuts of fish: it cooks the fish through quickly and helps seal in the juices.

SUGGESTED WINES

A sturdy Southern Rhône wine such as Gigondas, or a medium-bodied white Graves.

BOUILLABAISSE COLOMBE D'OR

Nothing can be said about bouillabaisse that has not been said before, except that every time I catch a whiff of that divine Mediterranean dish when one of our waiters brings it to a table, I think of Tétou, the restaurant in Golfe-Juan whose bouillabaisse has never been matched by any other.

To make bouillabaisse, it helps to be a fishwife, fisherman, or a professional cook. Barring these, it's a labor of love and, like everything born out of that sentiment, well worth the effort.

Bouillabaisse consists of four parts: fish soup (*soupe de poissons*), fish, croutons, and rouille or *aïoli*. Of these, only the fish and shellfish are cooked *à la minute*; everything else can be prepared in advance.

Since it takes time to prepare *soupe de poissons*, it pays to double or triple the recipe and keep portions of that precious soup in the freezer. Served piping hot, with a chunk of country bread, it will be appreciated at any time.

soupe de poissons

3 TO 4 POUNDS BONES, TRIMMINGS, AND HEAD FROM ANY LEAN FISH (SEE NOTE)

1 ONION

2 LEEKS

1 FENNEL BULB

3 MEDIUM TOMATOES (ABOUT ¾ POUND)

2 TABLESPOONS OLIVE OIL

¼ OUNCE SAFFRON

1 TEASPOON CAYENNE PEPPER

1 GARLIC HEAD, UNPEELED, HALVED

BOUQUET GARNI: SEVERAL PARSLEY SPRIGS, 3 SPRIGS OF THYME, 1 BAY LEAF, 5 BLACK PEPPERCORNS, A FEW FENNEL SEEDS, AND 2 PIECES OF DRIED ORANGE RIND, TIED IN CHEESECLOTH

1 10-OUNCE CAN TOMATO PURÉE

SALT AND FRESHLY GROUND BLACK PEPPER

1 TEASPOON PERNOD

228

fish and shellfish
....

1¼ POUNDS FIRM-FLESHED FISH
FILLETS (SUCH AS MONKFISH,
TILEFISH, OR BLACKFISH)

1¼ POUNDS MEDIUM-FLESHED
FISH FILLETS (SUCH AS COD
OR STRIPED BASS)

1¼ POUNDS FLAKY FISH FILLETS
(SUCH AS WEAKFISH, RED
SNAPPER, OR SEA BASS)

16 CLAMS

16 MUSSELS

16 SHRIMPS

3-4 LOBSTERS (1¼ POUNDS
EACH)

1 TABLESPOON OLIVE OIL

4 SHALLOTS, MINCED

2 GARLIC CLOVES, PEELED AND
MINCED

2 TABLESPOONS CHOPPED
PARSLEY

CROUTONS (2 PER SERVING;
SEE PAGE 888)

¼ CUP ROUILLE (SEE PAGE 888)

PREP SOUPE
DE POISSONS
....

1. Rinse the fish bones, trimmings, and heads under cold running water for 20 minutes to get rid of all the blood. Cut into big chunks. Drain and set aside.

2. Coarsely chop the onion, leeks, fennel, and tomatoes.

3. Heat the oil in a large stockpot. Add the vegetables and sweat until softened, about 5 minutes. Add the fish chunks. Raise the heat and cook for 15 minutes.

4. Add the saffron, cayenne pepper, garlic, and bouquet garni. Cover with cold water (about 2½ quarts); add the tomato purée. Mix well. Bring to a boil, stirring so that the bottom does not burn. Skim the foam that rises to the top.

5. Boil, uncovered, over medium heat for 2 hours.

6. Strain through a *chinois* or fine sieve lined with cheese cloth, crushing down the fish bones and shells to extract all the juices.

7. Season the soup with salt, pepper, and Pernod. (If the soup is to be stored, add the Pernod after the soup has been reheated.)

8. Let the soup cool. Store it in a sealed container in the refrigerator till ready to use. The soup will keep for 3 days.

PREP FISH AND
SHELLFISH
....

1. Trim the fish fillets. Cut to obtain 2 pieces per serving.

2. Wash the clams and mussels, and remove the beard from the mussels.

3. Devein and clean the shrimps, reserving the shells for future stock.

4. If using lobsters, remove the rubberbands from the lobster claws. Drop the lobsters in a large kettle of vigorously boiling salted water. Parboil for 2 minutes (just enough to kill the lobsters). Remove. Split the lobsters in half. Remove the dark green coral.

5. Preheat the oven to 500 degrees.

Arrange the lobster halves, shell side up, in a baking pan. Place in the oven for 12 minutes. Remove and set aside while finishing the fish and shellfish.

COOKING

. . . .

1. Heat the oil in a large saucepan. Add the shallots, garlic, and chopped parsley. Sauté for 4 minutes, or until translucent. Pour the soupe de poissons into the pan. Bring to a boil. Add the firm-fleshed and medium-fleshed fish and the clams. Boil, covered, for 5 minutes. Add the flaky fish and the mussels. Boil, covered, for another 4 to 5 minutes, adding the shrimps at the last minute.

PRESENTATION

. . . .

Lift the fish and shellfish out of the soup and arrange it on a large serving platter.

Crack the lobster claws and add the lobster to the platter. Pour a few ladles of the soup over the fish. Pour the rest of the soup into a warmed tureen. Float the croutons on top. You can serve the soup before the fish, or serve both dishes together. Either way they should be accompanied by a generous portion of the rouille. (At the restaurant, we cook and serve bouillabaisse in individual iron skillets. At home, I prefer to serve bouillabaisse family-style, which seems more in keeping with the simple origin of the dish.)

NOTE: At the restaurant, we always have plenty of fish bones, trimmings, and seafood shells on hand. So does your local fishmonger. Ask him to supply you with some of these items. Chances are he'll be impressed by your cooking prowess and flattered that you asked him.

SUGGESTED WINES

A Blanc de Blanc like Domaines Ott, a young, white Cassis, or a Côtes de Provence Rosé Château de Selle.

SEARED TUNA STEAK WITH BASIL-MINT OIL, YELLOW SQUASH, AND BEET FRITES

serves 4

I always think of this dish as East meeting West on a hot summer day. The barely seared tuna, recalling sashimi, has an encounter with Mediterranean-inspired basil-mint oil and American yellow squash. The result is a delight.

Don't let the fact that you may not have beet *frites* hold you back. The tuna works beautifully with any number of garnishes.

yellow squash

- 2 SMALL YELLOW SQUASH (ABOUT ¼ POUND)
- 1 TEASPOON PEANUT OIL
- SALT AND FRESHLY GROUND BLACK PEPPER

tuna

- 2 TEASPOONS BLACK PEPPERCORNS
- 1¼ POUNDS TUNA STEAKS, CUT INTO 2-INCH SQUARES
- SALT TO TASTE
- 2 TABLESPOONS PEANUT OIL
- ¼ CUP BASIL-MINT OIL (SEE PAGE ●●●)
- 4 GARNISH PORTIONS BEET FRITES (SEE PAGE ●●●)
- FRESH CHIVES, SNIPPED

PREP SQUASH

Peel the squash, and cut it into 1-inch cubes. Cook the squash in boiling salted water for 1 minute. Drain well. Moisten slightly with peanut oil, season with salt and pepper, and set aside.

COOKING

1. Spread the peppercorns between 2 sheets of wax paper. Crush them with a rolling pin.

2. Wipe the tuna dry and coat it with the crushed peppercorns. Season with salt.

3. Heat a large skillet until very hot. Add the peanut oil. When it is smoking hot, add the tuna. Sear the tuna for 10 seconds on all sides. Remove. Slice the cubes in half on the diagonal, to make triangles.

PRESENTATION

Ladle a small pool of basil-mint oil on each plate. Arrange 4 triangles of tuna, unseared side up, around it. Fill the center with a handful of beet *frites*. Toss 2 tablespoons of summer squash in between the tuna pieces. Sprinkle with chives. Serve immediately.

SUGGESTED WINES

A red Burgundy such as Auxey-Duresses, or a Chassagne-Montrachet Rouge.

231

SEA SCALLOPS WITH ORANGE-BRAISED ENDIVES AND BROCCOLI RABE

. . . .

serves 4

This dish could win first prize on appearance alone: fat and juicy scallops forming a circle around deep-green broccoli rabe, sitting in a puddle of orange butter dominated by a tall braised endive.

broccoli rabe
. . . .

1 BUNCH BROCCOLI RABE (ABOUT 1 POUND)

2 TABLESPOONS EXTRA VIRGIN OLIVE OIL

1 GARLIC CLOVE, PEELED

3 CRUSHED RED PEPPER FLAKES

SALT AND FRESHLY GROUND BLACK PEPPER

endive
. . . .

4 SMALL FAT ENDIVES

3 TABLESPOONS BUTTER

3 TABLESPOONS SWEET VERMOUTH

3 TABLESPOONS FRESH ORANGE JUICE

3 TABLESPOONS SUGAR

SALT AND FRESHLY GROUND WHITE PEPPER

scallops
. . . .

1½ POUNDS SEA SCALLOPS (ABOUT 6 SCALLOPS PER PERSON)

1½ TABLESPOONS BUTTER

SALT

PREP BROCCOLI RABE
. . . .

1. Remove the tough parts of the stems and large leaves of the broccoli rabe, keeping only the tender parts. Cut the remaining stalks and leaves into 1-inch pieces, leaving the buds intact. Blanch in salted boiling water for 2 minutes. Drain.

2. Heat the oil in a large saucepan. Sauté the garlic over medium heat for 2 minutes. Remove the garlic, and add the broccoli rabe and sauté lightly for a few minutes. Add the pepper flakes. Cook, covered, for 15 to 20 minutes, or until tender. Season with salt and pepper. Keep warm till ready to use.

PREP ENDIVE
. . . .

1. Remove any darkened leaves from the endives. Trim the ends. Leaving the endives intact, core the inside.

2. Heat 2 tablespoons of the butter in a shallow saucepan. Stir in the vermouth, orange juice, and sugar. Add the endives. Cover loosely with wax paper. Braise over medium heat until slightly brown and nutty, about 20 minutes, turning once.

Season to taste with salt and pepper. Remove the endives with a slotted spoon to a warm plate.

3. Deglaze the pan with the remaining butter. Cover loosely with wax paper and set the cooking liquid aside till ready to use.

COOKING

1. Clean the scallops and pat them dry on paper towels.

2. Heat a large nonstick pan over high heat. Add ½ tablespoon of the butter. When the sizzle subsides, add ⅓ of the scallops. Salt lightly. Cook for 2 minutes on one side ; turn and cook the other side for 1 more minute.

3. Remove to paper towels with a slotted spoon. Wipe out the pan and repeat the procedure until all the scallops are cooked.

PRESENTATION

Ladle a small pool of the reserved braised-endive liquid in the center of individual plates. Surround with a few pieces of the broccoli rabe. Arrange the scallops around the broccoli, 6 per serving. Place the endive in the middle, standing upright.

SUGGESTED WINES

A fragrant white Sancerre, or Clos de la Coulée de Serrant.

GRILLED SALMON WITH BRAISED RED CABBAGE AND CARROT CURLS

serves 4

Our salmon presentation is a symphony in red. Infinitely moist and flavorful, the dish is the number-one best-seller on our menu.

carrot curls

4 CARROTS

4 CUPS PEANUT OIL

mustard glaze and sauce

2 TABLESPOONS DRY MUSTARD

2 TABLESPOONS SUGAR

1½–2 TABLESPOONS WATER

⅛ CUP POMMERY GRAIN MUSTARD

⅛ CUP PEANUT OIL

salmon
. . . .

4 6-OUNCE BONELESS SALMON
FILLETS

PEANUT OIL TO COAT

SALT AND FRESHLY GROUND
BLACK PEPPER

BRAISED RED CABBAGE (SEE
PAGE ███)

PREP CARROT CURLS
. . . .

1. Peel the carrots and chafe in long strips, using a vegetable peeler.

2. Heat the oil to 350 degrees in a deep saucepan, using a deep-fry thermometer. Toss in the carrot strips, a few at a time, and deep-fry for 3 to 4 minutes. (Watch, because they burn very quickly.)

3. Remove the carrot curls with a wire-mesh spoon and let them rest on paper towels so they become crisp.

PREP MUSTARD GLAZE AND SAUCE
. . . .

1. Mix the dry mustard, sugar, and water together to create a paste for the glaze.

2. In a separate bowl, mix the Pommery mustard with the peanut oil until emulsified.

COOKING
. . . .

Preheat the grill.

Preheat the oven to 400 degrees.

1. Brush the fillets with peanut oil. Season them with salt and pepper. Put them on the grill for 3 minutes on one side only. (If you lack a grill, sauté the salmon in a very hot iron skillet and then transfer the salmon to the oven.) Remove the salmon, and brush the top with the mustard glaze.

2. Put the salmon in the preheated oven for 4 minutes for medium rare; 6 minutes for medium. Once the fish is cooked, slice the fillets in half on the bias.

PRESENTATION
. . . .

Place a mound of braised cabbage in the center of 4 individual plates. Arrange 2 salmon halves on top of each cabbage serving. Make a nice clean circle around the cabbage with the Pommery mustard sauce. Top with the carrot curls. Serve immediately.

SUGGESTED WINES

An elegant white burgundy such as Chassagne-Montrachet or Puligny-Montrachet, or a good white Graves like Château Haut-Brion.

MONKFISH

. . . .

theme and variations

When we first introduced monkfish at our restaurant in the late 1970s, few people this side of the Atlantic had ever heard of the fish. Monkfish is an ugly flat-bottom scavenger fish, and our waiters were embarrassed to describe it. Luckily, the media took a fancy to the maligned species and helped catapult it to stardom. Monkfish, *lotte* in French, became a fixture on our menu, undergoing various transformations depending on seasons and chefs.

Our first monkfish creation followed a recipe obtained from the chef of Le Petit Nice in Marseille, where we had first tasted the fish. In honor of that experience, we named the dish *lotte à la Marseillaise*. Served in a shining copper skillet, brimming with chunks of white fish in a green spinach-sorrel sauce, accompanied by wedges of toast and a fiery *aïoli*, the dish was a great success.

After that, monkfish appeared in Dijonaise sauce. There was summer monkfish with crunchy vegetables, pasta, and chervil, and cold-weather monkfish, clothed in a cornmeal crust with fennel and aïoli.

Rick Steffann dressed his monkfish in a saffron beurre blanc. When Paolo Penati joined our kitchen team, he gave the monkfish preparation a Cajun twist. Inspired by Paul Prudhomme, he all but blackened the fish by roasting it in an intensely flavored Provençal herbal crust.

Chef Wayne Nish, champion of an elegant blend of flavors, said boo to the strong and earthy flavors in our kitchen. Putting his stamp on monkfish, he transformed it into a refined dish, garnishing it with eggplant and *prosciutto di Parma*.

Mark May wrapped the fish in caul fat, which kept it wonderfully moist, and served the dish with lima bean purée and red pepper *coulis*.

The arrival of Naj Zougari in the early 1990s heralded the return to less fussy cooking. Naj's monkfish sautéed with tomatoes, fresh herbs, and fried leeks is in tune with the times and our food budget.

Following the styles of our various chefs, I offer four different monkfish preparations, freely mixing a decade of garnishes.

Monkfish always arrives minus its head, which is huge and unsightly. The remaining tail weighs from 4 to 10 pounds. We divide the tail into 2 fillets, cut from each side of the fish's central bone. Depending on the fish, single fillets run from ½ to 2 pounds. We consider the 2-pound fillets to be the best, because they provide uniformly thick cuts. Individual portions may be made by cutting slices, comparable to veal scaloppine, approximately ¾-inch thick, ideal for rolling and stuffing; or scallops, about 2 inches thick, good for sautéing and broiling; or cubes, to be cooked in stews or skewered for brochettes. One large fillet or 2 small ones trussed together make an admirable roast.

When planning a meal with monkfish, estimate 6 ounces to ½ pound per person.

serves 4

With this recipe, monkfish made its debut at La Colombe d'Or. Served over a bed of cooked greens, seasoned with Pernod, garnished with croutons, dollops of aïoli, and black olives, this is monkfish at its Provençal best.

bed of cooked greens

- 2 TABLESPOONS EXTRA VIRGIN OLIVE OIL

- 1 POUND FRESH SPINACH, WASHED, TRIMMED, DRIED, AND FINELY CHOPPED

- ¼ POUND SORREL, WASHED, TRIMMED, DRIED, AND FINELY CHOPPED

- 2 TEASPOONS CHOPPED FRESH FENNEL LEAVES

- 2 TEASPOONS CHOPPED FRESH CHERVIL

- 2 TEASPOONS CHOPPED ITALIAN PARSLEY

- 2 TABLESPOONS WHITE WINE

- 2 TABLESPOONS BUTTER, SOFTENED

- SALT AND FRESHLY GROUND BLACK PEPPER

- PINCH OF SUGAR

- 1 TEASPOON PERNOD

lotte

- ¼ CUP EXTRA VIRGIN OLIVE OIL

- 1¼ POUNDS MONKFISH FILLETS, CUT INTO 16 EVEN-SIZED CUBES

- OIL TO COAT THE FISH AND THE PAN

- SALT AND FRESHLY GROUND BLACK PEPPER

- 4 SLICES STALE FRENCH BREAD, TOASTED AND CUT INTO TRIANGLES

- ¼ CUP AÏOLI (SEE PAGE ███)

- 8 BLACK OLIVES, PITTED

- 4 LEMON WEDGES

PREP GREENS

1. Heat the olive oil in a large skillet. Sauté the spinach and sorrel over medium heat for about 2 minutes, until wilted. Add the fennel, chervil, and parsley. Stir in the wine.

2. Cook, uncovered, over high heat to completely reduce. Whisk in the butter. Remove the mixture from the heat. Season with salt, pepper, a pinch of sugar, and the Pernod. Cover until ready to serve.

COOKING

Preheat the oven to 375 degrees.

1. Heat the oil in a skillet. Sauté the monkfish cubes for 1 minute on each side to sear. Transfer to an ovenproof dish, coated with olive oil, and season with salt and pepper.

2. Braise, covered, in the oven for 15 to 20 minutes, or until cooked through. Let rest, uncovered, for 5 minutes before serving.

PRESENTATION

Put the greens into a deep serving dish, preferably a shining copper pot. Arrange the fish chunks on top of the vegetables. Place wedges of the toast, topped with dollops of *aïoli*, alongside, and garnish with olives and lemon wedges. Serve family-style.

```
SUGGESTED WINES
```

A white Châteauneuf-du-Pape, or a white Crozes-Hermitage.

MONKFISH IN TOMATO MARINADE WITH FRIED BABY ARTICHOKES

serves 4

I think of this preparation as summer monk—light, refreshing, with a bit of crunch provided by the crisp artichokes. The prep is done a day ahead; final cooking takes but a few minutes.

2 POUNDS MONKFISH FILLETS

marinade

4 TOMATOES, PEELED, SEEDED, AND DICED

2 TABLESPOONS SNIPPED CHIVES

1 TABLESPOON CHOPPED CHERVIL

¼ TEASPOON MINCED GARLIC

¼ CUP DRY WHITE WINE

SALT AND FRESHLY GROUND BLACK PEPPER

artichokes

1½ POUNDS BABY ARTICHOKES (12–16)

JUICE OF 2 LEMONS

4 CUPS PEANUT OIL

2 GARLIC CLOVES, PEELED

SALT AND FRESHLY GROUND WHITE PEPPER

¼ CUP EXTRA VIRGIN OLIVE OIL

PREP MONKFISH AND MARINADE

. . . .

Trim the monkfish, and slice it into 16 even medallions. Place them in a nonreactive container. Combine all the marinade ingredients, and pour them over the fish. Cover and refrigerate overnight.

PREP ARTICHOKES

. . . .

1. Trim the tops and bottoms of the artichokes. Remove the outer leaves and trim again. Cut the hearts into wedges. Soak them in water to cover with the lemon juice.

2. In a 4-quart saucepan, heat the peanut oil together with the garlic cloves to 350 degrees, using a deep-fry thermometer. Remove the garlic cloves when golden brown and discard.

3. Drain and dry the artichokes wedges. Fry them in the oil for about 2 minutes, or until golden brown. Remove with a slotted spoon and spread out on paper towels. Season with salt and pepper, and keep in a warm place until ready to use.

COOKING

. . . .

1. Remove the monkfish medallions from the marinade, and dry them on paper towels. Heat the marinade to a simmer over medium heat. Remove from the heat and whisk in ¼ cup of the olive oil. Set aside.

2. In a separate skillet, heat the remaining olive oil. Sauté the monkfish medallions over medium-high heat for 2 minutes on both sides.

PRESENTATION

. . . .

Divide the tomato marinade onto the center of 4 serving dishes. Arrange 4 monkfish medallions on each dish over the tomatoes. Sprinkle the artichoke quarters on top.

SUGGESTED WINE

. . . .

A lively white Rully or a nutty white Montagny.

238

MONKFISH SCALLOPS ON A BED OF LIMA BEAN PURÉE WITH BASIL PISTOU

serves 4

The name "monkfish," it has been said, derives from the fact that the lowly fish, also known as anglerfish, goosefish, frog belly, and sea devil, "mimics" the aristocratic lobster in taste and texture. Indeed, leftover cold monkfish can easily help stretch a lobster salad. In observant Jewish households, monkfish is an acceptable substitute for the taboo shellfish.

2 BAY LEAVES

1¼ CUPS KOSHER SALT

2 POUNDS MONKFISH, SLICED ON THE BIAS INTO 1¼ × 2½-INCH SCALLOPS (ABOUT 20 SCALLOPS)

BASIL PISTOU (SEE PAGE ■■■)

LIMA BEAN PURÉE (SEE PAGE ■■■)

1 TABLESPOON SNIPPED CHIVES

COOKING

In a medium saucepan, place enough water to cover the monkfish scallops. Add the bay leaves and salt, and bring to a boil. Reduce heat. Add the monkfish scallops, turning them with a wooden spatula. Poach uncovered for 2 minutes. Remove with a slotted spoon and spread out on a plate to prevent overcooking.

PRESENTATION

Make a circle about 4 inches round on 4 individual plates with the basil *pistou*. Fill the circle with 2 tablespoons of lima bean purée. Place 5 scallops per serving in the middle. Garnish with chives.

SUGGESTED WINE

A good Pouilly-Fumé such as Ladoucette.

MONKFISH ROAST WITH HERBS
POTATO–FAVA BEAN PURÉE
AND PEPPER COULIS

. . . .

serves 4

Here monkfish receives royal treatment: a whole fillet is roasted in a spice crust, which keeps the fish moist and juicy, perfumed with exotic spices. The dish is plated with a pale-green potato–fava bean purée and lush red pepper *coulis*.

Since fresh fava beans are at their best in spring, this would be a good time to offer monkfish in this fashion.

potato–fava bean purée
. . . .

4 RED BLISS POTATOES

2½ POUNDS FRESH FAVA BEANS

¼ CUP OLIVE OIL

SALT AND FRESHLY GROUND BLACK PEPPER

monkfish
. . . .

1 TEASPOON FENNEL SEEDS

1 TEASPOON CUMIN SEEDS

1 TEASPOON CORIANDER SEEDS

1 TEASPOON WHOLE WHITE PEPPER

2 TABLESPOONS EXTRA VIRGIN OLIVE OIL

2 POUNDS MONKFISH FILLETS

RED PEPPER COULIS (SEE PAGE ███)

1 TABLESPOON CHOPPED FRESH CHERVIL

240

PREP PURÉE

1. Boil the potatoes in salted water until soft, 15 to 20 minutes. Drain and peel them.

2. While the potatoes are cooking, shell the fava beans. Blanch the shelled beans in boiling salted water for 1 minute. Shock in ice water. Drain and remove the skins. Reserve ¼ cup of shelled beans for garnish.

3. Purée the remaining fava beans and potatoes in a food processor or blender, adding the oil. Season with salt and pepper. Store in a covered plastic container and refrigerate. When ready to use, reheat for 2 minutes in a microwave oven.

PREP MONKFISH

1. Put the fennel, cumin, and coriander seeds and pepper in a food processor and let the machine run for 2 minutes.

2. Wash and trim the monkfish fillets, and pat them dry.

COOKING

Preheat the oven to 400 degrees.

1. Heat the oil in a large skillet. Add the fish and sear it on both sides. Remove the fish and roll it in the spice seed mixture.

2. Place the fish in a lightly greased oven-proof dish and put it in the preheated oven. Roast for 15 to 20 minutes, depending on the thickness of the fish.

3. Let the fish rest for 5 minutes before slicing.

PRESENTATION

Place the potato–fava bean purée in the center of a large serving platter. Top with the reserved fava beans. Arrange monkfish slices around the purée. Surround the fish with red pepper *coulis*. Sprinkle the dish with chopped chervil, and serve family-style.

SUGGESTED WINES

A crisp Muscadet, such as Muscadet de Sèvre et Maine, or a white Châteauneuf-du-Pape.

POULET MAISON

serves 4

This was one of Rick Steffann's most popular creations back in 1982. The chicken breasts are rolled into roulades and filled with pesto, which gives the gentle chicken an unexpected punch and a lovely appearance. The beauty of this dish for the home cook is that it *must* be prepared ahead of time and then takes only 15 minutes to finish. Served with a French baguette and a mixed-green salad, it is the perfect summer dish. The pesto here is a lighter version than the basil *pistou* on page ▪▪▪. Either one, however, works well.

pesto

- 2 BUNCHES FRESH BASIL
- 2 BUNCHES FRESH PARSLEY
- 3 GARLIC CLOVES
- ¼ CUP PINE NUTS
- 2 TABLESPOONS EXTRA VIRGIN OLIVE OIL
- SALT AND FRESHLY GROUND BLACK PEPPER

chicken

- 3 WHOLE CHICKEN BREASTS, BONED AND SKINNED
- FLOUR TO DUST
- 2 EGGS, BEATEN
- 1 CUP BREAD CRUMBS, SEASONED LIGHTLY WITH SALT AND PEPPER
- ¼ CUP EXTRA VIRGIN OLIVE OIL
- SPRIGS OF PARSLEY

PREP PESTO

1. Trim the basil and parsley. Wash and pat dry. Peel and mince the garlic.

2. Combine all the pesto ingredients and process in a food processor. (Stored in a tightly covered jar, pesto will keep in the refrigerator for 1 week.)

PREP CHICKEN

1. Trim the chicken, pound it flat, and pat it dry. Cover one side with a thin layer of pesto; roll it, tucking the edges as you roll.

2. Dust the roulade lightly with flour; dip in the egg wash, and roll in the bread crumbs. Repeat with the other two breasts.

3. Wrap each roulade in plastic wrap. Refrigerate for several hours or overnight.

COOKING

Preheat the oven to 375 degrees.

1. In a skillet, heat the oil; remove the plastic wrap from the chicken and sauté the breasts to sear and brown. Remove and put them into a lightly greased ovenproof dish.

2. Bake the chicken in the preheated oven for 8 to 10 minutes. Remove the chicken from the oven and let it rest for 10 minutes.

PRESENTATION

Slice each rolled breast into half-inch slices on the diagonal. Arrange on a large serving platter. Surround with sprigs of parsley. Serve family-style.

NOTE: During the summer when basil is plentiful, I prepare batches of pesto, using it merrily in salads, with fish, and on pasta. I might even freeze small portions of pesto in suitable containers.

SUGGESTED WINES

A spicy Rosé such as a Tavel or a Beaujolais.

POACHED CHICKEN ROULADE WITH AÏOLI AND HARICOTS VERTS

serves 4

The beauty of this dish is manifold: poaching the chicken tightly secured in plastic wrap preserves its delicate flavor while keeping it moist and succulent; having to cook it in advance means it's ready whenever you are. The *aïoli* gives it a nice kick; slender *haricots verts* add color and crunch.

chicken

4 BONELESS SKINLESS CHICKEN BREASTS

4 CHICKEN LEGS

4 CHICKEN THIGHS

SALT AND FRESHLY GROUND WHITE PEPPER

haricots verts

. . . .

¼ POUND HARICOTS VERTS

1 TABLESPOON BUTTER

SALT AND FRESHLY GROUND
WHITE PEPPER

¼ CUP AÏOLI (SEE PAGE ███)

PREP CHICKEN
. . . .

1. Pound the chicken breasts to render them of even thickness. Bone the legs and thighs, leaving on the skin. Cut the boned legs in half.

2. Place 1 leg and 1 thigh on a board, skin side down. Season with salt and pepper. Place 1 chicken breast on top.

3. Roll the chicken tightly into a package, with the skin of the leg and thigh sealing the package. Tuck in the edges. Season the outside with salt and pepper.

4. Place the roulade on a square of plastic wrap and seal. Repeat with the remaining legs, thighs, and breasts.

5. Set the roulades on a steamer over boiling water. Steam, covered, for 20 minutes. Remove the roulades and let them cool in the plastic wrap. Then refrigerate for 4 hours or overnight.

PREP HARICOTS VERTS
. . . .

1. Wash the *haricots verts* and snap the ends off the beans. Drop them into rapidly boiling salted water and boil, uncovered, for 3 minutes, or until they are tender with a slight crunch.

2. Drain and shock the beans in cold water. Pat them dry and set aside until ready to use.

COOKING
. . . .

Heat the butter in a skillet. Add the beans; toss to coat well. Sauté for 2 minutes. Season with salt and pepper.

PRESENTATION
. . . .

Unwrap the chicken roulades and discard the plastic wrap. Slice the roulades on the diagonal into ½-inch slices. Arrange them on a serving platter. Surround the chicken with sautéed *haricots verts* and serve accompanied by *aïoli*.

SUGGESTED WINES

Youthful floral Pouilly-Fuissé, or a young robust red Côtes du Rhône or Côtes de Provence.

CHICKEN WITH ROASTED SHALLOTS AND TRUFFLED MASHED POTATOES

. . . .

serves 4

Two cannibals meet.
Says one cannibal to the other:
"I really hate my mother-in-law."
Says the other cannibal:
"Forget about your mother-in-law.
Eat your potatoes."

Mashed potatoes acquired status in the early 1990s, when every chef worth his toque put mashed potatoes on the menu. Not content with leaving the humble dish alone, chefs soon dressed it with black truffles, a gesture akin to bestowing knighthood on a commoner.

Potent as truffles are, this dish stands nicely on its own without the costly tuber. In fact, I often eat it without the mashed potatoes, truffled or otherwise, and put a mound of *mesclun* in the middle, napping it with a warm vinaigrette.

roasted shallots
. . . .

12 SHALLOTS

EXTRA VIRGIN OLIVE OIL TO COAT

SALT AND FRESHLY GROUND BLACK PEPPER

truffled mashed potatoes
. . . .

6 IDAHO OR RUSSET POTATOES (ABOUT 3 POUNDS)

8 TABLESPOONS (1 STICK) BUTTER

½ CUP HEAVY CREAM

SALT

1 TABLESPOON BLACK TRUFFLE SHAVINGS

chicken
. . . .

2 TO 3 TABLESPOONS EXTRA VIRGIN OLIVE OIL

8 MEDIUM BONELESS

CHICKEN BREASTS WITH SKIN, CUT IN HALVES, TRIMMED OF EXCESS FAT

SALT AND FRESHLY GROUND WHITE PEPPER

1 CUP RED WINE

1 CUP JUS DE POULET (SEE PAGE 000)

1 TABLESPOON BUTTER, SOFTENED

2 TEASPOONS SNIPPED CHIVES

245

PREP SHALLOTS

Preheat the oven to 400 degrees.

1. Peel shallots and coat lightly with oil; season with salt and pepper. Wrap in foil, and place in the preheated oven for 30 to 40 minutes, till soft.

2. Remove the foil. Transfer the shallots to a container; add oil to cover. Seal with plastic wrap and store till ready to use. (Roasted shallots will keep in the refrigerator for 1 week. When ready to use, reheat them in a microwave oven for 2 minutes.)

PREP POTATOES

1. Peel the potatoes, and cut them into 2-inch cubes. Rinse in cold water.

2. Boil the potatoes, uncovered, in salted water to cover for about 15 to 20 minutes, or until soft. Drain thoroughly. Purée through a food mill.

3. In a small saucepan, bring the butter and heavy cream to a boil. Whisk into the mashed potatoes while hot. Season with salt. Incorporate truffle shavings. Keep the potatoes in a warm covered bowl till ready to use. (The potatoes minus the truffle shavings can be prepared a few hours ahead of time and stored in a covered plastic container. Before serving, reheat, then whisk in the truffle shavings.)

COOKING

Preheat the oven to 500 degrees.

1. Heat the oil in a large skillet. Sauté the chicken breasts, skin side down, until golden and crisp, about 4 minutes. Transfer the chicken breasts to a baking sheet, skin side up. Season with salt and pepper.

2. Place the chicken in the preheated oven for 4 to 5 minutes, depending on the thickness of the breasts. Remove and let them rest for 2 minutes, then slice each breast on the diagonal into 3 portions.

3. While the chicken is baking, prepare the sauce: over high heat, reduce the wine by half. Add the *jus de poulet*, cooking it down a little further. Whisk in the butter. Season to taste.

PRESENTATION

Spoon individual portions of truffled mashed potatoes in the center of each serving plate. Arrange 6 portions of chicken around it. Top with 3 shallots. Spoon about 2 tablespoons sauce around the dish. Sprinkle with chives. Wipe the plates clean before serving.

SUGGESTED WINES

A fruity red from the Côte Chalonnaise, such as Mercurey, a St.-Emilion like Simar, or a Pomerol like Château Trotanoy.

246

DUCK: GRILLED BREAST AND THIGH CONFIT WITH SWEET AND AROMATIC SPICES

. . . .

serves 8

There's a lot going on here: mellow, tender duck *confit*, crisp and juicy breast; garlic-studded tomatoes, green asparagus stalks, pears poached in aromatic syrup; diverse textures and tastes brought together by a richly flavored sauce.

This is a very elegant duck presentation, ideal for festive occasions. Executing the dish calls for a fair amount of juggling; I kept wishing for a third hand. But with the *confit* and the pears prepped well ahead of time (a day or two before serving), the actual cooking can be accomplished within 30 minutes. (The asparagus should be prepped the day of serving.)

confit
. . . .

8 DUCK LEGS

ABOUT 6 TABLESPOONS KOSHER SALT

6 GARLIC HEADS

1¼ POUNDS DUCK FAT (ABOUT 3½ CUPS) (SEE NOTE)

1 SPRIG FRESH ROSEMARY

1 SPRIG DRIED SAGE

BOUQUET GARNI: ¼ CUP BLACK PEPPERCORNS, ¼ CUP HERBES DE PROVENCE (SEE PAGE 000) TIED IN CHEESECLOTH

poached pears
. . . .

4 PEARS

1 LEMON, HALVED

1½ TABLESPOON HONEY

BOUQUET GARNI: 1 CINNAMON STICK, 5 CORIANDER SEEDS, 5 WHOLE MACE TIED IN CHEESECLOTH

16 ASPARAGUS SPEARS (ABOUT 1 POUND)

duck breast
. . . .

4 DUCK BREASTS, SKINNED AND BONED

2 TEASPOONS PEANUT OIL

SALT

duck sauce
. . . .

2 CUPS DUCK STOCK (SEE PAGE 000)

2 TABLESPOONS HONEY

¼ CUP FRESH ORANGE JUICE

1 TEASPOON SHERRY VINEGAR

SALT AND FRESHLY GROUND BLACK PEPPER

8 ROASTED TOMATOES, HALVED (SEE PAGE 000)

PREP CONFIT

Preheat the oven to 400 degrees.

1. Trim the excess fat from the duck and break the joint between the leg and the thigh with a sharp kitchen knife (but keep the leg and thigh in one piece). Arrange the legs, skin side down, on a tray and coat them liberally with salt. Let them cure for 30 minutes, then wipe off the salt.

2. Cut the heads of garlic in half across their width, exposing all the cloves.

3. Melt the duck fat in a large, heavy ovenproof pan. Completely submerge the duck legs, garlic, rosemary and sage sprigs, and the bouquet garni in the melted fat. Bring to a slow boil.

4. Cover, and put into the preheated oven. (This can also be done on top of the stove.) Continue to boil in the oven for 20 minutes. Reduce the temperature to 325 degrees and cook slowly for 1½ to 2 hours the legs should be very soft without falling apart.

5. Remove the legs from the oven and let them cool for at least 45 minutes.

6. Using a pair of tongs, remove the legs and place them on a tray. Strain the duck fat, let it completely cool, and put it into a plastic container. Store tightly sealed in the refrigerator for future use.

7. Refrigerate the legs till firm, preferably overnight. Once the meat has cooled, chop off the bony knob at the end of the leg bone (best done with a cleaver).

(Stored in plastic wrap, prepped *confit* will keep in the refrigerator for 1 week.)

PREP PEARS

1. Peel the pears. Cut them in half and core. Put them in a small saucepan with cold water, together with the lemon halves, honey, and the bouquet garni. Bring to a boil. (Place a cloth napkin over the saucepan to seal in the spice-mixture aroma.) Reduce the heat and simmer slowly until the pears are soft, about 15 to 20 minutes.

2. Leave the pears in the liquid, with the bouquet garni. (The pears will absorb more flavor.) When the pears are completely cooled, refrigerate them in a covered container till ready to use.

PREP ASPARAGUS

Trim the asparagus stalks so that you have spears about 4 inches long. Peel the stalk end of the spears. Blanch in salted boiling water for about 2 minutes. Remove and drain. Keep in a warm place until ready to use.

COOKING

Preheat the oven to 450 degrees.

Preheat the grill.

1 Trim the excess fat from the *confit*. Flatten the pieces of *confit* with your hand to achieve an even thickness. In an ovenproof sauté pan, heat some of this reserved duck fat; sear the *confit*, skin side down, to brown nicely. Place the pan in the pre-

heated oven for 5 to 10 minutes. When you remove the *confit*, the skin should be crisp and the flesh moist.

2. Brush the duck breasts lightly with oil. Sprinkle with salt. Place on the preheated grill or in a very hot skillet for 2 minutes on each side for medium-rare. Remove the breasts and let them rest for 3 to 5 minutes.

3. Drain the poached pears and sauté to brown in the same skillet.

4. Heat the duck stock, then whisk in the honey, orange juice, and sherry vinegar. Season with salt and pepper.

PRESENTATION
. . . .
Place half of a roasted tomato in the center of each plate. Top with 2 asparagus spears. Slice the duck breasts in half and arrange them, one per person, together with 1 *confit*, on each plate. Place one halved pear next to the *confit*. Nap the plate with ⅓ cup of the duck sauce.

NOTE: Duck fat is a good investment for the serious cook. Properly handled, it can be reused many times. Extremely flavorful, duck fat can be heated to a higher temperature than butter, which makes it ideal for sautéing potatoes and braising cabbage, kale, or any other winter vegetable.

You can make your own duck fat (Paula Wolfert has a good recipe for it in her book, *The Cooking of Southwest France*). Or you can order it from D'Artagnan: 1-800 Dartagn.

Once you have embarked on making *confit*, you may consider prepping double portions, particularly if you contemplate a future cassoulet.

Leftover *confit* makes a delectable winter salad. Serve it with braised *radicchio* or any other hardy vegetable tossed in a warm vinaigrette.

SUGGESTED WINE

A St.-Emilion Grand Cru Classé such as Château L'Angélus.

249

BRAISED SQUAB WITH TURNIP PEAR PURÉE AND BLACK FIGS IN HONEY-THYME VINAIGRETTE

serves 4

This dish, I am convinced, was invented in heaven for what could be more divine than the harmony among the dark and tender meat of the squab, tart turnips, gentle pear, and luscious black figs, embraced by a honey-and-thyme vinaigrette?

The turnip-pear purée is so good that I suggest you double the recipe and use it to garnish other fowl preparations.

turnip-pear purée

1¼ POUNDS SMALL WHITE TURNIPS (ABOUT 8)

1 RIPE PEAR

2 BAY LEAVES

ABOUT 1½ CUPS MILK

1 TABLESPOON HEAVY CREAM

2 TABLESPOONS BUTTER

SALT

squab

4 1-POUND SQUAB

SALT AND FRESHLY GROUND BLACK PEPPER

2 CUPS CHICKEN STOCK

BOUQUET GARNI: 10 CORIANDER SEEDS, 1 BAY LEAF TIED IN CHEESECLOTH

2 TEASPOONS EXTRA VIRGIN OLIVE OIL

1 TEASPOON FRESH THYME LEAVES

honey-thyme vinaigrette

2 TABLESPOONS JUS DE POULET (SEE PAGE ███)

1 TABLESPOON HONEY

¼ CUP EXTRA VIRGIN OLIVE OIL

1 TABLESPOON RICE VINEGAR

SALT AND FRESHLY GROUND BLACK PEPPER

1 TEASPOON FRESH THYME LEAVES

4 FRESH CALIFORNIA BLACK MISSION FIGS, QUARTERED

PREP TURNIP-PEAR PURÉE

1. Peel the turnips and cut them into small pieces. Peel and core the pear and cut it into small pieces.

2. Place the turnips, pear, and bay leaves in a small saucepan. Pour on enough of the milk to barely cover. Place wax paper over the pan. Bring to a boil. Reduce and simmer the mixture over low heat for 25 to 30 minutes, until the turnips are soft.

3. Drain and remove the bay leaves. Purée the mixture with the heavy cream in a food processor. Whisk in the butter. Season with salt. Put in 4 small individual molds. Cover with plastic wrap and store in the refrigerator till ready to use. (The flavor of the purée will intensify if done 1 or 2 days ahead.) Reheat when ready to serve.

PREP SQUAB

1. Remove the legs from the squab, leaving them whole. Separate and remove the breast of the squab from the back.

2. Bone the breasts, slice in half, remove the skin, and make 3 incisions on the back of each breast. Season with salt and pepper.

COOKING

1. In a saucepan bring the stock and bouquet garni to a gentle boil. Add the squab legs. Reduce the heat and cook very slowly over moderate heat for 20 to 30 minutes, or until the legs are tender. Transfer the legs to a warm plate.

2. Heat a heavy-bottomed skillet to very hot. Coat the skillet with the 2 teaspoons olive oil. Sear the breasts over high heat, 2 minutes per side for medium-rare.

3. Remove the breasts, season again, with salt and pepper, sprinkle with thyme, and let them rest for 5 minutes.

4. While the squab is resting, prepare the vinaigrette. Heat the *jus de poulet* in a small saucepan over medium heat. Whisk in the honey. Remove the mixture from the heat and slowly whisk in the oil and the vinegar. (The sauce should be thick enough to coat a spoon.)

5. Season the vinaigrette with the salt, pepper, and thyme.

PRESENTATION

Unmold the reheated turnip-pear purée in the center of 4 individual plates. Place 4 fig quarters around the purée on each plate. Arrange 2 legs and 2 breast halves next to the figs. Dribble the honey-thyme vinaigrette over the squab. Serve immediately.

SUGGESTED WINES

A velvety red Burgundy such as a Gevrey-Chambertin, or a Grand Cru Pauillac, or a St.-Emilion.

GRILLED SPRING LAMB CHOPS WITH ZUCCHINI CHUTNEY AND ROSEMARY POTATOES

serves 4

This recipe, which looks complicated, is a perfect example of the virtue of *mis en place*. With flavored bread crumbs and mustard paste prepped ahead of time, anyone who has ever grilled a chop and cooked potatoes can successfully execute this festive dish.

flavored bread crumbs
. . . .

1 2-OUNCE CAN ANCHOVY FILLETS, RINSED AND DRAINED

¼ CUP DRAINED CAPERS

2 TABLESPOONS GARLIC PURÉE (SEE PAGE ███)

TABASCO TO TASTE

1 BUNCH PARSLEY, STEMMED

1 TABLESPOON CHOPPED FRESH ROSEMARY LEAVES

SALT AND FRESHLY GROUND BLACK PEPPER

1¼ CUPS BREAD CRUMBS

english mustard paste
. . . .

2 TABLESPOONS DRY MUSTARD

2 TABLESPOONS SUGAR

WATER

rosemary potatoes
. . . .

8 SMALL RED BLISS POTATOES (ABOUT 1 POUND), UNPEELED

¼ CUP EXTRA VIRGIN OLIVE OIL

SALT AND FRESHLY GROUND BLACK PEPPER

1 TEASPOON MINCED FRESH ROSEMARY LEAVES, OR ¼ TEASPOON DRIED ROSEMARY

1 TEASPOON MINCED GARLIC

1 TEASPOON BUTTER

252

lamb
· · · ·

2 3¼-POUND WHOLE RACKS OF
LAMB, CUT INTO 16 DOUBLE
CHOPS

SALT AND FRESHLY GROUND
BLACK PEPPER

PEANUT OIL

4 GARNISH PORTIONS OF
ZUCCHINI CHUTNEY (SEE
PAGE ■■■)

PREP BREAD CRUMBS
· ·

1. Put all the ingredients except the bread crumbs in a food processor. Pulse until the mixture becomes a paste.

2. Remove to a mixing bowl and fold in the bread crumbs. (The bread crumbs will keep in a sealed tin for 3 days.)

PREP MUSTARD PASTE
· ·

Mix the dry mustard and sugar together, adding enough water to make a thick paste. Set aside until ready to use.

COOKING
· · · · · · · · · · ·

Preheat the oven to 550 degrees.

1. Scrub the potatoes with cold water. Pat them dry.

2. Heat the oil to very hot in an ovenproof skillet. Sautée the potatoes to brown, for about 10 minutes, shaking the pan back and forth to prevent the potatoes from sticking to the bottom. Sprinkle with salt and pepper.

3. Put the potatoes in preheated oven for 10 minutes, or until cooked through.

4. Remove the potatoes from the oven. Add the rosemary, garlic, and butter. Shake vigorously and return the potatoes to the oven for 3 minutes. (This helps to intensify the garlic-rosemary flavor.) Remove and keep in a warm place.

5. Raise the oven temperature to 450 degrees and preheat the grill. Trim the lamb chops. Season them with salt and pepper. Coat lightly with oil.

6. Put the lamb chops on the grill and sear for 2 minutes per side, or dry-sauté lamb chops in a very hot skillet, 2 minutes on each side.

7. Brush the chops with the mustard paste. Pat the bread crumb mixture on top. Put the lamb chops on a roasting sheet in the preheated oven, and bake for 4 to 5 minutes (bake on 1 side only for medium-rare).

8. Remove the lamb from the oven and let it rest for 2 minutes.

PRESENTATION
· · · · · · · · · · · · · · · · · · ·

Place a mound of zucchini chutney in the center of 4 individual plates. Arrange 4 double chops around the chutney and surround with rosemary potatoes.

SUGGESTED WINE

A Côtes de Nuits such as a Chambolle-Musigny.

GIGOT D'AGNEAU WITH CHESTNUT POLENTA AND RAISIN—PINE NUT SPINACH

. . . .

serves 6

This dish has become an honored tradition at our annual Napoleon's Birthday Dinner. The chestnut polenta is a tribute to Napoleon's birthplace, Corsica, where chestnut trees grow in abundance. In contrast to the soupy polenta that accompanies our rabbit stew, this polenta is cooked thick enough to be sautéed. For Napoleon's Birthday Dinner in midsummer, we use canned chestnuts. When we serve the gigot in the winter—fresh chestnut season —we roast our own.

chestnut polenta
. . . .

6 1/2 CUPS WATER

1 TABLESPOON SALT

2 CUPS COARSE-GRAINED CORNMEAL

1/2 POUND ROASTED FRESH CHESTNUTS, FINELY DICED, OR 1/2 POUND CANNED VACUUM-PACKED FRENCH CHESTNUTS, DRAINED, CLEANED, AND FINELY DICED (SEE NOTE)

1 1/2 TABLESPOONS PEANUT OIL OR EXTRA VIRGIN OLIVE OIL

raisin-pine nut spinach
. . . .

2 POUNDS SPINACH

2 TABLESPOONS BLACK RAISINS

1 TABLESPOON EXTRA VIRGIN OLIVE OIL

1/4 CUP PINE NUTS, ROASTED

1 TEASPOON GARLIC CONFIT (SEE PAGE 355)

SALT AND FRESHLY GROUND BLACK PEPPER

lamb
. . . .

1 5-POUND LEG OF LAMB, AT ROOM TEMPERATURE, BONED AND TIED

SALT AND FRESHLY GROUND BLACK PEPPER

3 GARLIC CLOVES, PEELED AND SLIVERED

2 TABLESPOONS PEANUT OIL

1 SPRIG ROSEMARY

2 SPRIGS THYME

1 CUP HOT WATER

1 CUP WHITE WINE

PREP POLENTA

1. Bring the water to a boil in a large heavy saucepan. Add the salt; reduce the heat to medium-low so that the water is just simmering. Sprinkle in the cornmeal in a very thin stream, stirring constantly with a wooden spoon. (The stream of cornmeal should be so thin that you can see the individual grains. A good way to do this is to let a fistful of cornmeal run through nearly closed fingers.)

2. Continue stirring for 20 minutes after all the cornmeal has been added. The polenta is done when it pulls away from the sides of the pot as you stir. In the last few minutes, add the diced chestnuts.

3. Pour the polenta onto a large tray. Allow it to cool. Brush the top lightly with ½ tablespoon oil. (This may be done a day ahead of time and stored in the refrigerator.)

PREP SPINACH

1. Pick over the spinach, removing the large stems. Thoroughly wash and drain well. Blanch the spinach in a pot of boiling salted water for 1 minute. Plunge the blanched spinach in ice water. Drain, and squeeze out the excess water. Put aside.

2. Soak the raisins in cold water for 5 minutes. Drain and set aside.

COOKING

Preheat the oven to 450 degrees.

1. Season the lamb with salt and pepper. Make a few slits in the lamb and push the garlic slivers into the slits.

2. Heat the peanut oil over high heat in a roasting pan large enough to hold the lamb. Add the lamb, rosemary, and thyme and put it into the preheated oven. Sear the lamb on all sides to brown evenly, about 20 minutes.

3. Reduce the oven temperature to 375 degrees and roast the lamb for 30 to 40 minutes, turning and basting it several times. When the lamb is cooked to the desired doneness (8 to 10 minutes per pound for medium-rare, 10 to 15 minutes for medium), remove it and place it on a carving board. Remove the twine, rosemary, and thyme sprigs. Season the lamb again with salt and pepper.

4. Cover the lamb loosely with aluminum foil and let it rest in the turned-off oven for up to 35 minutes while you finish the dish.

5. Deglaze the pan on top of the stove with 2 tablespoons of the hot water, scraping up the coagulated pan juices. Bring to a slow boil, add the rest of the water, and reduce by half. Pour in the wine and boil down to 1 cup. Whisk in the butter. Season to taste.

6. To finish the polenta, cut the cooled polenta into 1½-inch squares. Heat the remaining 1 tablespoon of olive oil in a large pan. Sauté the polenta until slightly brown on both sides.

255

7. To finish the spinach, heat the 1 tablespoon of olive oil in a large skillet, and sauté the spinach over high heat until just wilted. Add the pine nuts, raisins, and the garlic *confit*. Season with salt and pepper.

PRESENTATION
. . . .
Use 4 or 5 slices of lamb per serving. Place them on a serving dish, and garnish with polenta and spinach. Pour a little of the sauce on top. (Make sure that it is hot.)

NOTE: To roast chestnuts: With a sharp knife, slit an X on the round side of each chestnut. Place the chestnuts on a baking sheet and roast in a preheated 400-degree oven or broiler for 30 to 45 minutes. Peel the chestnuts while they are still hot. When cooled, cut into dice.

Serve roasted chestnuts at special dinner parties, particularly around Thanksgiving and Christmas. Your guests will adore you.

| SUGGESTED WINE |

A big, full-flavored Châteauneuf-du-Pape such as Vieux Télégraphe.

RABBIT WITH POLENTA
. . . .
serves 6

When our friend Ed Giobbi prepared this dish for us at his home in Katonah, we were so taken with it, that we asked Ed if he would cook it one day at the restaurant. "Love to," said Ed. On the scheduled day, George and Ed went shopping at the Italian market on Arthur Avenue in the Bronx. They arrived at the restaurant with 12 rabbits, enough to feed a small army. We offered Ed's rabbit as a *plat du jour*. The dish was such a hit that we sold all but 2 portions. These I promptly took home and froze. Three weeks later, George and I had a repeat performance—as memorable as the first.

rabbit
. . . .

2 TABLESPOONS VEGETABLE OIL

1 3½ TO 4-POUND RABBIT, DRESSED AND CUT INTO SERVING PIECES

3 GARLIC CLOVES, UNPEELED

1 LARGE ONION, STUDDED WITH 4 CLOVES

1 CUP DRY WHITE WINE

1 TEASPOON CHOPPED FRESH ROSEMARY LEAVES

SALT AND FRESHLY GROUND BLACK PEPPER

2 TABLESPOONS
CHOPPED FRESH BASIL
LEAVES

2 CARROTS, PEELED AND
CUT INTO 1¼-INCH
PIECES

1 THICK CELERY RIB,
CUT INTO 1-INCH
PIECES

3 TABLESPOONS TOMATO
PASTE

4 CUPS CULTIVATED OR
WILD MUSHROOMS

1 OUNCE DRIED PORCINI,
SOAKED IN WARM
WATER FOR 15
MINUTES AND DRAINED

polenta
. . . .

6 CUPS WATER

4 TEASPOONS KOSHER
SALT

1¼ TO 1¾ CUPS FINE CORNMEAL

COOKING

1. Heat the oil in a shallow pot that is large enough to hold the rabbit pieces without overlapping. Add the rabbit (including the liver) and brown on all sides over high heat, about 10 minutes.

2. Lower the heat, push the rabbit to one side, and add the garlic and onion. Brown lightly. Remove the liver and set aside.

3. Add the wine, rosemary, salt, pepper, and basil. Cover and let simmer over low heat until the wine has evaporated. Add the carrots and celery. Stir in the tomato paste. Boil gently, covered, for 1½ hours, stirring constantly.

4. Toss in the mushrooms and continue to simmer for an additional hour, adding the liver the last 15 minutes.

5. Remove the garlic. Slice the liver and add it to the dish. Adjust the seasonings. Keep the rabbit warm while making the polenta. (Better yet, make the rabbit 1 or 2 days in advance, and then reheat it while you cook the polenta.)

6. Add the salt to the water and bring to a gentle boil in a 2-quart heavy saucepan. Add the cornmeal gradually by letting it trickle from your hand in a slow, steady stream while stirring constantly with a wooden spoon in your other hand.

7. Continue until you have used as much of the cornmeal as necessary to make a polenta that is the consistency of thick porridge. (If you use fine cornmeal, it will be done by the time you have added the final grains. If you use coarse cornmeal, the olenta needs to cook, uncovered, for 20 minutes.)

PRESENTATION

Ladle the polenta onto hot plates. Add a serving of sauce and 1 or 2 pieces of rabbit on top of each. Serve immediately.

SUGGESTED WINE

A rich and earthy Cahors or a Cornas.

257

GRILLED CALF'S LIVER WITH CARROT PURÉE AND GRILLED ONIONS

serves 4

People who dislike liver have been known to become instant converts once they taste the first morsel of this dish. In the summer months, we garnish the liver with carrot purée and grilled onions; in the winter, we switch to onion compote.

grilled onions

· · · ·

2 LARGE RED ONIONS

1 TABLESPOON OLIVE OIL

SALT AND FRESHLY GROUND BLACK PEPPER

liver

· · · ·

2½ POUNDS CALF'S LIVER, METICULOUSLY TRIMMED

1 TABLESPOON EXTRA VIRGIN OLIVE OIL

SALT AND FRESHLY GROUND BLACK PEPPER

Vinaigrette

· · · ·

1 CUP BALSAMIC VINEGAR

1 CUP CHICKEN STOCK

1 TEASPOON BUTTER, SOFTENED

CARROT PURÉE (SEE PAGE ███)

PREP ONIONS

· ·

Trim the bottom ends of the onions, peel and cut into quarters. Rub the quarters with oil; season with salt and pepper.

PREP LIVER

· ·

Cut the liver into long strips, about ¾ inch thick. Brush lightly with oil. Season with salt and pepper.

COOKING

· · · · · · · · · · · ·

Preheat the grill (see Note).

1. Place the onion quarters on the preheated grill and grill for 10 to 20 minutes, or until glossy brown. Remove and set aside. (At the restaurant, where grilling space is at a premium during service, we grill the onions for 5 minutes, just enough to mark them all around, and finish cooking them in a 375-degree preheated oven, which takes 10 to 15 minutes.)

2. Grill the liver for 1½ minutes on each side for medium-rare. Remove and let it rest for 2 minutes.

3. Heat the vinegar in a small saucepan. Cook over high heat to reduce the liquid by half. Add the chicken stock and reduce by three-quarters. Whisk in the softened butter.

PRESENTATION
. . . .

Mold the carrot purée in individual dome-shaped portions and invert in the center of each plate. Slice the liver into small diamond shapes and arrange around the garnish. Surround with grilled onion quarters. Sauce the plates. Serve immediately.

NOTE: If you don't have a grill, sauté the onions in a very hot cast-iron skillet over high heat for approximately the same length of time as per grilling instructions. Do the same with the liver. Without the grill marks, the effect will not be the same, but the onions will still be nice and nutty, and the liver succulent.

```
SUGGESTED WINE
```

A firm, racy "Cru Bourgeois" of Pomerol, such as Château Lagrange.

CASSOULET
. . . .

serves 8 to 10

I used to think that tackling cassoulet was beyond me. But Naj Zougari, our dauntless chef, said, "Nonsense. I bet you can." And thus encouraged by his confidence, I did. I still think cassoulet is a heavy-duty job: there are so many steps involved. But stripped of its mystique, cassoulet, like much of cooking, is simply a matter of prepping and cooking choice ingredients in logical sequence. As an extra help, the beans may be done a day ahead of time and stored in the refrigerator.

Since there are 3 different types of cassoulet—depending on whether it uses duck or goose, pork or duck, or only pork, and what type of sausages—there is no point fretting over the authenticity of your or anyone else's version.

The following is "ours." It invites changes. At the restaurant we prepare individual portions by distributing the ingredients in white porcelain crocks. The beauty of offering cassoulet at home is to serve it home style—which allows guests to fish out their own morsels.

beans

. . . .

2¼ POUNDS CANNELLINI BEANS

1 LARGE SPANISH ONION,
PEELED, HALVED, AND
STUDDED WITH 4 CLOVES

2 LARGE CARROTS, PEELED AND
HALVED LENGTHWISE

2 BAY LEAVES

3 OR 4 SPRIGS THYME

1 GARLIC HEAD, UNPEELED,
HALVED

¾ POUND SMOKED PORK BELLY,
CUT INTO BIG CHUNKS

¼ CUP DUCK FAT (SEE NOTE ON
PAGE ███)

½ SPANISH ONION, PEELED AND
MINCED

4 GARLIC CLOVES, PEELED AND
MINCED

1 TABLESPOON HERBES DE
PROVENCE (SEE PAGE ███)

1 15-OUNCE CAN TOMATO PURÉE

SALT AND FRESHLY GROUND
BLACK PEPPER

1¼ POUNDS LAMB-AND-
ROSEMARY SAUSAGE

1 POUND GARLIC SAUSAGE

1¼ POUND CHIPOLATA (PORK
SAUSAGE), CUT UP

1 CUP BREAD CRUMBS

4 DUCK CONFIT (SEE PAGE ███)

1 CUP DUCK CRACKLINGS
(OPTIONAL)

PREP BEANS

. . . .

1. Rinse the beans 3 times in cold water.
(Soaking beans reduces their flavor and
actually causes them to begin to ferment.
Only beans that are more than 3 years old
need to be soaked. To avoid buying old
beans, shop at a busy place that moves
their merchandise quickly.)

2. Fill a large pot ¾ full with cold water.
Add the onion, carrots, bay leaves, thyme
sprigs, garlic heads, smoked pork belly,
and beans. Bring to a boil.

3. Lower the heat and let the beans simmer, uncovered, for about 1 hour, or until
they are soft, occasionally skimming off
the foam that rises to the top.

4. Strain the stock and reserve. Discard
everything except the pork belly and the
beans. Put aside.

COOKING

. . . .

Preheat the oven to 450 degrees.

1. Heat the duck fat in a large casserole.
Sweat the minced onion and garlic in the
fat till they are translucent. Toss in the
herbes de Provence. Add the cooked beans
and pork belly. Stir in the tomato purée.
Season generously with salt and pepper.

2. Add the reserved bean stock and all the
sausages. Stir well. Sprinkle the top with
¾ cup of the bread crumbs.

3. Bake in the preheated oven, uncovered,
for 1 to 1½ hours.

PRESENTATION
. . . .
Preheat the oven to 500 degrees.

1. Discard the pork belly. Fish out the sausages. Remove the skin from the garlic sausage and cut the sausage into large slices. Slice the lamb and pork sausages into 2-inch chunks.

2. Split the duck *confit* in half, and remove the bone.

3. Fill the bottom of a casserole dish with half of the cooked beans. Arrange the sausage meats and duck *confit* on top. Cover with the remaining beans.

4. Just before serving, sprinkle duck cracklings and the remaining bread crumbs on top. Place into the preheated oven for 10 minutes to brown.

5. If the beans seem too dry, push the crust down with a large spoon and add some duck stock, braising juices, reserved bean liquid, or plain water to the beans before sprinkling the duck cracklings and bread crumbs on top.

NOTE: I like to recycle cassoulet in 2 stages: once by serving all meats as a separate dish, accompanied by a warm potato or lentil salad, and on another occasion by offering the cassoulet sans meat, accompanied by a crisp, green salad—my version of a vegetarian meal.

NOTE: Crunchy duck cracklings sprinkled on top of cassoulet before the final reheating add further zest to the dish. *To make cracklings:* Reserve the skin of 1 duck. Cover the skin with cold water and bring to a boil. Reduce the heat and cook, uncovered, over low heat for 15 minutes, or until the skin turns soft. Remove the skin and submerge it in duck fat. Cook slowly, uncovered, over medium-high heat for 30 minutes, or until golden brown, stirring frequently. Drain the skin and sprinkle it liberally with salt. When it is cool enough to handle, cut the skin into ½-inch pieces. Covered with wax paper, cracklings will keep 1 week in the refrigerator.

SUGGESTED WINES

A sturdy red from the Languedoc such as a Minervois, Madiran, or Corbières.

BOUDIN NOIR WITH CARAMELIZED APPLES, MASHED POTATOES, AND FRIED LEEKS

serves 4

This is old-fashioned French peasant fare. Served with plenty of Dijon mustard, it was a common bistro item years ago. Getting a bad rap from health-food fanatics, abetted by apostles of nouvelle cuisine, *boudin noir* and its cousin, *boudin blanc*, all but disappeared from the menu. Luckily, common sense triumphed: *boudin* is back in favor, although some of our younger clients are still skeptical.

"Blood sausage?" they ask.

"Try it," say our equally young waiters. "It's really good."

apples

2 TART APPLES, PREFERABLY GRANNY SMITH

SUGAR

2 TABLESPOONS BUTTER

boudin

8 BOUDIN NOIR

2 TABLESPOONS OIL

MASHED POTATOES (SEE PAGE ●●●), MINUS THE TRUFFLE SHAVINGS

FRIED LEEKS (SEE PAGE ●●●)

PREP APPLES

1. Peel and core the apples. Cut them into cubes.

2. Heat a sauté pan, and coat the bottom with sugar. Add the butter, and let caramelize without burning.

3. Add the apples. Sauté till browned and soft, about 5 to 7 minutes. Remove the apples and set them aside till ready to use. (Stored in a closed container the apples will keep in the refrigerator for 3 days. If they have drawn too much water, cook to reduce while reheating.)

COOKING

Preheat the oven to 550 degrees.

Brush the *boudin* with oil. Oil the bottom of a sheet pan and place the *boudin* in the pan. Bake the *boudin* in the preheated oven for 5 to 7 minutes.

PRESENTATION

Slice the *boudin* into 1-inch chunks. Put a mound of mashed potatoes in the center of each plate. Arrange *boudin* slices around the potatoes. Top with 1 tablespoon apples and a handful of fried leeks.

SUGGESTED WINES

A big, meaty red from the Midi, such as a Corbières, or a French beer or hard cider.

DESSERTS

PARIS-BREST

serves 8 to 10

It's been said that this delightful French dessert (which used to make our waitresses blush because they thought it was called Paris-Breast) was created by a pastry chef in honor of a bicycle race between Paris and Brest. The cake consists of a baked almond-topped *choux* pastry ring (patterned after a bicycle tire), layered with praline butter and whipped cream. It is rich enough to prompt partakers to engage in a little race on their exercise bikes.

pastry cream
(crème pâlissière)
. . . .

4 EGG YOLKS

¼ CUP SUGAR

1 TEASPOON VANILLA EXTRACT

2 TABLESPOONS CORNSTARCH

1¼ CUPS MILK

ALMOND PRALINES (SEE PAGE 000)

cream-puff pastry
(pâte à choux)
. . . .

1 CUP WATER

4 TABLESPOONS BUTTER (½ STICK), CUT INTO SMALL PIECES

PINCH OF SALT

1 CUP SIFTED ALL-PURPOSE FLOUR

4 EGGS

1 EGG, BEATEN WITH A TOUCH OF MILK

whipped cream
. . . .

2 CUPS HEAVY CREAM

3 TABLESPOONS CONFECTIONERS' SUGAR

1 TEASPOON DARK RUM

PREP PASTRY CREAM

1. Combine the yolks, sugar, and vanilla extract in a bowl. Whisk together for a few minutes until the mixture forms a ribbon. Add the cornstarch and mix until blended.

2. In a heavy saucepan bring the milk to a boil. Pour half of the hot milk into the sugar-yolk mixture. Mix with a whisk until smooth.

3. Pour the mixture back into the saucepan. Bring to a gentle boil over medium heat, stirring constantly, until the cream is thick. Pour into a bowl, cover with plastic wrap, and let cool.

4. When cooled, fold in the almond pralines. Set aside.

PREP CREAM-PUFF PASTRY

1. Place the water, butter, and salt in a heavy saucepan. Bring to a slow boil. As soon as the butter is melted, remove the saucepan from the heat and add the flour all at once, mixing well. Return to medium-high heat and mix vigorously with a wooden spatula. Stir until the mixture forms a ball and can be pulled away from the sides of the pan.

2. Transfer the dough to another bowl. Let it cool for 5 minutes before adding the eggs, one at a time, always beating between each addition until the mixture is smooth.

3. Place the dough in a pastry bag with a star tube (number 6). Make a large ring of dough on a buttered cookie sheet. Make another ring inside and against the first one. Make a third ring on top and in between the first 2 rings. (You now have 3 rings, one against the other.) Let the dough dry for 10 minutes.

COOKING

Preheat the oven to 425 degrees.

1. Bake the cream-puff pastry in the preheated oven for 10 minutes. Lower the heat to 350 degrees. Continue to bake for 30 minutes. Remove from oven and gently brush the top with the egg wash. Return to oven and bake for another 10 minutes. The pastry should puff to double its size, feel hollow inside, and be lightly browned.

2. Remove the pastry from the oven and let it cool to lukewarm. Split it in half by cutting the lower half from the 2 smaller tiers.

3. Whip the cream, and when it starts to thicken, beat in 2 tablespoons of the sugar. Continue whipping until stiff. Fold in the rum.

PRESENTATION

Spread the pastry cream on the bottom half of the cake. Put the whipped cream in a pastry bag with a fluted tube. Pipe the whipped cream over the pastry cream. Cover the top half of the cake, and press down slightly. Sprinkle the top with the remaining powdered sugar.

GÂTEAU VICTOIRE

serves 8

Chocolate fanciers dote on this cake, which has been in our repertoire from the beginning. The cake looks awesome, but it is easy to make. Deep brown and velvet in texture, it contains no flour, a point our waiters teasingly love to stress when clients protest the cake might be too rich. The ice cream actually helps to cut some of the richness of the cake, in addition to offering a pleasant contrast.

1 POUND BELGIAN BITTERSWEET CHOCOLATE

6 LARGE EGGS

1 OUNCE VANILLA EXTRACT

1 OUNCE DARK JAMAICAN RUM

1¼ CUPS HEAVY CREAM

PINCH OF SALT

VANILLA ICE CREAM (OPTIONAL)

CHOCOLATE SHAVINGS (OPTIONAL)

COOKING

Preheat the oven to 350 degrees.

1. Melt the chocolate in a *bain-marie*.

2. Mix the eggs, vanilla, and rum together in a small metal bowl. Set over a double boiler over medium heat. Beat mixture by hand for 5 minutes till creamy.

3. Add the mixture to the melted chocolate. Whisk in heavy cream and a pinch of salt.

4. Line a 12 x 3-inch cake pan with parchment or wax paper. Pour the cake mixture into the pan.

5. Set the cake pan in a water bath and bake in the preheated oven for 45 minutes.

6. Remove the cake from the oven, and let it cool to room temperature before ummolding. Since ovens are hotter in the back than in front, turn the cake pan after 20 minutes to allow for even baking.

PRESENTATION

Cut 2 thin slices per person. If desired, put a scoop of vanilla ice cream in the center. Top with chocolate shavings. The cake will keep in the refrigerator for 2 weeks.

DESSERTS

beverages

What to serve with dessert, even more than what to serve with a meal, is foremost a matter of personal taste, mood, and occasion. It could be a Brut, Extra Dry, or Demi-Sec Champagne, a white or rosé Crémant. Then again, it could be a young Sauterne, a perfumed Muscat, a port-like Banyuls, or a spicy, late-vintage Gerwürztraminer.

265

WALNUT TART

serv_es 12

This rich and heavenly walnut tart is best made a day before serving, since it takes 6 hours for it to cool. The recipe serves 12. Because the tart keeps for 2 to 3 weeks in the refrigerator, you may as well make it in this quantity. It doesn't take any more time, and it certainly pays off to have this yummy and chewy dessert on hand. In fact, one of our cooks told me that when he made this walnut tart at home, it never reached the table because his family devoured the entire tart before it had a chance to cool.

sweet pastry
(pâte sucrée)
....

1 CUP (2 STICKS) BUTTER

1 CUP GRANULATED SUGAR

2 EGGS

3 EGG YOLKS

4³/₄ CUPS ALL-PURPOSE FLOUR

¹/₂ TEASPOON SALT

walnut topping
....

1 POUND LIGHT BROWN SUGAR (2¹/₄ CUPS)

¹/₄ CUP GRANULATED SUGAR

1 CUP HONEY

2 CUPS (4 STICKS) BUTTER, CUT INTO PIECES

PINCH OF SALT

¹/₂ CUP HEAVY CREAM

3 POUNDS SHELLED WALNUTS

VANILLA ICE CREAM

PREP PASTRY
....

1. Blend the butter and sugar together with a mixer or in a food processor. Add the eggs and the egg yolks. Incorporate the flour and the salt. Do not overprocess.

2. Gather the dough together and transfer it to a sheet of wax paper. Gently push it into a ball. Wrap and refrigerate the dough for at least 1 hour or overnight.

3. Bring the dough up to room temperature. Place the dough on a sheet of wax paper or plastic wrap at least 2 inches larger on all sides than a 13 x 18-inch sheet pan. Cover it with a second sheet of the same size. Roll the dough out between these two sheets into a rectangle that is 1½ inches larger on all sides than the sheet pan. (Use the sheet pan to get the right size.)

4. Remove the top wrap. Invert the sheet pan over the dough and flip it over. Remove the remaining wrap, and fold over and trim the edges of the dough. Smooth out the bottom.

5. Cover the dough with plastic wrap. Refrigerate for at least 30 minutes or overnight. (This resting period is important—otherwise the dough will shrink.)

6. Preheat the oven to 425 degrees. Bring the dough up to room temperature. Prick the bottom of the dough with a fork. Blind bake (bake unfilled) for 10 minutes in the preheated oven.

COOKING

Preheat the oven to 350 degrees.

1. In a mixing bowl, combine the 2 sugars and the honey. (If the honey is slightly warm, it will be easier to work with.)

2. Add the butter and the salt.

3. Bring the mixture to a boil, stirring constantly. Continue to let it boil until the mixture thickens and caramelizes, turning darker in color, about 5 minutes.

4. Add the cream, and continue to boil the mixture for 2 minutes. Remove and incorporate the walnuts. Stir well.

5. Pour the topping mixture onto the partially baked dough. Distribute it evenly to get the caramel into every nook and cranny of the tart.

6. Bake in the preheated oven for 30 to 40 minutes. (Put a larger sheet pan under the baking pan to catch the caramel drippings.)

7. Remove the tart from the oven. When it has slightly cooled, cover the top with wax paper and press down with a heavy pan or skillet to distribute the mixture evenly. Cool the tart completely, for about 6 hours.

PRESENTATION

Cut the completely cooled tart into 2-inch squares. Serve 3 squares per person, topped with vanilla ice cream.

LEMON SABAYON TART

serves 6 to 8

A wonderful, refreshing tart that can be assembled in a short time. The pie shell actually benefits from being prepared a day ahead of time, but once you have embarked on the sabayon, there is no turning back.

In the restaurant, we serve the lemon tart with lemon *confit*. However, the lemon tart will still be a success without the benefit of the *confit*. Simply sprinkle the top with sifted confectioners' sugar.

lemon confit

- 1 LEMON
- ⅓ CUP SUGAR
- ¼ CUP WATER

pastry

- 1 CUP (2 STICKS) BUTTER, SOFTENED
- 2 TEASPOONS SUGAR
- 1 EGG, LIGHTLY BEATEN
- 1 CUP ALL-PURPOSE FLOUR
- 1 CUP SEMOLINA FLOUR
- ⅛ TEASPOON SALT
- 3 TO 4 TEASPOONS COLD WATER

lemon sabayon

- ⅓ CUP FRESH SQUEEZED LEMON JUICE
- ZEST OF 1 LEMON
- 3 EGGS
- 3 EGG YOLKS
- ½ CUP SUGAR
- 6 TABLESPOONS BUTTER, SOFTENED

PREP CONFIT

1. Cut the lemon into 8 thin slices. Remove the seeds.

2. Put the lemon into a saucepan, together with the sugar and water. Cover with wax paper, trimmed to fit the size of the pan. (This prevents the lemon slices from becoming too dry.)

3. Set over the lowest possible heat. Simmer for 10 to 15 minutes. Cool to room temperature.

4. Refrigerate in a covered container till ready to use. (Refrigerated *confit* of lemon, covered with plastic wrap, will keep for at least 1 month.)

PREP PASTRY

1. In a food processor, cream the butter and sugar together. Mix in the egg, flours, and salt, adding water as needed.

2. Let the dough rest for 30 minutes before rolling it out to fit into a 10-inch pie plate. Refrigerate the pie shell overnight.

3. When ready to bake the pie shell, preheat the oven to 350. Prick the unbaked pie shell with a fork. Blind bake (bake unfilled) in the preheated oven for 15 to 20 minutes, or till lightly browned. Remove from the oven, and let cool completely before adding lemon sabayon.

COOKING

1. Make the sabayon by combining the lemon juice and zest in a mixing bowl. Beat the eggs and egg yolks into it. Whisk in the sugar.

2. Set the mixing bowl over a pot of rapidly boiling water. Start to beat the mixture slowly at first (to avoid getting air into it). Then continue beating vigorously till the mixture has thickened and resembles the consistency of a hollandaise. This may take from 5 to 15 minutes.

3. Add the softened butter. Continue stirring till the butter has completely dissolved.

4. Remove from the heat and immediately pour the sabayon into the pie shell. Shake to distribute the mixture evenly.

5. Let the tart rest for at least half an hour before serving.

PRESENTATION

Cut the lemon tart into serving portions. Have the lemon *confit* at room temperature. Remove individual slices from the syrup and place on the tart portions.

NOTE: The finished tart will not keep, not even in the refrigerator. Leftover pie dough, however, makes delectable cookies.

serves 4

The kitchen prepares from 7 to 10 apple tarts per service. Since the tart bakes in 3 minutes, the cooks will whip up 2 or 3 more tarts in no time. The apples can be prepared days in advance. Getting the hang of working with the fragile phyllo dough is a matter of practice.

apple filling

. . . .

6 TO 8 MEDIUM GRANNY SMITH APPLES

1 TABLESPOON BLACK SEEDLESS RAISINS

1 TABLESPOON PINE NUTS

2 TABLESPOONS BUTTER

¾ CUP SUGAR

pastry

. . . .

2 TABLESPOONS BUTTER

5 SHEETS PHYLLO OR STRUDEL PASTRY LEAVES

¼ CUP ALMOND PRALINES (SEE PAGE 888)

CINNAMON ICE CREAM

PREP APPLES

1. Peel and core the apples. Cut them into quarters and dice. (If the apples aren't used immediately, toss with some lemon juice to prevent discoloring.)

2. Soak the raisins in warm water to cover.

3. Roast the pine nuts in a preheated 300 degree oven or in a nonstick sauté pan for about 10 min-tes. (Stand by and watch because they burn easily.)

4. Melt the butter in a skillet over medium high heat. Add 2 tablespoons of the sugar, shaking the pan to let the mixture caramelize, about 3 minutes.

5. Add the apples, shaking the pan and tossing them. (They start browning immediately.) Add more sugar if needed. Sauté for 5 to 10 minutes, depending on the water content of the apples.

6. Remove the pan from the heat. Drain the raisins and mix them into the apples, together with the roasted pine nuts. Pack the mixture tightly into a glass bowl. Set aside till ready to use. (Covered with plastic wrap, the apples will keep in the refrigerator for 1 week.)

COOKING

Preheat the oven to 550 degrees.

1. Melt the butter. Place a cotton cloth on a work table. Sprinkle it with cold water to moisten slightly.

2. Gently place 1 sheet of phyllo dough onto the cloth. Dab the center with a mere touch of melted butter. Sprinkle with ½ teaspoon of pralines.

3. Put another sheet of dough across the first, to form a cross. Repeat this procedure with 3 additional sheets, placing each sheet at a different angle.

4. Invert the apple mixture on the center of the last sheet. (The apple mixture should not be wet. Strain if necessary.) Gather the edges of the dough and squeeze it together at the center to make the tart look like a flower in bloom.

5. Spray an iron sauté pan or glass baking pan with Pam.

6. Gently pick up the apple tart and place it in the baking pan. Spray the tart with Pam. Sprinkle the rest of the pralines over the top and on the sides. Bake in the preheated oven for 2 to 3 minutes. Let the tart cool.

PRESENTATION

Cut the tart into 4 portions. Serve with cinnamon ice cream.

BREAD PUDDING WITH PEAR COULIS AND CHOCOLATE SAUCE

serves 6

Just as a frugal housewife doesn't let any food go to waste, we take care of much of the bread that we have left over by making bread pudding. The rest of the bread, made into bread crumbs, is used for cassoulet, lamb chops, and an occasional saffron soup special.

I love to watch a man's reaction to finding bread pudding on the menu.

"Ah, bread pudding," he'll say, looking like a delighted boy.

I know how he feels. The bread pudding —leftover bread or not—was George's idea. It's his favorite dessert.

pear coulis

3 ANJOU PEARS

2 TABLESPOONS WHITE WINE

¼ CUP HEAVY CREAM

1 TABLESPOON HONEY

¼ TEASPOON VANILLA EXTRACT

bread pudding

4 TABLESPOONS (½ STICK) BUTTER

1 CUP LIGHT BROWN SUGAR

4 EGGS, BEATEN

1 TABLESPOON VANILLA EXTRACT

1 TEASPOON FRESHLY GRATED NUTMEG

1 TABLESPOON CINNAMON

1 CUP HEAVY CREAM

¼ CUP MILK

3 RIPE BANANAS

¼ CUP RUM

4 CUPS 1-INCH STALE BREAD CUBES

chocolate sauce

6 OUNCES SEMISWEET CHOCOLATE, CUT INTO SMALL PIECES

1 CUP HEAVY CREAM

2 TABLESPOONS CHOCOLATE SHAVINGS

PREP PEAR COULIS

1. Peel the pears, core them, and cut them in half. Poach the pears in the wine and enough water to cover for 15 minutes, or until soft.

2. In a separate pan, bring the cream to a boil.

3. Purée the poached pears, honey, and vanilla extract in a food processor, gradually adding the hot cream. (The *coulis* will have the consistency of a fairly thick sauce.) Let the mixture cool. (Properly stored, pear *coulis* will keep 1 or 2 days in the refrigerator.)

COOKING

Preheat the oven to 350 degrees.

1. Cream the butter and brown sugar together. Gradually beat the eggs into this mixture. Add the vanilla extract, nutmeg, and cinnamon. Mix in the heavy cream and milk.

2. Purée 2 of the bananas with the rum. Add the purée to the cream mixture.

3. Soak the bread cubes in the pudding mixture for a half hour.

4. Slice the remaining banana into 6 pieces, and place 1 banana slice in the bottom of 6 individual 8-ounce ovenproof molds that have been lightly buttered. Spoon the pudding into the molds. Place in a water bath and bake in the preheated oven for 40 minutes. Raise the heat to 425 degrees and bake for an additional 10 minutes. Remove and set aside till ready to use. (Covered with plastic wrap, the bread pudding will keep in the refrigerator for 1 to 2 days. Reheat in the microwave oven or in a *bain-marie*.)

5. When ready to serve, bring the cream to a slow boil and pour the hot cream over the semisweet chocolate pieces, stirring evenly for 2 to 3 minutes (not to lose shine).

PRESENTATION

Put 1 tablespoon of pear *coulis* on the bottom of each dessert plate. Invert the pudding over it. Make a ring of the chocolate sauce around it. Design with a knife. Sprinkle the top with chocolate shavings.

GOAT-CHEESE CAKE WITH BLACK CURRANT COULIS

serves 8 to 12

This uncommon and rather sophisticated goat-cheese cake was born the day the kitchen inherited a large amount of goat cheese, leftover from our ill-fated demo-cheese dinner, mentioned on page 000. Ever since then, it has been part of our standard dessert repertoire. The black-currant *coulis* also is an excellent glaze for cherry and peach tarts.

black currant coulis
. . . .

1 CUP DRAINED BLACK CURRANTS IN SYRUP

⅛ TEASPOON BALSAMIC VINEGAR

SUGAR TO TASTE

⅛ CUP ALMOND PRALINES (SEE PAGE 000)

goat-cheese cake
. . . .

4 EGGS

1 CUP SUGAR

⅛ TEASPOON VANILLA EXTRACT, OR 2 VANILLA BEANS

1 TEASPOON AMARETTO

1 POUND CREAMY GOAT CHEESE, SUCH AS MONTRACHET OR SILVER GOAT

⅛ POUND RICOTTA CHEESE

1⅛ CUPS BROKEN-UP GRAHAM CRACKERS (ABOUT 22 CRACKERS)

1 TABLESPOON MELTED BUTTER

PREP COULIS
. . . .

Pour the black currants into a blender. Add the vinegar and purée. Sweeten with sugar to taste. Strain through a fine sieve. (Stored in a tightly covered container, the refrigerated *coulis* will keep for at least 1 month.)

COOKING
. . . .

Preheat the oven to 325 degrees.

1. Beat the eggs till lemony in color. Gradually add the sugar, vanilla, and amaretto. (If using vanilla beans, flatten the beans, cut them in half lengthwise, and scrape out the seeds. In a small bowl, mash the seeds in the amaretto.)

2. Break the goat cheese in small pieces and add them to the mixture. Add the ricotta cheese. Mix until smooth.

3. In a blender or food processor, process the graham crackers coarsely. Mix them with the melted butter.

4. Press the graham cracker mixture into a 10-inch spring mold. Top with the cheese mixture. Bake in the preheated oven for

1 to 1¼ hours. To check for doneness, insert a tooth pick in the center of the cake. If it comes out clean, the cake is cooked. Let the cake cool completely before serving.

PRESENTATION
. . . .
Unmold the goat-cheese cake. Glaze the top with 2 tablespoons of black currant *coulis*. Sprinkle with almond pralines. Serve with additional *coulis* on the side.

GRAPEFRUIT SECTIONS WITH FRESH RASPBERRIES AND SORBET
. . . .

serves 4

This refreshing dessert is popular with clients who want something light after their meal. The best grapefruit to use is the Star Ruby, either from Florida or Texas. When raspberries are not available, try it with pomegranate seeds: it looks stunning and presents an intriguing texture contrast.

grapefruit sections
. . . .

2 GRAPEFRUITS (5 SECTIONS PER SERVING)

¾ CUP SUGAR

¾ CUP GIN

1 PINT RASPBERRY SORBET

1 BOX FRESH RASPBERRIES

4 SPRIGS MINT, CUT INTO JULIENNE

PREP GRAPEFRUITS
. . . .
1. Remove grapefruit peel with a utility knife. With a very sharp carving knife, section the grapefruits by cutting between the membrane. (It's best to do this over a bowl to catch all the juice.) Reserve the juice.

2. Heat equal amounts of grapefruit juice and sugar in a saucepan. (Since grapefruits vary in sweetness, the amount of sugar should be adjusted accordingly.) Remove from the heat. Add the gin. When the syrup has cooled, add the grapefruit sections. Let macerate overnight.

PRESENTATION
. . . .
When ready to serve, bring the dish up to room temperature. Place 5 grapefruit sections in a spiral form in a glass bowl. Place a scoop of raspberry sorbet in the middle. Arrange the raspberries in between the grapefruit sections. Spoon the syrup over it. Garnish with julienne of mint.

. . . .

dining room terms & kitchen jargon

À LA MINUTE. Cooked to order.

BACK OF THE HOUSE. The kitchen.

BAIN-MARIE. A shallow pan of hot water into which a container with food is placed, allowing that food to cook gently and evenly. It can also be used to keep the cooked food warm.

BÂTONNET. A garnish of vegetables cut into small sticks.

BREAKDOWN. Time for the kitchen to close, meaning every single food item is properly stored away and the entire kitchen is scrubbed down.

BRUNOISE. Small-diced vegetables.

CHINOIS. Also called china cap, a conical, deep sieve with an extremely fine mesh, used for straining and pureeing.

CONFIT. A preserved preparation. This can be anything from lemon slices to garlic cloves. *Confit de canard*, or duck *confit*, is duck cooked and preserved in its own fat.

COULIS. A liquid purée of cooked vegetables, shellfish, or raw or cooked fruit (from the French *couler*, "to flow").

COVERS. Number of diners served during a particular shift.

DUPE. An ordering slip, consisting of several copies, on which waiters note their customers' orders in prescribed menu language to be presented to the kitchen.

86. Kitchen term for a sold-out dish.

EXPEDITER. The person stationed in the kitchen in charge of processing the flow between the dining room and kitchen.

FIRE. The term, used by the chef, expediter, runner, or other person in charge, to start cooking a particular order.

FONDUE. The French word for "melt," frequently referring to cheeses but also to finely chopped vegetables that have "melted" together by lengthy and slow cooking.

FRONT OF THE HOUSE. The dining room.

JUS DE POULET. A concentrated chicken jelly, similar to *glace de viande*, obtained by a series of reductions.

LINE. The stations where the chef and his crew work. A line cook is somebody who works on the line.

MANDOLINE. A hand-operated machine with adjustable blades for finely slicing and French-fry cutting raw vegetables with tremendous precision and uniformity.

MIS EN PLACE. The prep, or kitchen work that takes place before meal service; also the assembling of all required utensils and whatever else is needed before meal service begins.

NO-SHOW. A table reservation that has not been honored.

PICKUP. A term meaning that the order for a particular table has been cooked and plated and is now ready to be served.

PLAT DU JOUR. Special of the day.

PRIX FIXE. A complete meal offered at

PROVENÇAL. A French term relating to the cuisine inspired by the bounty of herbs and spices, fruits, vegetables, olives, oil, and garlic that thrive in the sunny climate of Provence.

RUNNER. The server who "runs," or brings the food from the kitchen to the guests' table.